The Celtic Revolution

PETER BERRESFORD ELLIS, historian, literary biographer and novelist, has published 40 books to date under his own name and that of his pseudonym, Peter Tremayne. Born in Coventry, Warwickshire, in 1943, of Irish descent, he became interested in the Celtic countries at an early age. As a journalist, he wrote on ethnic minority problems for a wide variety of newspapers and magazines during the 1960's and was deputy-editor of an Irish weekly newspaper, before becoming editor of a weekly magazine in London. Joining the Celtic League in the mid-1960's, he was chairman of the League's publicity committee in 1969-70 and still holds an active membership of the League. Writing a highly controversial fortnightly column, 'Celtica Today', in the bilingual Scottish newspaper *Sruth* during 1969-70, he preached a fundamentalist attitude towards political and cultural freedom.

A History of the Irish Working Class, was first published by Victor Gollancz in 1972, and has just been reissued in paperback by Pluto Press, 1985, and is already regarded as a classic. His interest in the practicalities of language revival was demonstrated in *The Problem of Language Revival* (Club Leabhar, Inverness, 1971), co-authored with Seumas Mac a' Ghobhainn. Ned Thomas (author of *The Welsh Extremist*) hailed it as "a book for the activist or potential activist, not for the academic bookshelf". *The Cornish Language and its Literature* (Routledge & Kegan Paul, 1974) remains the definitive history of the language.

The Scottish Insurrection of 1820 (Victor Gollancz, 1970), also co-authored with Seumas Mac a' Ghobhainn, has not been out of print since it appeared and is also becoming accepted as a classic of radical history. His other works include *Celtic Inheritance* (Muller, 1985) and *Hell or Connaught! The Cromwellian Colonization of Ireland 1652-60* (Hamish Hamilton, 1975); *MacBeth: High King of Scotland 1040-57 AD* (Muller, 1980); and *The Boyne Water: The Battle of the Boyne 1690* (Hamish Hamilton, 1976). He introduced and edited the Penguin *James Connolly: Selected Writings* (1973) and his highly praised, historical novel, *The Liberty Tree* (Michael Joseph, 1982), had a setting which culminated with the French landings at Carreg Wastad in Pembrokeshire in 1797.

As 'Peter Tremayne', his fantasy novels and short stories, frequently utilizing Celtic themes, have won him popular acclaim and honours on both sides of the Atlantic and have been translated into several European languages.

As well as in the Celtic countries, he has lectured in America, Canada, France and in England.

The Celtic Revolution

A Study in Anti-Imperialism

PETER BERRESFORD ELLIS

First impression: 1985
Fifth impression: 2000

Jacket design: Y Lolfa Cyf.

ISBN: 0 86243 096 8

Published in Wales by Y LolfaCyf.,
and printed on acid-free and partly recycled paper
by Y Lolfa Cyf., Talybont, Ceredigion SY24 5AP
e-mail ylolfa@ylolfa.com
internet http://ylolfa.com
tel (01970) 832 304
fax 832 782
isdn 832 813

CONTENTS

	Introduction	9
1	The Celts	12
2	Alba (Scotland)	28
3	Breizh (Brittany)	54
4	Cymru (Wales)	76
5	Éire (Ireland)	98
6	Kernow (Cornwall)	134
7	Mannin (Isle of Mann)	149
8	The Celtic Diaspora	165
9	Celtic Unity	187
10	Celtic Nationalism	199
	Further Reading	215

'Tugaigí oideachas ionas go mbeidh sibh fuascailte.'
'Educate that you might be free.'
—Thomas Osborne Davis (1814-1856),
Irish poet and revolutionary

For Alan Heusaff,
Secretary-General of The Celtic League;
a tribute to his years of selfless endeavour
on behalf of the Celtic peoples.

Introduction

The past twenty years have seen a significant rise in 'Celtic consciousness'; in the recognition of a common identity by the Celtic peoples; in the awareness of shared national and social problems from which common lessons could be learned. Yet a few years ago, when giving a lecture at the New School Graduate Faculty of New York University, I was asked a question that I found, to my surprise, I could not answer. I was asked where one could find, in a single volume, a brief outline of the Celtic struggles' of who the Celts are, their place in history, their current situation and their aspirations for the future? Although I could recommend entire libraries of books covering these subjects, I realized that no single comprehensive volume existed. There was an obvious need for a 'Celtic primer', not only as a means of informing non-Celts about the Celtic world but for informing Celts about their fellow Celts. This is my attempt to supply that primer.

When I speak of 'The Celtic Revolution', I am referring to change in attitudes among the Celtic peoples towards themselves and their place in the world; to the growing awareness of what it means to be Celtic and what they, as Celts, could offer their fellow human beings. Among a people assimilated almost to the point of extinction, even that step is a tremendous political revolution.

This is the story of a people, now divided into six small nations, who constituted an ancient civilization; a bright thread in the tapestry of European development; a people who fell before conquerors who ruthlessly imposed their will and, more importantly, their languages and cultures upon them. It is a story of how, after centuries of oppressive colonialism, in which Celtic culture has all but perished, this people still has not gone down into the abyss and is struggling to survive in the modern world and carve for themselves a valid role for the future.

I have sometimes been accused by academics of 'undue piety' towards the Celts in my writing. I make no apology for any piety that may creep into this volume. I find it hard to be otherwise when examining a people who stand on the verge of extinction; a people who, within a few generations, may be spoken of as we, today, speak of the Etruscans or Phoenicians. Unlike many so-called 'objective' historians and commentators, I prefer to state my bias at the outset. I write as someone who fully supports Celtic cultural, political and economic independence. Nor do I disguise the fact that I am a socialist.

I believe in mankind and that human dignity and individuality are of paramount importance; that the exploitation of man by man, and nation by nation, is an evil thing and that the world must be rid of such exploitation and the social conditions that lead to it.

In my view, nationalism, by which I mean the advocacy of the freedom of national communities from the cultural, political and economic exploitation of other nations, is inseparable from the achievement of a true socialist society. National and social freedoms are not two separate and unrelated issues. They are two sides of one great democratic principle, each being incomplete without the other.

The way to a sound internationalism lies through the recognition, not the repudiation, of the fact of nationality. The solidarity of the peoples of the world must rest upon a pact between national units, associated in a common purpose and destiny. No state can be regarded as progressive and 'peace-loving' while it seeks to dominate the nationalities within or without its state boundaries.

Therefore, I reiterate that the principal condition for securing a lasting world peace and prosperity is that every nationality, without exception, all over the world, should obtain freedom and the opportunity to decide for itself its future, as part of the human family. In that context, the Celtic struggle is part of the world struggle of peoples in which their humanity is being driven inexorably towards extinction because of the evils of big-state politics and of centralism, in which man loses touch with his humanity and where individuals no longer count. It will only be through individualism, through the role of small nations on the world stage, that the world will eventually find a path to peace.

Peter Berresford Ellis

'Lios na nAislingí',
August, 1984.

Chapter One
The Celts

Today, on the north western seaboard of Europe, the descendants of the ancient Celtic civilization still live on, a people struggling hard to survive and maintain their individuality in these days of increasing cultural uniformity and deadly sameness of life. The Welsh, Cornish and the Bretons make up the Brythonic-speaking group whilst the Irish, Manx and Scots constitute the Goidelic or Gaelic-speaking people. Six small nationalities, with their rapidly disappearing latter-day offshoots—the Welsh-speaking area of Patagonia in Argentina and the Scottish Gaelic-speaking area in Nova Scotia, Canada—who, through their ancient languages and cultures, are the inheritors of nearly three thousand years of unbroken cultural tradition.

The Celts were the first Transalpine people to emerge into recorded history. It was the ancient Greek chroniclers who first designated them as *Keltoi*. It has been suggested that the word means 'hidden people' because of Celtic reluctance to commit their vast store of scholarship and knowledge to written records. The etymology of the word may well be from the same root which gives us *ceilt*, an act of concealment, and also the word *kilt*, the short male skirt of traditional Celtic dress.

What must be made clear from the outset is that the Celts were a linguistic group and not a racial one. Professor Eoin Mac Neill has explained that there is no such thing as a Celtic 'race' anymore than we can speak about a Latin race, a Germanic race or a Slavic race. The peoples of Europe are mixtures of several races, for the most part of the same races for, when we speak of *race*, we are talking in terms of physical attributes which is a dangerous path to tread. As there is little biological difference between a Scandinavian and an African, to talk of race is usually meaningless and delusory. The mixture of physical attributes among the Celts was as evident in ancient times as it is today. Thus early writers could describe the 'typical' Celts as the swarthy, stocky Silurian, or, equally, as the tall, gangling, blond Gaul. Only language, with its attendant culture, distinguishes the Celtic peoples from the rest of European society. Therefore, a Celtic people is by definition a people who speak, or were known to have spoken, in modern historical times, a Celtic language. Once the Celtic languages are entirely dead, with no hope of resuscitation, the Celtic peoples will have ceased to exist.

Reference has been made to the two branches of Celtic—Brythonic and Goidelic, both deriving in some long-gone epoch from a common root. The main differences between the two branches is that the Brythonic languages have simplified themselves in their case endings and in the losing of the neuter gender and dual number. The two groups also differ in the matter of initial mutation and aspiration. There is the famous substitution of P for Q in the Brythonic languages. This was the sound which, in Indo-European, from which Celtic along with the majority of other European languages descends, gave us *qu* (*kw*). This sound in Goidelic later became represented by *c* and in Brythonic by *p*. For example:

English	son	head	worm	feather	everyone
Welsh (P)	ap	pen	pryv	pluv	paup
Irish (Q)	mac	cenn	cruiv	cluv	cách

At the start of the first millenium BC, the Celts possessed great skill in metal work, especially in the use of iron, a metal only then becoming known to the craftsmen of the 'Classical' world. By the 6th Century BC, their formidable armament of spears, swords, axes and agricultural implements rendered the Celts militarily superior to their neighbours. Their billhooks and axes enabled them to open roadways through the previously impenetrable forests of Europe, and to make extensive clearances and till the land with comparative ease. An ancient Irish word for road, avenue or pathway, which is still in use, is *slighe* from the word *sligim*—I hew. It was the Celts, not the Romans, who were the original road builders of the ancient world, a fact slowly being accepted by scholars in the light of new archaeological finds. To the thoughtful historian, the evidence has always been there, especially in the writings of Juluis Caesar. Among the many Celtic loan-words adopted into Latin, one observes the preponderance of words connected with transportation, names of various types of chariot and cart—*carpentum* (from which derives both car and carpenter), *carruca*, *currus* and *essedum*.

By 900 BC, the Celts had settled extensively in southern France, crossed into the Iberian peninsula and established themselves in settlements as far south as modern Portugal. It is generally thought that the first Celtic migrations to the British Isles took place during this period, but some modern scholarship suggests that the first Celtic peoples may well have arrived as early as 2000 BC and definitely not later than 1000 BC. The last series of migrations of Celtic tribes to Britain occurred in the 2nd Century BC, when the Belgic tribes arrived in the south of the country, migrating from the territory which is still named after them—Belgium.

By 600 BC, the Celts began to cross the Alps into the fertile valleys of the River Po in what is modern Italy. They had firmly settled in the area when the city state of Rome began its expansion, pushing into the territory of its northern neighbour, Etruria. Celt and Roman soon came into conflict and on July 18th, 390 BC, they faced each other across the River Allia within a few miles of Rome itself. The Romans were defeated and the City fell to the Celts. However, they did not occupy it for long, preferring to return to their own territories. That most trustworthy of ancient historians, Polybius, tells us that is was not until 349 BC that Rome was strong enough to resume further aggressive action against the Celts. The Celtic territory, known as Cisalpine Gaul, stretched across northern Italy from Liguria to as far south as Senigallia, near Ancona. Senigallia is still easily recognizable as the town of the Senones Gauls. We are reminded that the names of Celt, Gaul and Galatian are all synonymous.

For centuries during the Roman expansion through Italy, the Celts proved to be a tough opposition, making alliances with the Etruscans, Samnites and finally with Hannibal himself who would not have achieved fame without his Celtic allies. Following the end of the Carthaginian Wars, Rome turned its attention to quelling the only people who stood in its way to a complete domination of the Italian peninsula. A campaign of conquest against the Celts was undertaken in 196 BC, which was not really concluded until the last Ligurian Celtic tribes surrendered in 180 BC, thus bringing the territory of Cisalpine Gaul into the Roman fold.

The Italian Celts were in evidence down to Imperial times, leaving their mark in many place-names such as Trevi, Bologna, Treviso, Treviglio, Reno, Trebia, and countless others. Venice itself was the tribal capital of the Veneti; another Veneti tribe gave its name to Vannes in Brittany and was made famous by Caesar's battles with them.

It has not yet been fully demonstrated just how much the Celts influenced the struggling Latin culture. Loan-words from Celtic appear in Latin during this period, particularly words concerned with weaponry, transport and philosophy. Celtic influence on Latin literature has yet to be studied; that there was such an influence is demonstrated by a study of Livy, whose histories are epic and fabulous in Celtic tradition and contain episodes of pure Celtic religious symbolism. Livy, significantly, was raised in the territory of Cisalpine Gaul, as were the poets Vergil and Gallus (the latter bearing an obviously Celtic name). Cornelius Nepos, the writer and friend of Catullus, was proud of the fact that he was an Insubrian Celt from the Po Valley. Trogus Pompeius acknowledged himself to be a Vocontii, also from Cisalpine Gaul. There are a number of early Celtic names which begin with *trog* and it is interesting to make a momentary digression to contemplate a possible connection with the Irish *tróg* or Welsh *tru* which means 'miserable'.

It is from northern Italy that we find one of the earliest surviving Celtic texts. While the Celts refrained from writing extensively in their own languages at this period, not from lack of literacy but because of a firm policy, there appear many inscriptions from Celtic sources (mainly in Greek, sometimes in Latin) usually identified as Celtic by the written names. Some of the first surviving inscriptions which give Celtic words as well as names are the Todi and Saigon inscriptions and the Briona stone, all dated to the 2nd Century BC. An even earlier text was found at Botorrita in Spain and continuing work by continental Celtic scholars, such as K.H.Schmidt, M.Lejune, A.Tovar and Enrico Campanile, are pushing back the date of known Celtic literacy to a surprising degree.

The Celts continued as a threat to Roman expansion for many years and it is ironic, perhaps, that the first time the Germanic peoples (ancestors of the English and French) emerge into recorded history, they are seen fighting for the Celts. "Undoubtedly as hired troops or as forces levied on a subject territory", comments Professor Mac Neill who, with Professor Carl Marstrander of Oslo, has pointed to the number of words of Celtic origin which are to be found in the whole group of Germanic languages. "Some of these words are especially indicative of Celtic political predominance at the time of their adoption into Germanic speech." For example, the German *Reich* comes from the Celtic *rigion*; and *Amt* (public office) from *ambactus*, which the Romans borrowed from the Celtic and which has now emerged as the English (and French) word *ambassador*. The Germanic peoples first emerged into recorded history in the Roman *acta triumphalia* for the year 222 BC, when the consul Marcellus defeated Virdumarus and his Celts at Clastidium (Casteggio).

In the 2nd Century BC, the western Transalpine Celts inflicted five major defeats on the Romans. Finally, in 104 BC, Caius Marius was elected consul and set about the reorganization of the Roman army. It was he who created the ruthless legionary fighting force that became so well known—a creation, ironically, necessitated by the military success of the Celts. By 101 BC, Marius was making punitive expeditions into Transalpine Gaul and, forty years later, Julius Caesar was to assert Roman domination over the territory.

At the same time as the Celtic expansion into northern Italy, other Celtic tribes were pushing further east into the Balkan Peninsula. The Macedonians who, a generation before, had conquered the world for Alexander, were unable to impede their progress. The Celts divided into three armies and began to advance into the Greek interior in 280 BC. Cerethrios led the eastern wing through what is now modern Bulgaria; the western army, led by Bologios, defeated the Macedonians and slew their king Ptolemy Cereaunos (once Alexander's favourite general). The central army advanced successfully against Haemos and Thessaly. This army was commanded by Brennus and Achichorius. Brennus, incidentally, could simply be the Celtic name Bran (raven) or just a title, as *brennin* remains the word for 'king' in modern Welsh. Brennus and Achichorius scattered the Greek armies. They came to Thermopylae where they faced the Athenian armies and routed them. Then they turned on Aetollia and Callion, others coming through the gorges of Parnassos to sack the temple of Apollo's oracle (the Pythia) at Delphi. A fabulous treasure was taken by the Tectosages which was later discovered at their tribal capital of Tolosa (Toulouse). The Roman consul Quintus Servillius Caepio was charged with taking it to Rome but the sight of the wealth proved too much for him and he disappeared with it! While the Greeks turned back the Celtic invasion, Thrace remained a Celtic kingdom until 193 BC. This contact also resulted in Celtic loanwords being adopted into Greek.

About the same time, Celtic tribes moved into Egypt to take service with Ptolemy II Philadelphos (circa 277 BC). He used a Celtic symbol on some of his coinage. It seems there was a plot in which the Celts tried to overthrow the Greek rulers of Egypt, according to Pausanias and, on its failure, the Celts were imprisoned on an island in the Sebennytic arm of the Nile where they all perished. This did not deter Ptolemy III and Ptolemy IV from recruiting more Celtic mercenaries who were encouraged to settle in Egypt with their families. Some fascinating Celtic graffitti can be seen in the Temple of Seti I in Upper Egypt, resembling an early version of the 'Kilroy was here' message.

Nicomedes, king of Bithynia, was also quick to see the potential of the Celtic warriors as mercenary troops and he invited certain tribes into Asia Minor to serve in his army. These tribes were led by Leonarios and Lutarios and, we are told, they consisted of 20,000 warriors with their women and children. Having served the king of Bithynia for a while, the Celts decided to carve out their own kingdom in what became modern Turkey. For a while, they simply wandered the area sacking such cities as Troy, Ephesos, Miletos and other. Then, in 270 BC, Antiochos Soter of Syria soundly defeated them but allowed them to settle in the region of what is now the modern Turkish capital—Ankara. The country was called Galatia and what we know of this state gives us our first knowledge of Celtic political organization. Galatia was governed by an assembly of 300 elected clan chieftains who met at their capital Drunemeton ('the sacred oak grove').

Galatia lost total independence during the Roman campaigns in Asia Minor in 197-6 BC and, from 25 BC, it was recognized as a Roman province ruled by a *propraetor*. The Galatians were the first group of Celts to accept Christianity, being converted by Paul of Tarsus. They achieved a form of immortality through Paul's famous letter to them which is now part of the New Testament. Although the Galatians were surrounded on all sides by Hellenistic cultural influence, they clung tenaciously to their language and culture and, as late as the 5th century AD, St Jerome reported that the Galatians spoke an offshoot of Gaulish and compared their dialect to that of the Belgic tribe called the Treviri.

Ancient Celtic civilization achieved its biggest expansion from Asia Minor in the east to Ireland in the west in the 3rd Century BC. It was a very sophisticated society. The Celts were among the first to evolve a doctrine on the immortality of the soul and their philosophers were highly regarded in the ancient world. Aristotle, Sotion and Clement of Alexandria all state that early Greek philosophers borrowed much from the Celts. The similarity of druidic ideas on immortality and Pythagorean philosophy has frequently been remarked upon. While Clement says that Pythagoras and the Greeks acquired the philosophy from the Celts, Hippolytus claims that it was a slave of Pythagoras who took it to the Celts. "He, after the death of Pythagoras, having made his way there, became the founder of this philosophy for them." Yet Hippolytus was obviously wrong because the Celtic belief in immortality was entrenched long before the time of Pythagoras who died about 497 BC.

The belief in immortality was simple: the druids taught that death was only a changing of place and that life went on with all its forms and goods in another world, the fabled Otherworld. A constant exchange of souls took place between the two worlds. When a soul died in this world, it was reborn in the Otherworld; when a soul died in the Otherworld, it was reborn in this one. Julius Caesar cynically remarked: "The druids' chief doctrine is that the soul of man does not perish but passes after death from one person to another. They hold that this is the best of all incitements to courage as banishing fear."

The druids, the Celtic priesthood, remind one of Buddhist monks or Zen masters. They dwelt in a firm communication with

Nature, believing in the consciousness of all things. Trees, fountains, rivers and even weapons and implements were possessed of an indwelling spirit. Everything was but a fragment of one cosmic whole. Thus, in Celtic myth, could Mananán Mac Lir's boat know a man's thoughts; or the sword of Conaire Mór sing; or the Lia Fáil (Stone of Destiny) cry out for joy when it felt the touch of a righteous ruler's feet.

A lot of nonsense has been written about the druids, of human sacrifices and dark practices. Many writers have fallen hook, line and sinker for the propaganda of Julius Caesar. A conquering soldier, however brilliant, is not the most reliable source from which to discuss the social customs and culture of the people whose civilization he is in the process of destroying. Lt. General Lord Chelmsford, for example, would not have made the ideal authority on Zulu society and culture. Most of the 'classical' writers simply tried to equate Celtic religion with Greek or Roman parallels. Therefore most of the Celtic gods can only be viewed through Greek and Roman masks. They were basically ancient heroes and the ancestors of the people rather than their creators. Celtic mythology is thoroughly heroic as the Celts made their heroes into gods and their gods into heroes. In the lives of these gods and heroes, the lives of the people and the essence of their religious traditions are mirrored.

Celtic mythology, embodied in the early Irish and Welsh manuscripts, is certainly every bit the equal of its Greek and Latin counterparts. The final commitment of the ancient oral literary tradition of the Celts was first made by the Irish. Thus, Professor Calvert Watkins of Harvard University can argue that "Irish has the oldest vernacular literature of Europe". He argues that the literature contained in Greek and Latin was written in languages which were a *lingua franca* and not a *lingua materna*. Whilst it is an interesting argument, Irish certainly has claim to be one of Europe's oldest literary languages, the third literary language of Europe.

At this time, Celtic society displayed a primitive communism, or community-ism which, by the 5th Century AD, when the laws of Ireland (known as the Brehon Laws from *breitheamh*—a judge) were first codified, was an extremely sophisticated and complex system. We can assume that the same social system prevailed throughout the entire Celtic world from a comparison of the Brehon Laws with the Welsh law tracts known as the Laws of Hywel Dda, which were codified in the 9th Century AD; as well as the Breton laws embodied in the Treaty of 1532 AD, which brought Brittany under French suzereignty.

The Celtic law system was very complex and one finds its closest parallel in the tradition of Hindu law. Election was provided for every office from High King down to the lowest sub-chieftain. There was no such concept as primogeniture nor of absolute private ownership. Lack of understanding of this basic concept has led many English and French-orientated historians into pitfalls in their analysis. On discussing the succession of Celtic Scottish High Kings, one historian could blandly remark: "This must have been a bloody business, for hardly ever did a son succeed his father to the throne!" This viewing of things from an alien culture can totally distort the realities of the society one is examining. Thus one can be warned against the acceptance of Greek and Roman assumptions about early Celtic society.

The Gaulish Celts felt the might of Rome, in the person of Julius Caesar, in the 1st Century BC. Then, in the 5th Century AD, came Athauf's Visigoths and the Franks of Clovis. Nevertheless, the generally accepted notion that the Gaulish language was dead by the 3rd Century AD is wrong. Latin had not displaced the Celtic tongue but had been adopted as a *lingua franca*. Apollinarius Sidonius, bishop of the Averni tribe (d. 479 AD), in a letter to his brother-in-law Ecdicius comments that, during this time, "leading families, in their efforts to throw off the scurf of Celtic speech" were making efforts to learn literary Latin. If Celtic was still strong among Gaul's 'leading families' in the late 5th Century AD, how much stronger would it have been among the ordinary people?

It has been argued that the Celtic speech of Gaul did not 'disappear' and that a great deal of it was simply incorporated into Low Latin which, in turn, emerged as French. Certainly, there is a large Celtic loan-word vocabulary in French. The *Dictionnaire Général* (1890-1900) admitted to 400 Celtic words in general use, ranging from ***bar***, ***barque***, ***beret***, ***charpentier***, ***chemin***, ***cheminée***, ***cloque*** and so on, may of which have made their way into English. Celtic scholars Henri Hubert and Georges Dottin believed a far more extensive Celtic vocabulary could be found in Low Latin and French. However, by the 5th Century AD, Gaulish was certainly in decline and a few centuries later the language had vanished along with its sister tongue in Galatia. Soon, the only Celtic spoken on the European mainland was that of the Armorican peninsula of Gaul (Brittany).

Whilst the island of Ireland had never been part of the Roman Empire, Britain had been twice visited by the Romans commanded by Caesar. The British Celts had repulsed his two expeditions but in 43 AD, nearly a hundred years later, Rome gained a foothold on the island. Gradually, their administration and influence spread across the lowlands of the country. In the 5th Century AD, a more ruthless threat to the British Celts came with the arrival of the Jutes, Angles and Saxons. It is recorded that a king named Vortigern (Celtic for 'overlord') invited the Jutes to serve him as mercenaries but they turned on him and seized the kingdom for themselves. For the next few centuries, native Celt and invading German battled across Britain. It was the age of the legendary Celtic hero Arthur. By the 8th Century AD, the Celts had been pushed into the western peninsulas and to the north of the island and the modern Celtic countries began to take on their geographical boundaries.

As the ancestors of the English began to push into Britain, driving the Celts back, many Celtic tribes decided that migration was the only escape from the barbarian hordes now flooding the country. Some went to the north west of the Iberian peninsula and settled on the northern seaboard, mainly in Asturias, between Lugo and Oviedo. Their settlements were recognized at the Council of Lugo in 567 AD as constituting the Christian See of Bretona whose bishop, Mahiloc, signed the *acta* of the 2nd Council of Braga in 572 AD. The settlers bequeathed a name to the country—Galicia, which it is argued comes from the same root as Galatia. But the Celtic settlements in Galicia were quickly absorbed and even the Celtic Church's influence ceased when Roman orthodoxy was accepted at the Council of Toledo in 633 AD.

Galicia, which received a form of home rule within the Spanish state in 1980, is not a Celtic country. This must be made plain owing to the confusion created by a curious programme broadcast in the Channel 4 television series 'How to be Celtic' (September, 1983) which made the claim for Galicia. (The same claim was reiterated in a booklet *How to be Celtic* published by Channel 4 as a companion to the programme.) What increased confusion was that this series totally ignored the Celtic people of Ellan Vannin, the Isle of Mann. Galician musicians and cultural delegations had been making their presence felt at several Celtic gatherings, such as the Inter-Celtic Festival at Lorient and the annual Pan-Celtic Week at Killarney. In April, 1984, Galicia was even allowed to submit films for the Fifth Celtic Film and Television Festival in Cardiff and, astonishingly, the Festival programme book showed Galicia on a map as one of the Celtic countries. While it is flattering to the Celtic peoples that the Galicians have such respect for their Celtic connection, it must be emphasized that they are not a Celtic people.

The Galician language, which is now spoken by 80 per cent of Galicia's two million population, and is being reintroduced into schools after nearly 50 years of ruthless persecution under Franco's Fascist state, is a Romance language. It derives from the same Hispanic dialect as Portugese, with Portugese crystallizing into a literary language distinct from Castillian Spanish in the 16th Century. One can observe a few survivals of Celtic words in Galician vocabulary, such as *llerdu*, heavy or dull, recognizable in the Celtic llurd; *mel*, honey; *parar*, to halt or stop; *soga*, rope; *terco*, stubborn and so forth. There are far more Celtic survivals in French or, indeed, loan-words in modern English, and one presumes the next step to recognition of the Galicians as Celts would be to recognize both the French and English also.

The only criteria for recognition of a Celtic people is a linguistic one. Therefore, any adoption of the Galicians into the Celtic fold would be detrimental to the national claims of the genuine Celts.

Other British Celtic migrants went to Armorica and soon renamed the peninsula Brittany—little Britain. Some modern Celtic scholars, such as Nora Chadwick, maintain that this migration was not to escape the attacks of the Angles and Saxons but to escape the Irish raids on the west coast of Britain. However, Gildas, our earliest authority for the migration, speaks clearly of the *ferocissimi Saxones* and holds them responsible. Whatever may be the case, by the 6th Century AD, Armorica no longer existed but Brittany had emerged speaking a British Celtic language. Again, we enter into scholastic dispute for it has been suggested that the indigenous Armoricans retained their Gaulish speech, not too far removed from British, while the immigrants were absorbed into this ethos. Professor Kenneth Jackson leads the contrary argument saying that British predominated and that Breton is not a survival of Gaulish. What is abundantly clear, however, is that the British Celts did not invade Armorica as military conquerors. All the evidence suggests that they settled peacefully and indigenous Gauls and migrant Britons soon merged into the Breton nation.

The Franks, now dominating the territory to which they would give their name, tried to expand into the Breton peninsula on many occasions. Weroc'h II of Brittany (577-94 AD) demonstrated, by a brilliant defensive military campaign, that the Franks would have a difficult time in maintaining a conquest. Finally, Louis the Pious succeeded in a temporary conquest with his defeat of Wiomarc'h (822-25 AD), when he appointed a personable Breton chieftain named Nominoë as 'duke' of Brittany. Nominoë was an astute political leader and took the opportunity of an uneasy peace with the Franks to build up Breton resources. On the death of Louis the Pious, he struck and declared Brittany independent again. Charles the Bald's attempts to reconquer the Bretons came to nothing. Nominoë defeated him at Ballon on November 22, in 845 AD. Brittany was to be one of th foremost trading countries of Europe, until the end of the 15th Century when the Breton armies were finally defeated.

The Angles and Saxons had now succeeded in pushing the insular Celts back to the western and northern parts of Britain. Some scholars have proposed that intermarriage took place. Such was emphatically not the case and this may be demonstrated by the lack of Celtic loan-words from this period. The conquest of the Celtic population led not to intermarriage but to an almost complete extermination either by death or by forced migration. Ironically, however, geographical names and place-names have survived, especially names of rivers, hills and towns; even the English capital of London still retains its Celtic name (Lugh's dun or fortress) which straddles the Thames (*tamesis*—dark river).

The famous port of Dover, where rivers meet, can be translated through the Welsh *dwfr*; Cornish *dovr* and Breton *dour*, all meaning water. But apart from place-names, and words of geographical significance such as *combe* (valley), *dun* (fort), *avon* (river) etc, and a few religious loan-words, the majority of Celtic loan-words in modern English date mainly from the 19th Century.

The spread of the ancestors of the English in the island resulted in the establishment of the kingdom of Dumnonia (Devon and Cornwall) for a brief while, which eventually crumbled back to the River Tamar and the new country became Cornwall—its Celtic name being *Kernow*. The English called it the 'land of the Kern-wealh' or 'foreign Kerns', hence Cornwall. It lasted as an independent kingdom until 930 AD, when it succumbed to Athelstan's conquest.

Other British Celts were cut off in the area which the Anglo-Saxons called the 'land of foreigners'—*wealh/welisc* meaning 'foreigners', hence Wales. The Welsh called their country 'the land of comrades'—*Cymru*. The name was also applied to a north-western Celtic territory and survived in English phonetics as Cumbria and Cumberland. This Brtish-speaking area lost its independence to Scotland in the 9th Century AD and was finally annexed by the English in the 12th Century AD. Nevertheless, Celtic speech survived there until the 14th Century AD, as Cumbrian place-names can bear witness.

Ireland was to remain free of Anglo-Saxon expansionism although, in the 8th and 9th Centuries, the Danes (Viking bands) settled on parts of the Irish coast and founded city-states such as Dublin. Culturally, they tended to merge with the native Irish, and Norse power was finally broken at Clontarf in 1014, when the Irish High King Brían Boroimhe smashed the combined Norse armies. It was not until 1169, that the Anglo-Normans began to gain a foothold in the country.

During these years of struggle, the remarkable phenomenon of the Celtic Church developed. The Celts had been quick to accept Christianity because Christian philosophy was not completely alien to the Celtic religious concepts. It is interesting to observe that early Celtic 'saints' were also acknowledged as druids. Illtyd of Wales is so designated in the earliest extant life of a Celtic saint—that of Samson, written in the 6th Century.

It has already been my contention in *The Celtic Inheritance* that Christianity was absorbed by the druids, and druidism was not simply displaced by Christianity. For example, the idea of the Holy Trinity, a remarkable concept, is not Judaic, nor does it occur in Greek myth. Why, then, does it occur in Christianity? The first significant work on the Holy Trinity was written by a Gaulish Celt, Hilary of Poitier, who wrote *De Trinitate* during his exile in Phrygia about 356-360 AD. Trinity, the significance of the number three, is an ancient Celtic philosophical symbol. It is known that the druids taught by means of triads.

The term 'Celtic Church' is not a strictly accurate one because the early Christian churches among the Celtic peoples, in most essentials, were part of the Roman Catholic Church. Neither was the Celtic Church an identifiable organization with a central leadership. Nevertheless, during the early Christian era, for a period of 150 years, the insular Celts of the British Isles were cut off from strict Roman influence. While Rome began to reform many of its customs during the 5th Century, especially the dating of Easter, the Celts clung to the old computations and freely mixed many pre-Christian traditions and social concepts into their Christianity, thus developing as a distinct entity within the wider Christian movement.

It was a singular cultural entity, delineated by its practices, social concepts and art forms. These individualistic practices, the observances and customs, its asceticism, monastic extremism, its attitude to social order, views on land tenure, lack of hereditary rights and so forth, brought it into an early conflict with Rome. Absorption was inevitable because of its very individualism, lack of cohesion and natural anarchism. Nevertheless, it was not until the 12th Century that one could say that the majority of Celts adopted Roman orthodoxy.

During the years of conflict, the Celtic monks and scholars began to take their Christian individualism out of their own lands to preach to others. The Irish, in particular, were seized by a *peregrinatio pro Christo*. It was Irish monks who converted the pagan English: it was Irish monks who made their way to the mainland of Europe, establishing monastic centres, churches and hospices as far east as Kiev, the capital of the Ukraine, south to the Mediterranean and north to the Faroes and Iceland. The *Book of*

Lismore, which contains the first Life of St Brendan the Voyager, who founded the monastery of Clonfert in 560 AD, contains a story that Brendan voyaged seven years in the Atlantic. Some scholars have suggested that Brendan actually landed on the American continent. A new dimension to this theory was provided in 1976 when a Harvard Professor, Tim Severin, and a small group of companions, constructed a boat in the style of an 8th Century Irish craft, named it after the saint and sailed across the North Atlantic. Astonishingly, their voyage compared well with many incidents recounted in the ancient text, and they encountered similar landscapes, animals and marine phenomena. Professor Severin has therefore proved it possible that Brendan and his monks could have reached America centuries before Columbus.

The phenomenon of the Celtic Church was, without doubt, one of the most important cultural influences in Europe during the 'Dark Ages' which, for the Celts, was a Golden Age of scholarship and learning. Without the Celtic scholastic foundations, the Celtic love of literacy and their great libraries, it can be argued that an enormous amount of Europe's cultural heritage would have perished in the destructive ravages of their more warlike neighbours. It was an age of great Celtic philosophers, geographers, poets and musicians, and men of medicine.

In the mediaeval period, even in an age of destruction in Europe, the Celtic peoples achieved a great deal. Ireland was the centre of literacy and learning, the medical centre of Europe and the bright jewel in Christendom's crown; Brittany was an independent, prosperous sea-trading nation; Wales, too, held a society that loved literacy and law; Scotland was emerging as a powerful Christian bastion against the ever-threatening pagan Norse; the Isle of Mann had fallen to a Norse ruling class but was showing signs of recovering, absorbing Norse concepts of government and mingling them with Celtic philosophy in a more vigorous way of life; and only Cornwall seemed to be buckling beneath the weight of the English onslaught—yet even little Cornwall had its respected centres of learning. The Celts of the mediaeval period seemed to have much to look forward to.

Yet, one by one, the Celtic nations fell; one after another they were conquered and their futures were to be characterized by ruthless suppression and colonization. Over the centuries, the English and French have treated their Celtic neighbours with military mercilessness and savage mockery, with a curious 'racial' hatred and it is almost impossible to analyze it or to discover its origins. The Celts have been subjected to a remorseless colonization which has all but destroyed their heritage, their languages and cultures.

Today, on the edge of north-west Europe, the Celts are reaching the ultimate crisis in their long march through history. By the end of this century, it will be possible to judge if they are to be destroyed by the centuries of savage repression they have suffered; whether they will be erased by the very progress to which they, as a civilization, have contributed so much, or whether they will be able to survive and carve a valid future for themselves.

It has been my intention, in this opening chapter, to demonstrate the answer to the frequently asked question—who are the Celts? If nothing else, I hope that I have countered the fallacious notion that the Celts were a bizarre barbarian horde, illiterate and uncivilized; or a group of primitive rustics who had no culture of their own. They are an old, sophisticated and highly literate civilization to which European progress owes more than a little thanks.

Chapter Two
Alba (Scotland)

Scotland is the only Celtic country in which a large portion of its inhabitants refuse to recognize the Celtic origins of the nation. Scots have been imbued with the myth which proposes that the country has always contained two distinct nationalities; the 'Highlanders' who are Goidelic or Gaelic Celtic in speech and the 'Lowlanders' who are Teutonic in speech, using a dialect of Northern English which they call 'Lallans' (Lowlands) or 'Scots', which has been developed into a serious literary medium during this century. This belief started life as long ago as the 15th Century and has been so often repeated, especially through the medium of state education, that most Scots, presented with contrary evidence, will simply refuse to listen. Even the modern Scottish national movement is divided on the importance of 'Celticness' as the basis for their national differences from the English. To many, being Scottish does not necessarily mean being Celtic.

In all other Celtic countries, however Anglicized or Frenchified, the Celtic language of that country is recognized as the national language. For example, no Welshman, however hostile to the Celtic language spoken in Wales, would think of calling it by any other name in English than *Welsh*. Try telling the average Scot, even if he is well educated, that the Gaelic language of his country was the national language and deserved to be called, in English, *Scottish*, and he would be totally hostile to the concept. The current Scottish Language Society, based in Kinross, in Perthshire, is a promotional body for 'Lallans' and not Scottish Gaelic. The Scottish National Party's Member of the European Parliament, and a former Westminster MP, Mrs Winifred Ewing, once told a bemused gathering of Scottish Gaelic language enthusiasts: 'I'm learning *your* language!' While it was laudable that Mrs Ewing was learning Scottish Gaelic, the unfortunate comment was illustrative of prevailing Scottish attitudes.

In fairness to Mrs Ewing, she has since expunged her 'sin of ignorance'. In July, 1984, Mary Banotti, an Irish Member of the European Parliament, began to make her maiden speech to the Parliament in Irish. Since Ireland's entry into the EEC in 1973, Irish has been an *official* EEC language although not one of the seven *working* languages. The Acting-President, the English leader of the Tory group in the Parliament, Lady Elles, claimed: "I do not know what language you are speaking, but I would ask you to continue your speech in one of the seven official laguages of the Community." Mary Banotti then continued her speech in Italian. However, Mrs Ewing intervened to point out that Irish was an 'official language' and asked that Mrs Banotti be allowed to continue. "Irish has been given recognition by the Community. The EEC treaties have been translated into Irish. I wish the same recognition had been given to the language of the country I come from—Scottish Gaelic."

Therefore, it seems that Mrs Ewing is now clear that Scottish Gaelic is the language of Scotland.

Yet how could this 'two nation' myth gain such credence?

Until the 11th Century, the entire population of Alba, by which name Scotland is still known in modern Gaelic, was Celtic in speech and culture. North of the Rivers Clyde and Forth, the people spoke Goidelic or Gaelic. South of this line, however, they spoke Brythonic Celtic. But, during this same period, these southern areas were being rapidly absorbed into the Gaelic-speaking majority and most of the Brythonic place-names were Gaelicized. Gaelic at this time was the *lingua franca* of the entire country—the language of the royal court, of administration, of law, of literature and even of religious worship.

I say 'the entire country' bearing in mind that the Orkneys were not annexed to Scotland until the reign of James III in 1471. Here, the people were Norse in speech and culture as were their settlements on the mainland in Caithness and Sutherland, though the settlers tended to intermarry with the native Gaelic-speaking population and soon made the linguistic change to Celtic. Similarly, the Hebrides, ceded to Scotland in the 13th Century, had a Gaelic-speaking population ruled firstly by the Norse jarls of the Orkneys and later by the Kings of Mannin.

It is somewhat ironic that this 'Norse territory' is now the stronghold of modern Gaelic. The Shetland Islands, also mortgaged to Scotland in 1471, were not Celtic by tradition and now, quite rightly, have their own Shetland Movement for self-government.

North of the Clyde and Forth, 11th Century Scotland was divided into six administrative units which had been carved out of the territorial union of the Picts and Scots in the 9th Century. The Picts were the earliest Celtic inhabitants of Scotland, so called from the Latin *Picti* or 'painted people'. For many years, Scots were enouraged to think that the Picts constituted a separate national identity to the Celts. Early Celtic scholars such as Whitley Stokes, Kuno Meyer, Arbois de Jubainville, Joseph Loth and Alexander MacBain identified the Pict as Celtic but considered them as Brythonic Celts. William F.Skene, perhaps the most notable of early Scottish Celtic scholars, maintained that they were Goidelic. Of the Pictish personal names mentioned by classical writers, most tend to show an affinity to Brythonic rather than Goidelic, although the names appear in both Brythonic and Goidelic form.

All scholars agree on the fact that Gaelic was the common language of the Picts as far back as scholastic research can penetrate. In view of the comparatively unimportant part played by the Dalriada settlement in the early years, it seems incredible that the Pictish language, had it been anything other than a branch of Goidelic, would have vanished so quickly. A branch of the Picts is recorded as dwelling in mid and northern Ireland for many centuries; the last reference to these Irish Picts occurs in the *Annals of Ulster* in 809. In Scotland, the Latin-named Pictavia was called Cruithne-tuath by the Picts themselves, meaning the tribes of Cruithne, the semi-mythical warrior who was said to have founded the Pictish monarchy.

The 3rd Century saw a migration of Celts from Ireland—people called by the Romans Hiberni, Attecotti and Scotti. The Brythonic-speaking Celts called them Gwyddell, hence the mutation into 'Goidel' and 'Gael'. Of the names given to this migratory people, it was the name Scotti which became the most popular and by which the entire country became known in modern times. The

Scotti settled on the Argyll coast (*Airer Ghàidheal*—seaboard of the Gaels). They called their settlement Dalriada (*Dál*—a territory) after their leader Cairbre Riada, son of Conaire II of Munster who had been driven north by a famine in the southern Irish kingdom. Cairbre had initially established a settlement in Antrim in the north of Ireland but he and his followers quarrelled and some settlers followed him to Argyll. It was a descendant of these Dalriadans, Kenneth Mac Alpin, who succeeded in forming a union between the Picts of the Cruithne-tuath and Dalriada. This became the kingdom of Alba with its capital at Sgàin (Scone in Perthshire).

This kingdom was divided into six provinces and they were called *An Mhaorine*—'the stewardry'—the designation surviving in one instance today in the Anglicized form of Mearns. Each province was governed by a *mór-mhaor* (Mormaer of High Steward), answerable only to the *Ard Righ* or High King. These provinces were Moireabh (Moray), which stretched across Scotland from the east coast of modern Aberdeenshire to the west coast of Argyll and was the biggest of all the provinces; and then there was Fótla or Athfhótla which is anglicized as Atholl. This name means 'new Ireland' and the province stretched from Scone in the east to the Mull of Kintyre in the west, and also included the islands of Arran, Jura, Islay and Mull as well as the holy island of Iona, where Colmcille had founded his monastery. There was also the smaller province of Círech, the territory of Angus and Mearns; the province of Cé, modern Marr and Buchan; the province of Fíobh, easily recognizable as Fife; and the province of Fortiriu or Fortrenn, synonyms for Ireland, which covered Strathearn, bridging the Firth of Clyde and the Firth of Forth. (Strathearn is a valley around Loch Earn, originally Loch Éireann or the Lake of Ireland.)

To the south of the Clyde and Forth, the Brythonic-speaking territories had a different relationship to the High King. They were not governed by mormaers (*mor-mhaor*) but by petty kings under the suzereignty of Sgàin (Scone). The first kingdom was that of Clóta or Strathclyde which had its capital at Alcluyd, a town which eventually became known by its Gaelic name Dùn Breatann (Dumbarton), 'the fortress of the Britons'. Strathclyde came under the rule of Sgàin during the reign of Constantine Mac-

Beth (900-942 AD). The second kingdom of Cymru (not to be confused with modern day Cymru—Wales), lay south of the Solway Firth and extended down the west coast of Britain to a point above Barrow-in-Furness. The English retained the name after their annexation of it, pronouncing it in English phonetics—Cum-ree, and the kingdom became Cumbria. Its capital was at Caer Lliwelydd (Carlisle) and it appears to have come under the rule of Sgàin about the same time as Clóta or Strathclyde. It is interesting to note that, in the 11th Century, its petty king displayed a perfect piece of bilingualism between the two branches of Celtic...his name was Owain Mac Domhnull.

It is also fascinating to recall that the earliest surviving poetry in the language we now call Welsh was written in southern Scotland near Edinburgh. Edinburgh was a Brythonic Celtic township called Dinas Eidyn, later Gaelicized to Dùn Éadainn and then Anglicised to Edinburgh. It was Symeon of Durham who miswrote the name as Edwinesburgh and started a popular legend that the town was founded by Angles under a king of that name. Dinas Eidyn was, in fact, the capital of a Celtic tribe called the Gododdin. One of the first surviving 'Welsh' poems comes down to us in the *Llyfr Aneurin* (The book of Aneurin), entitled *Y Gododdin*. Aneurin was a 6th Century poet living at the court of Mynddawg Mwynvawr, the king of the tribe. Aneurin tells how 300 warriors of his people went to attack Caertraeth (Catterick in Yorkshire) to reclaim it from the invading Angles. The attack failed and the warriors were slain. Other famous 'Welsh' poets of the 6th Century, Taliesin and Llywarch Hen, were actually born and brought up in southern Scotland.

It was in the 6th Century that groups of Angles and Flemings began to settle around the mouth of the River Tweed and impose their rule on the native Brythonic Celts. They established a small kingdom which they called Bernica and which the Celts called Lleudduniawn (Lothian). By the end of the 10th Century, this small kingdom with its ruling class of Angles and its peasant class of Celts, had become part of the earldom of Northumbria. Bernica did not stretch much beyond the Lammermuir Hills and it certainly did not cover the major part of southern Scotland, as the popular myth maintains.

It was in 1018 that Malcolm II decided to seize the territory of

Bernica for Scotland. The territory was of strategic importance against attacks from England but the majority of the population was Celtic and resentful of life under an alien feudal system. Malcolm's army met the Northumbrian army of Eadulf Cudel at Carham, a few miles above Coldstream, and won the day. Henceforth, the territory of Bernica north of the Tweed became an integral part of Scottish territory. Professor Kenneth Jackson, in *The Celtic Aftermath in the Islands*, affirms that "in consequence of this (Carham) the whole of Scotland became for a time Gaelic in speech". Professor W.J.Watson in "The Position of Gaelic in Scotland" (his inaugural address at Edinburgh University) comfirms that "Gaelic attained its greatest extent in the Eleventh Century when at the time of Carham in 1018 it ran from Tweed and Solway to Pentland Firth".

How, then, has Gaelic been reduced to the confused place in history with which modern Scots view it?

The tragedy of MacBeth marks the turning point of Celtic Scotland. But we must forget the Macbeth of Shakespeare if we are to fully understand the situation. MacBeth Mac Findlaech was elected High King of Scotland in August, 1040, according to the Celtic law system which did not recognize primogeniture. He was 35 years-old and had just overthrown in battle his despotic cousin, Duncan Mac Crinan, his senior by four years, who had been one of Scotland's most unpopular rulers, having led them in six years of inept rule during which he had suffered defeat after defeat by the English and the Norse forces. For seventeen years, MacBeth ruled Scotland wisely and well, without embarking on any wars of aggression. So stable and peaceful did Scotland become that MacBeth was able to go on pilgrimage to Rome in 1050, without any fear of being overthrown in his absence.

However, Duncan Mac Crinan had three sons, the eldest of whom, Maol-Callum (St Colm's Servant), Malcolm, had been taken to the English court by his Danish mother. Malcolm grew up entrenched in the English theory of hereditary right and primogeniture and believing, therefore, that he was rightfully King of Scotland. In 1054, having grown to manhood, he persuaded the English to give him an army to contest the claim. It took Malcolm three long years of warfare before MacBeth was 'slain by strategem', a sure sign that he was assassinated rather than slain in battle. Even so, Scotland rejected Malcolm's claim and Lulach, the son of MacBeth's cousin, Gillecomgáin, was elected High King. Lulach, in continuing the warfare against Malcolm, was eventually slain in battle in 1058.

Malcolm, by force of arms, had made himself Malcolm III of Scotland and became known as Callum *a' chinn mhòr,* Malcolm Canmore or Malcolm the Bighead. He could not have been opposed initially to Gaelic—after all, it was the language of the country, of the court, of administration, law, literature and religious worship. Contemporary chroniclers agree that Gaelic was his native tongue but he had also grown up proficient in Danish (his mother's language) and in the Norman-French of his English royal mentor, Edward the Confessor. He would also have learned Anglo-Saxon, and having grown up in England, he would have inherited social concepts that were alien to the Celtic system, which was already under pressure from the Roman Church's orthodoxy.

Malcolm, whose first wife, Ingibjorg of the Orkneys, had died, then married Margaret, the sister of Edgar Aetheling, claimant to the English throne now that William the Conqueror had removed the Anglo-Saxon royal house and taken England for himself. It is another myth of Scottish history that Margaret was supposed to have made the Scottish Court speak English, and so initiated the decline of Gaelic as the language of the ruling class. Yet Margaret's father, Edward the Outlaw, had lived all his life in Hungary and had married a Hungarian princess. When her brother, Edgar Aetheling, came to England, the chroniclers state that he was not seriously considered as a suitable candidate for the English succession because he could not speak English. It was unlikely that his sister Margaret, who went to England with him, was any more proficient in the tongue.

It is certainly true that Margaret protested against the use of Gaelic in the churches of Scotland, where she claimed that mass was celebrated in the vulgar tongue "with I know not what barbaric rites". Margaret instigated a debate on the state of the Scottish Church and invited three Benedictine monks from Canterbury to dispute with the Scottish monks and clergy on the merits of changing from Celtic to Roman usage. The result was that the Scottish Church was forced to fall in line with Rome and adopt

Latin as the language of worship.

Malcolm was killed in fighting his former allies, the English, in 1093. Margaret survived him by only three days. The people of Scotland saw an opportunity to break away from the 'alien rule' of Malcolm and Margaret and return to the old Celtic system. Malcolm had a young brother called Domhnall Bàn (Fair Donald) who had been raised in the Hebrides while his brother was being educated in England. Domhnall Bàn was entirely Celtic in attitude. So, at the age of 63 years, he was elected High King in the traditional manner. According to the *Anglo-Saxon Chronicle*: "The Scots drove out all the English who were with King Malcolm before".

The return of an independent Gaelic Scotland was not a prospect desired by William Rufus of England. He wanted to see Scotland ruled by a man who would acknowledge English suzerainty and so he backed Duncan, Malcolm III's son by his first wife Ingibjorg, who had grown up as a Norman knight at the English court. Duncan set off for Scotland with an English army to gain the throne. By May, 1094, Duncan and his army had established themselves in Edinburgh and he became the first Scottish King to style himself thus: "I, Duncan, son of King Malcolm, *by hereditary right* King of Scotia!" Duncan did not rule for long. He was slain on November 12th, 1094, by Maol Peadar Mac Leon, the mormaer of Círech. Domhnall Bàn returned in triumph. He ruled Scotland for three years, attempting to return all the Celtic customs and laws which Malcolm and Margaret had rejected.

In October, 1097, Edgar, a son of Malcolm and Margaret, with another English army, invaded Scotland and took Domhnall Bàn prisoner, proclaiming himself king. Edgar had the eyes of Domhnall Bàn struck out and the old king died at Roscobie in Forfar. With the ascendancy of Malcolm and Margaret's children as rulers of Scotland, the end of the Celtic laws and customs was only a matter of time. Edgar, Alexander and David, who were to succeed each other to the Scottish throne, had been raised in an Anglo-Norman environment and encouraged the settlement of Anglo-Normans amongst the ruling class in Scotland. So it is feasible to argue that in MacBeth, Scotland had its last great Gaelic ruler and that he represented the native order, as opposed to the foreign feudal order which began with the coming of Malcolm III to the Scottish throne.

From the 12th Century, the language of the Scottish Court became firstly Norman-Frech and subsequently English. It took many centuries for Gaelic to be pushed out of southern Scotland; in fact in Galloway it did not recede until the 18th Century. Many times, over the centuries, historians have attacked the popular myths that Gaelic was never spoken in the 'Lowlands' of Scotland. Evan MacLeod Barron in *The Scottish War of Independence: A Critical Study*, 1914, wrote:

> It is high time, indeed, that the English myth in Scotland was exploded once and for all. The only people of English blood who are found in any numbers in Scotland are the people of Lothian...Moreover, all recent research goes to show that in the thirteenth century the language of the bulk of the people outside Lothian was Celtic. In the district to the south of the Forth and Clyde as well as to the north, Celtic, save in Lothian, was the popular tongue.

It must be pointed out that the term 'Lothian' referred to Bernica and not the modern and recently created 'Lothian' counties.

One would have thought that Professor W.J. Watson's excellent work, *History of the Celtic Place Names of Scotland*, Blackwood, 1926, would have exploded the myth for all time. All over the south of Scotland, Gaelic place-names are found in such profusion that it is obvious that they were not given by invading skirmishers from the 'Highlands' but by generations of Gaelic-speaking inhabitants. Take Peebles, for example, where there are ninety-nine pure Gaelic place-names such as Fingland from *Fhionn Ghleann*, the bright glen; Achingall from *Achadh nan Gall*, the field of strangers; and Kilduff, south-east of Edinburgh, from Coille Dubh, the black wood. Dalry, now part of the city of Edinburgh, could have come from *Dail an Righ*, the king's meadow, or *Dail Fhraoigh*, heather meadow. Gilmerton, near Edinburgh, comes from *Gille Mhuire*, Mary's servant. The Braid Hills themselves are named from *Braghaid*, a dative of *Braighe*, meaning upper park. Glencourse, written Glencrosk in the 14th Century, means glen of the crossings, in the area. Drumsheugh (written Drumselch in 1507) comes from Drum Seileach or willow ridge. Currie is taken from the dative of Curach—a wet place. Craighentinnie comes from *Creag an tSionneaigh*—the fox's rock. Close by Castellan of Dumbar is a knoll called Knockenhair from *Cnoc an h-Aire*, the watch hill. One could go on indefinitely wandering the 'lowlands' and deciphering their Gaelic place-names. Galloway, in south-west Scotland, remained Gaelic in speech until the 18th Century.

Blind Harry, a Scottish poet, presents us with evidence that the redoubtable William Wallace, who became Guardian of Scotland during the Second Interregnum in 1296-1306, spoke Gaelic while Robert the Bruce is on record as holding a parliament at St Modan's Priory, Ardchattan, in 1308 AD, in which all business was conducted in Gaelic. In 1315, Robert Bruce sent a message to the Irish chieftains and petty kings:

> Whereas we and you, and our people, free since ancient times, share the same national ancestry and are urged to come together more eagerly and joyfully in Friendship by a common language and by common custom, we have sent over to you our beloved kinsmen, the bearers of this letter, to negotiate with you in our name about permanently strengthening and maintaining inviolate the special friendship between us and you, so that with God's will your nation may be able to recover her ancient liberty.

The result was Robert's brother Edward Bruce was crowned King of Ireland in 1316 and was subsequently invited by the Welsh chieftains to assume the title of Prince of Wales.

Senor Ayala, the Spanish ambassador to the Scottish Court, recorded that James IV (1488-1513) was the last Scottish monarch to speak Gaelic.

According to Andrew Trevisano, the Venetian ambassador, writing about 1500:

> The language of the Scots is the same as that of the Irish, and very different from the English; but many of the Scottish people speak English extremely well in consequence of the intercourse they have with each other on the borders.

Hector Boece, writing about 1527, and probably more responsible than any man for the creation of the Macbeth of Shakespeare's vision, admitted that "those of us who live on the borders of England have forsaken our mother tongue (Gaelic) and learned English being driven thereto by wars and commerce". Another historian of the time, John Major, in *The History of Greater Britain*, 1521, also admitted that the majority of Scottish people had spoken Gaelic only "a short time ago" and that the language was still in fairly widespread use. This was confirmed by the historian George Buchanan who mentions the widespread use of the language in southern Scotland during the 16th Century.

Towards the end of the 15th Century, two notable poets had clashed in literary battle. One of them was Walter Kennedy, son of Gilbert, Lord Kennedy of Carrick, a Gaelic poet. The other was William Dunbar who represented the new 'Inglis'-speaking order in Scotland. In a long poem, *The Flyting, or Scalding, of Dunbar and Kennedy* (*circa* 1460-1508), Dunbar accuses Kennedy of being too Gaelic and contrasts the characteristics of the Gaels with those of the 'Inglis'-speakers to whom he belongs. Kennedy, who was born and raised in Dunure, Ayrshire, condemns Dunbar's superior attitudes and answers that Gaelic was the only language for anyone who called himself a Scotsman. "It was the good language of this land and caused Scotland to multiply and spread", he said.

An English official, preparing a report between 1563-66 on the possibility of the military occupation of Carrick, Kyle and Cunningham by an English army, wrote of the town of Carrick: "The people for the moste parte spekenht Erische". *Galloway Gossip*, 1901, quotes a report that as late as 1762 the parish of Barr in Carrick had advertised for a schoolmaster and it was particularly requested "that he budst be able tae speak Gaelic (and) the man they took was frae aboot the Lennox". The same records show that during the 1715 and 1745 insurrections in Scotland, 'Highland' troops passed through the area. "Forbye whun the Rebels wus passin' through Gallowa' and Carrick in 1715 and 1745 the Hielanmen wus able tae converse freely with the natives, but naither the natives nor the Hielanmen could talk wi' the Erische auxiliaries for their Gaelic wus that different they cud hardly mak them oot". Margaret MacMurray of Cultzeon, near Maybole, who died about 1760, was generally accredited with having been the last native speaker of Gaelic in Carrick. Be it remembered that Robert Burns was born near Ayr 'on the Carrick border' in 1759.

In 1725, the English traveller Edward Burt, writing in *Letters from a Gentleman in the North of Scotland*, observed that Gaelic was current in Fife, just opposite Edinburgh, until the early 18th Century. He says that, until the Union of 1707, it was made a condition that when a boy or girl was bound as an apprentice on the Edinburgh side of the Forth, he or she had to be taught English. Burt also says that Sir James Foulis of Colington had informed him "he had it from an old man, who spoke Gaelic, that even in his time it was the universal language of Fife".

So it was in the 15th Century that a clear change in linguistic thinking took place in Scotland which created the 'Highland'/ 'Lowland' division. Previously, writers such as John of Fordun (d.1384 AD) had made it clear that the new language spoken by the ruling class and growing merchant class in southern Scotland was 'Inglis' or English, and that the Gaelic spoken by the majority of the people was 'Scottish'. But it was the 'Inglis'-speaking ruling class which had led wars of independence against the English. To tell them that they were speaking the language of the enemy would not do. A similar problem had arisen in England during its Hundred Years' War with France; the Norman-French ruling class had changed its language from Norman-French to English, as a means of encouraging the English-speaking peasantry to fight against the French on a national basis, without becoming confused about their allegiance. With Scotland, the problem was resolved in a different way.

So that they could retain their Scottish nationality without becoming Scottish in speech, the Anglicized Scots and descendants of the Norman and English settlers began to call the Scottish language Yrisch, Ersch and Irish (today, it is simply called Gaelic); and their own English speech was designated as Scots, Scottish or sometimes 'Lallans'. Gavin Douglas (1457-1577) was the first writer to call the Scottish dialect of English 'Scots'. Thus the first major wedge was driven detween the Gaelic-speaking Scot and the Anglicized Scot. The 'two nation' myth was formed.

A further blow, about this time, was the Scottish Reformation during which there came into being, in Scotland, an anti-Gaelic government dedicated to the total extirpation of Gaelic. Gaelic was seen as an obstacle to the spread of Protestant ideas and "English schools for rooting out the Irish language and other pious uses" were created. These institutions, still strangely regarded as a progressive education system by modern Scottish historians, were merely instruments of a sustained policy of cultural genocide in Scotland. The problem was that they were created by a native Scottish government before the union of the Scottish monarchy with that of England.

The Reformation can be blamed for the lack of old literature in Gaelic. James Loch, an architect of the 19th Century genocidal 'clearances', tried to justify his policy of stamping out the language by saying that nothing had ever been written in Gaelic, and therefore it was a worthless language. Even today, responsible historians like George Pryde seem to propagate this weird theory. But there are remains and, such Gaelic literature that has come down to us from the Pre-Reformation period, meagre evidence though it may be, shows that the Scottish Celts were heirs to an extremely ancient and sophisticated learning.

Libraries full of Gaelic works must have been destroyed by the anti-Gaelic administrators of the country. One such complete library of Gaelic books was seen and catalogued by the Celtic scholar Edward Lhuyd in 1699: the catalogue survived but the library was destroyed. It is sad to reflect on the wealth of literature which must have perished. All that is left is *The Book of Deer* with its Gaelic notations from the 9th Century, an 11th Century poem, and then there is a surprising gap before we find the Islay Charter of 1408. This Charter not only demonstrates a sophisticated literary medium, the obvious product of a long tradition of writing in the language, but also proves that Gaelic was still being used as the language of administration, for which it was absolutely necessary.

From the purely literary viewpoint, the most important surviving manuscript is the *Book of the Dean of Lismore* compiled between 1512 and 1526, containing an anthology of Gaelic poetry. The first known printed Gaelic book was Bishop John Carswell's *Form na h-Ordaigh*, 1567, a prayer book which translated John Knox's liturgy. And yet, such is the disrepute in which Gaelic is now held, that as recently as 1961 a Scottish historian, George Pryde, in *A New History of Scotland*, could solemnly assure his readers that the first book was not printed in Gaelic until the late 18th Century AD...in spite of the fact that the entire Bible was published in Gaelic in 1690.

Dr I.F.Grant, in his *History of the Clan MacLeod* asks a pertinent question: "There are no rent rolls, deeds of fosterage or similar documents as early as Rory Mór MacLeod of Dunvegan, d.1626). Can it have been that they were all destroyed?" The simple answer is—yes. The destruction was almost complete but, pathetic though the remnants are, they are evidence of a wealth of literature and records in Gaelic which were unacceptable to the anti-Gaelic reformers.

The linguistic persecutions of the 16th Century have had a profound effect on the country's understanding of its past and this is the explanation behind the 'two nation' myth. Unfortunately, even some of the friends of Gaelic and its culture have led the Scottish people further into the mire of this myth, by the instigation of the 20th Century 'Scots Revival' of literature in the Scottish dialect of English. Hugh MacDiarmid (C.M.Grieve) now regarded as Scotland's greatest poet, was chief architect of what was called the 'Scottish Renaissance'. Yet MacDiarmid did not subscribe to the 'two nation' myth and he clearly recognized Gaelic as the Scottish, or national, language. As late as 1935, in his pamphlet *Scotland in 1980*, MacDiarmid stated that his hope lay in the restoration of Gaelic with "eighty per cent of all the creative literature of any value" in Scotland being written in the language. He repeated this and his ideal for the re-establishment of a Gaelic Commonwealth in Scotland in his auto-biography *Lucky Poet* (Methuen, 1943). MacDiarmid, too, was an early adherent to the pan-Celtic idea and, until his death, he never ceased to propagate his determination to "work for the establishment of Workers' Republics in Scotland, Ireland, Wales and Cornwall, and, indeed, make a sort of Celtic union of Socialist Soviet Republics in the British Isles". Unfortunately, aside from adopting a more obviously Celtic name, Hugh MacDiarmid did not lend his literary genius to writing in the language he recognized to be his national tongue and which he wished to see restored across the country. He felt it was asking too much of the bulk of Scottish people to get them to accept Gaelic, whereas the acceptance of 'Lallans' might be a *first step*. Unfortunately, those who followed him, adherents of the 'Scottish Renaissance', saw it as the *only step* and it became a further entrenchment of the 'two nation' myth.

Under its Anglicized and anti-Celtic monarchy and government, Scotland remained independent until 1603, when the English Privy Council invited James VI of Scotland to succeed Elizabeth I of England. Thus James became James I of England and a Union of Crowns took place. James immediately started to press for a union of parliaments but he met strong opposition from both nations. The English Parliament rejected the proposal by an overwhelming vote in 1607 AD. From 1603, however, the citizens of both countries enjoyed the same citizenship rights and the political commitment that, when England went to war, so too did Scotland. Nothing was said of any reverse commitment. To all intents and purposes, Scotland had become a semi-independent province. The Scottish Parliament continued its anti-Gaelic policies which, after the Union of Crowns became, if anything, more vicious. In 1609, the suppression of bards was strictly enforced. Chieftains were made to send their children to English-speaking schools and, in 1616, an Act was passed seeking to totally suppress Gaelic. This act was confirmed again by the Scottish Parliament in 1631, again in 1649, and yet again in 1696.

By the end of the 17th Century, however, Scotland's ruling class was feeling politically impotent. Professor J.MacKinnon in his *The Union Between England and Scotland* sums up the position in these words:

> A century of English interference, religious dissension and international friction, had reduced the country to beggary and impotence. Contemporary writers are unanimous in charging the political system established in 1603 as the main cause of the national depression that culminated in the poverty and misery of the last decades of the 17th and the opening years of the 18th Centuries, Misgovernment, with its adjuncts of civil and religious strife, was the fruit of a system which placed the fate of Scotland in the hands of an Anglified Monarch whose Scottish Ministers were more or less the tools of English influence and interests.

With the removal of the Stuart family from the English throne, Scottish antipathy towards England heightened. William IV did little to gain the respect of the Scots and is remembered for his signing of the order for the infamous Massacre of Glencoe of February 13th, 1692, a fact conveniently overlooked by Scots who support the archaic Orange Order. In 1693, the Scottish Parliament passed an Act which led to the establishment of the Company of Scotland Trading to Africa and the Indies. The Scots decided to establish their own colonies and trade links. On July 21st, 1698, the Scottish Parliament established a colony on the isthmus of Darien (Panama). Illness broke out, the Spanish attacked them and the English in the West Indies were under the specific orders of their government to refuse assistance and shelter. Some 2,000 Scottish settlers' lives were lost. There were anti-English riots in Scotland when the facts became known.

In 1703, the Scottish Parliament enraged England by passing an 'Act Anent Peace and War' which stipulated that no sovereign could declare war on Scotland's behalf without the consent of the Scottish Parliament. Further Acts were passed in direct opposition to English trade regulations. Finally, the first move towards a severance from the English monarchy was made. In 1701, just before Queen Anne came to the throne, the English Parliament had passed an Act of Settlement declaring the Crown should go to Sophia, Electress of Hanover, on Anne's death, so that there would be no chance of a Stuart Restoration. In 1704, the Scottish Parliament passed an Act of Security which enforced Scotland's right to choose her own monarch after Anne's death. This alarmed the English Parliament which passed an Alien Act, declaring that if Scotland did not agree to England's choice of monarch, Scots would be treated as aliens and would no longer enjoy dual citizenship.

Behind the scenes, England's politicians were worried at the possible severance of the union of crowns. They sent an agent in the person of Daniel Defoe (author of *Robinson Crusoe*) to Edinburgh, to dispense bribes in order to persuade Scottish Parliament members to agree to a union of Parliaments. It was a difficult task and Defoe did not hold out any hopes—after all, popular opinion in Scotland was for greater independence not for greater union. But the bribes worked. After a three-month debate, the question was put to the vote. The voting was 110 for the union and 69 against. The theory was that Scotland and England would become co-equal partners, that the names 'Scotland' and 'England' would disappear, to be replaced by the name 'Great Britain'. The Treaty of Union of 1707 was, in fact, the written consitution of the new state. Within a short time, England began to break the provisions of the Treaty and the Scots, duped into sending 16 peers and 45 commoners to the Parliament in London, had no powers to protest.

The first Self-Government for Scotland Bill was introduced in Westminster in 1714. English reaction was predictable. The Speaker of the House of Commons said: "The English had catcht Scotland and would keep her fast". The Lord Treasurer commented: "Have we not *bought* the Scots and the right to tax them?" Daniel Defoe made no bones about the situation as he saw it: "If ever a nation gained by being conquered it was here". England had conquered Scotland and of that they were in no doubt. Within a few years, Scotland was left in no doubt of its conquest.

The people of Scotland decided to put their faith in a restoration of the Stuart monarchy but the first attempted insurrection in 1708 was abortive. Then came the more famous uprising of 1715, minor risings in 1719 and 1720 and, the most famous of all, in 1745. After the 1745 rebellion a 'pacification' of the Gaelic-speaking areas, whose support for the insurrections had been total, was carried out with the extreme ruthlessness. Not only the language was vigorously crushed but the visible signs of Celtic culture, such as the wearing of the kilt, the tartan, and the playing of bagpipes. The social structure of the old clan system, was broken down. In 1777, the Gaelic Society of London was formed and became successful in securing the repeal of some of these genocidal measures in 1782 and 1784 AD. The Gaelic Society of London still exists.

The insurrections between 1708 and 1745 have been passed off by historians as Jacobite manifestations. The point is that the Stuarts would have had no support in Scotland had they not made the dissolution of the Union of 1707 one of their prime policies. When the Stuart cause failed, the new creed of republicanism pointed the way for the Scots.

The movements of the 1790's, such as the 'Friends of the People' and the more shadowy 'United Scotsmen', sought to establish a Scottish Republic. The Scots made an attempt to convince the new French Republic to aid them. The French were giving similar aid to Ireland. In 1796, the French Committee of Public Safety sent Citoyen Mengaud, as their emissary to the revolutionary movement in Scotland, and he reported back that the Scots were much disposed to revolution and "this feeling had existed since the

Union of England and Scotland". But the carefully planned uprising was triggered off prematurely by the enforcement of the Militia (Conscription) Ballot Act in 1797. Only in Perthshire did the United Scotsmen, under Angus Cameron, have any success, capturing the Castle Menzies, taking prisoner the Duke of Atholl and Sir John Menzies. It was reported that Cameron had 16,000 men in the field. The uprising was crushed and the United Scotsmen were vigorously suppressed. Nevertheless, the United Scotsmen movement continued its existence into the early years of the 19th Century.

In 1820, another major uprising took place, mainly confined to Renfrew, Dumbarton, Ayr, Stirling and Lanark. It was radical in politics and gregarian in spirit. Its leaders also saw the dissolution of the Union as a prime objective, planning to establish a Scottish Parliament. The uprising resulted in 88 trials for high treason, three executions, and 22 transportations for life, as well as numerous jail sentences.

Agitation, including a near insurrection swiftly crushed in 1848, continued throughout the 19th Century. In 1889, as a result of the agitation for the dissolution of the Union, the first Scottish Self-Government Bill since 1714 was introduced at Westminster. Since then, there have been no less than 26 Self-Goverment motions and bills, all of which have been vetoed by the English majority in Parliament. It is interesting to note that of those motions and bills which have come to a vote in Parliament, the majority of Scottish members have always been in favour.

With the formation of a National Association for the Vindication of Scottish Rights in 1853, the Scottish people put their faith in constitutional means to obtain self-government. "We must demand a Scottish Parliament on Scottish soil", argued Lord Eglington, chairman of the Association. From this movement grew the Scottish Home Rule Association, founded in 1886 and supported by the Edinburgh newspaper *The Scotsman* which, in the following year, published a Charter of Home Rule. At first, the Liberal Party pledged themselves to Home Rule, only to drop the idea when coming to power. Later, the Labour Party supported it—also dropping the idea when in power.

Of the many Scottish national organizations founded in the late 19th Century, it was Comunn an Fhearainn, the Highland Land

League, which kept to the radical aims of the 1820 insurrectionists and was active between 1883 and 1895, born in the wake of the terrible Highland Clearances when landlords found that sheep were worth more than people, and cleared large areas of Gaelic-speakers from their estates in order to replace them with sheep runs. Many thousands of Scots were forced to migrate and the Clearances were yet another genocidal blow against Gaelic. Comunn an Fhearainn was re-established in the early 20th Century and sought the establishment of a Scottish Parliament, and the restoration of Gaelic as the national language of all Scotland. It was the Hon. Ruaraidh Erskine of Marr, founder of the Gaelic periodical *Guth na Bliadhna* (Voice of the Year) who helped reactivate the movement with the aim "that Scotland may become again an independent nation".

The early decades of the 20th Century saw the emergence of many Scottish 'fundamentalists' such as Erskine—men who saw beyond the 'two nation' myth. Seumas Mac Garaidh was an unrepentant Gaelic republican until his death in exile, in California, USA, in 1966, aged 81. There was the great Scottish radical, and friend of James Connolly, John MacLean, who formed a Scottish Workers' Republican Party in 1920 and stood as a parliamentary candidate for Gorbals, Glasgow, in 1922, expressing his faith in a Scottish Workers' Republic. MacLean died on November 30th, 1923, at the early age of 44 from pneumonia attributed to the severe hardships he had suffered while imprisoned for his beliefs during the First World War. Some 40,000 Scots followed his funeral cortège. MacLean was deeply committed to supporting the struggle of Scotland's fellow Celts in Ireland and many shared his view. Grahame Mackenzie-Kennedy of Inverness joined the Irish Volunteers in 1916, learned Irish, fought for the IRA in the War of Independence and, still serving in the West Cork Brigade, he fell defending the Republic in the Irish Civil War in August, 1922. A Glaswegian, S.Reeder, commanded a Scottish Brigade of the IRA in 1919-21.

Eventually, in 1928, the various Scottish national movements tried to submerge their differences and join together into a Scottish National Party but, within a few years, fragmentation occurred again. Nevertheless, the Scottish National Party emerged to remain the foremost of the Scottish political bodies seeking independence. The SNP's first election success came in 1945 when Dr Robert M.MacIntyre was elected to Parliament for Motherwell. A more spectacular election victory was that of Mrs Winifred Ewing who took the seat at Hamilton on Novermber 2nd, 1967. In the 1970 General Election, the SNP increased its representation even further and the Gaelic-speaking Western Isles returned Donald Stewart to represent them. In the General Election of 1974, SNP won an even greater success with the return of eleven MP's to Parliament. This success caused the British Labour Government to make proposals for a Scottish Devolution Bill which would establish a Scottish Assembly. It was to be simply a 'talking shop', lacking in fiscal powers. Many Scots saw this as a necessary 'first step'. In March, 1979, the Government declared a referendum on the subject. Some 1,230,-937 voters (52 per cent of the votes polled) voted in favour of a Scottish Assembly, while 1,153,502 (48 per cent of the votes polled) voted against. However, it was declared that Westminster needed a two-thirds 'yes' majority before they would establish such an assembly. While the majority had been in favour, the idea was dropped.

Later that year, Margaret Thatcher and the Conservative Party came to power. It was the first General Election in which the new 'British' Social Democratic Party stood, causing many voting splits. The SNP lost the majority of the seats it had gained earlier although, that same year, in the first elections for the European Parliament, Winifred Ewing won the seat for the Western Islands. In the 1983 General Election, SNP managed to hang on to only two seats, in the Western Islands and in Dundee East. Against a background of falling membership and dropping income, SNP continued to do well at local council elections and remain the third largest party in Scotland in terms of votes. The 1984 European Parliament elections saw Mrs Ewing hold her seat with an increased majority. While SNP continued to be the major national political party, it tended to concentrate on economics rather than the fundamentals of national freedom.

One year after the referendum which declared in favour of a Scottish Assembly, a Campaign for a Scottish Assembly was formed, trying to gain all-party support. Its first National Convention was held in 1981 and became an annual event. A 'Blueprint for Scotland' was published at the 2nd National Convention. At the same time, *The Scotsman* published an opinion poll's results, showing that 69 per cent of the Scottish electorate wanted a Scottish Parliament in some form or other. In the 1983 General Election, the Conservatives had won only 21 of the 72 Scottish seats, holding 20 of them on a minority vote. All other candidates declared a commitment to some form of 'devolution'. The Campaign therefore declared, in 1984, that the pro-Assembly parties form local arrangements, to put forward one candidate as a pro-Scottish Assembly candidate to achieve the establishment of such an assembly.

On December 14th, 1983, Archie Kirkwood MP had moved in the House of Commons to introduce a bill seeking to establish a Scottish Parliament. It was the 26th such motion in the past one hundred years. Out of the 355 members who voted, 111 voted for the motion and 244 voted against it. Of the 72 Scottish MP's, the majority voted in favour. This 'undemocratic' fact was pointed out to the Speaker but he ruled that he had no power to restrict the vote to Scottish members. The constitutional position of Scotland remained the same; no matter how many times a majority of Scottish Members of Parliament voted for self-government, they were always over-ruled by the majority of English Members of Parliament.

Frustration at the blocking of the 'constitutional' path to independence has tended to show itself from time to time by the emergence of various manifestations of Scottish Liberation Armies. Throughout the 1970's and early 1980's, there were many trials of alleged members; many of the prosecutions were clearly demonstrated to be the result of agent provocateurs and of police political harassment. In March, 1972, members of the Workers' Party of Scotland were given lengthy jail sentences for armed bank robberies by which, the prosecution alleged, they intended to fund guerilla warfare. Matt Lygate, Chairman of the Party, who had stood as a parliamentary candidate in 1969, and was editor of the Party's journal *Scottish Vanguard*, received 24 years' jail; Colin Lawson, party treasurer, also received 24 years; William MacPherson, Vice-Chairman of the Party, received 26 years'—which was then the longest prison sentence ever given in Scotland at that date, and Ian Doran received 25 years. Many others have followed them to jail since then.

Returning to the question of *nationality*, unlike the situation in other Celtic countries, the language has not been the basis of the national movement in Scotland because of the 'two nation' myth so strongly accepted even among so-called 'nationalists'. That the Scottish Gaelic language has survived at all is a matter of surprise. In spite of the persecutions of the Scottish Reformation and the anti-Gaelic policies of the 17th Century, as well as the repression of the 18th Century, the language had produced a highly cultured and lively literary medium, with the works of poets such as Iain Lom, Alasdair Mac Mhaighistir Alasdair, Iain Mac Codrum, Donnachadh Bàn Mac an tSaoir, Rob Donn Mac Aoidh, Màiri Ni Ghean, Alasdair Ruadh and others.

In spite of the anti-Gaelic policies, the Society for Propagating Christian Knowledge (SPCK) found that they had to use Gaelic as a means of instruction and this lead to the publishing of new versions of the New Testament in 1767 and of the Old Testament in 1801. (The complete Bible, a Scottish version of Bedell's Irish Bible, had already been printed in Gaelic in 1690 AD.) At this time, it is estimated that there were at least 300,000 people who could not speak English and so, in 1824, Gaelic textbooks were introduced in SPCK schools. So, in spite of attempts to eradicate the language, a new literacey was actually springing up with Gaelic publishing houses and two weekly newspapers *An Gàidhael* (The Gael) and *Mac Talla* (The Echo), the latter an import from the Gaelic-speaking area of Nova Scotia, Canada—both achieving wide circulations.

From 1881, the Government Census carried a question on the language and discovered that 254,415 people spoke Gaelic, 6.84 per cent of the population. By 1901, there were 230,813 Gaelic-speakers with 28,106 who spoke no English. The Gaelic-speaking population continued to decline rapidly and, by the 1961 Census, the figure had reached 1.66 per cent of the population, some 80,978 people. Then, against the background of a new enthusiasm in the Celtic world, there came an incredible development. The 1971 Census showed there to be 88,415 speakers of the language, or 1.8 per cent of the population. Publication of the Census volume was delayed while the figures were checked. Scotland had become unique in being the only Celtic country to show a significant increase in the number of native speakers of its language. The 1981 Census showed a decrease again to 79,307 (1.6 per cent) but a foreward added that 3,313 persons claimed to be able to read and write the language but not speak it. These had been deleted as literacy questions were not valid. Of course, such census figures do not show Gaelic-speakers domiciled outside of Scotland.

After education became firmly controlled by the State in 1870, Gaelic was not allowed to be used in schools, either as a medium of instruction or as a subject in itself in the Gaelic-speaking areas. In 1899, An Comunn Gàidhealach was founded, in order to promote the language and its use, growing out of the Gaelic Society of Inverness which had been formed in 1871. Both movements were active in asking that Gaelic be used and recognized for teaching purposes in the Gaelic-speaking areas. An Comunn Gàidhealach became the 'established' language movement, even receiving a small Government pittance to promote annual musical and literary festivals, providing a focus of cultural activity, acting as a pressure group and as a publishing agency. For a while, in the late 1960's and early 1970's, it published its own bilingual fortnightly newspaper *Sruth*.

The 1918 Education Act instructed local authorities to make "adequate provision for teaching Gaelic in Gaelic-speaking areas". In spite of this, persecution of the language continued. Right up to the 1960's many Scots could recount experiences with the *Maidhe crochaidh* or 'beating stick' which was hung around his or her neck if he or she were overheard speaking Gaelic. The idea was that the child heard speaking the language would have the stick placed around their neck and, when they heard another child speak the language, they would pass it on, and so on. At the end of the day, the teacher called for the stick and began to systematically flog each child who had worn it during the day. Even in the 1950's, there was a psychologically-shattering case of a schoolteacher in Lewis who used to hang a human skull around the neck of the child who dared speak in Gaelic.

Some years ago, the Scottish Council for Research in Education published a report which stated that Gaelic was being systematically destroyed in Scotland by "the state system of compulsory education in English".

In October, 1969, a new language movement was launched by the Scottish author and journalist, Seumas Mac a' Ghobhainn. It was to be a fundamentalist movement on the lines of the Welsh Language Society. He called it Comunn na Cànain Albannaich—the Scottish Language Society. In justifying why the CNCA was needed, when An Communn Gàidhealch had been in existence since 1899, a statement was issued saying:

> Mòds and other festivals are all right, but they will not stop the ordinary man from being forced to use English in order to earn a living. Neither will they stop the criminal destruction of the Scottish Gaelic-speaking communities in North and South Uist.

At the time, the British Government was establishing rocket-testing ranges on the Uist islands and importing a thousand English soldiers into the area with their families. Children of these families were sent to local schools and their presence in the classrooms forced the medium of education to be changed from Gaelic to English.

Comunn na Cànain Albannaich started in a small way, attracting members and building up a detailed account of the exact position of Gaelic in all walks of Scottish society. it was felt unwise to launch immediate campaigns of civil disobedience along the lines of the Welsh model. Minor campaigns were undertaken such as sending letters addressed in Gaelic through the mail. The Post Office steadfastly refused to deliver such letters. CNCA followed this by a poster and sticker campaign, drawing attention to the plight of Gaelic.

In October, 1971, CNCA was able to hold its first public meeting in Glasgow at which Seumas Mac a' Ghobhainn stepped down to continue his researches into the history of the language. CNCA continued to be active during the 1970's, achieving a small victory by getting a change of heart at the Post Office, securing bilingual road signs in certain areas and achieving a marginal increase in the amount of hours devoted to broadcasting in the language. In 1972, after being pressed about the appallingly low percentage of broadcasting in Gaelic, the BBC proposed a local Gaelic radio station but it was discovered that only for 13 hours a week would there be broadcasts in the language. After some protests, this has been increased and Radio nan Eilean now broadcasts from Stornoway on Lewis. BBC Radio Highlands, based in

Inverness, also uses some Gaelic.

Support for CNCA was sporadic and not widespread. Most language enthusiasts preferred to stick with An Comunn Gàidhealach, although the emergence of CNCA did have the effect of making An Comunn Gàidhealach more radical in attitudes. From 1972, a 'Western Isles Regional Council' of An Communn was established, based in Stornoway, which began the practice of actually holding its meetings in the language! It has subsequently carried on the CNCA demands of campaigning to improve the position and use of the language in public life.

The main breakthrough on the language front occurred when the Western Isles' local government authority adopted an official bilingual policy in all its public dealings. Comhairle nan Eilean, as the authority is now officially called, also adopted a bilingual education policy. In pressing for an official recognition of the language in public life, the Scottish National Party's MP for the Western Isles, Donald Stewart, played a prominent role, although the SNP itself had been slow to support the language. It was not until 1968 that the Party agreed to set up a Gaelic Secretariat; and it was not until 1974 that it undertook to develop a Gaelic policy, introducing the language throughout Scotland and not just in those areas where it was still spoken.

The publishing scene is far from satisfactory. Gaelic does not lack talent in its modern writers or poets; it simply lacks outlets through which work written in Gaelic might find an audience. The names of Somhairle MacGill-Eain, Iain C.Mac a' Ghobhainn, Deòrsa Caimbeul Hay, Derick S.Thomson, Ruaraidh Mac Thomais, Murchadh Moireach, Catriona NicDhomhnaill and Morag NicLeòid head a list of writers of considerable reputation. Yet there is no all-Gaelic newspaper. The *Stornoway Gazette* (Lewis) and the *West Highland Free Press* (Skye) used Gaelic in their columns. The *West Highland Free Press* does issue a monthly newspaper supplement—*Crùisgean*. Several newspapers, such as *The Scotsman* and *The Oban Times* include lively Gaelic columns. Literary magazines and other journals come and go with sad irregularity and *Gairm*, founded in 1952, edited by Professor Derick S.Thomson, remains the most senior and respected Gaelic magazine. Other regular magazines, such as *Crann*, *Ossian*, and *Tocher* tend to be published by the universities. There is a significant number of books published in the language, and such publishing is carefully catalogued and details issued by Leabhraichean Gàidhlig (Gaelic Books Council) at the University of Glasgow both in catalogue form and in a bi-annual magazine entitled *Facal air an Fhacal.*

Individual enterprises cause one to have hope, such as the establishment in 1972 of small-scale economic enterprises in Skye by Iain Noble, using Gaelic as the language of business and economic transactions as well as the community. In 1973, Iain Noble was able to finance Sabhal Mór Ostaig, a Gaelic college which serves as a cultural institution and entertainment centre. The main hope in creating a barrier to the decline of the language within the present Gàidhealtachd, or Gaelic-speaking areas, has been the new attitudes emanating from Comhairle nan Eilean, the local government authority.

Kenneth MacKinnon, in his excellent book *The Lion's Tongue* (1974), has said: "The immediate task of the promoters of Gaelic in national life is to get over the view that Gaelic is above all the Scottish language...However, before Gaelic is capable of becoming a political issue capable of uniting Scots, even within the Gàidhealtachd, grassroots work in the cultural re-education of the nation will be necessary. Indeed, five hundred years of myth-making has to be halted and reversed." There is one formidable enemy working against those who believe in a Celtic Scotland—time. Yet there are still many who share the hope of the 18th Century poet, Alasdair Mac Mhaighstir Alasdair, expressed in his stirring poem *Moladh an Ughdair do 'n t-sean Chànain Ghàidhealach (The author's praise of the Gaelic language):*

Mhair i fòs
Is cha téid a glòir air chall
Dh'aindeon gò
Is mìoruin mhóir nan Gall.

It (Gaelic) continues—
And its glory will not be lost
in spite of the vilification
and the great malice of the strangers (English-speakers).

Chapter Three
Breizh (Brittany)

On November 22nd, 845 AD, the Breton ruler Nominoë inflicted a crushing defeat on the invading Franks led by Charles the Bald. That defeat caused the Franks to recognize the independence of Brittany. Six years later, Nominoë was dead but his successors, Erispoe (851-857), and Saloman (857-874), consolidated the Breton state and Alan Barvak (c. 937) managed to turn back a Norse threat to independence. Brittany, with its powerful merchant fleet, became one of the most prosperous countries in mediaeval Europe. Commerce was thriving; the arts and literature flourished; and social laws were evolved. The Breton rulers governed with the aid of an annual parliament, a representative assembly without which no important decision concerning policy or finance could be reached.

This prosperous little country was, of course, the envy of both French and English expansionists—both countries trying to involve themselves in Breton affairs. Alan Fergent defeated William I (The Conqueror) in England's attempt to annex Brittany to his empire in 1085. Conan IV, 'The Black', (1156-1169) tried to form an alliance by marrying his daughter Constance to Geoffrey, the son of Henry II, as Conan had no son. Constance and Geoffrey ruled from 1169-1186 and, in spite of Geoffrey's family connections, they kept Brittany independent. Geoffrey's son, Arthur I, was murdered by John I of England in 1187 but Arthur's sister Alix succeeded in keeping Brittany out of England's clutches. During the 14th Century, England and France managed to bring about a civil war in Brittany over the succession, each side trying to put forward a candidate to the Breton throne. England successfully supported Jean de Montfort, Earl of Richmond, while the French supported Charles de Blois, who was killed at the Battle of Aurey in 1341. But, surprisingly, while the de Montforts became rulers of Brittany, they did not align Brittany with England.

The Church had done much to undermine Breton independence during this period by seeking to incorporate it, for ecclesiastical purposes, with the Frankish Church, ordering the Breton bishops to submit to the See of Tours. Brittany was a bastion of the Celtic Church and had, for centuries, refused to recognize the jurisdiction of Tours, claiming Dol as their primacy. When Pope Leo IX appointed Aurard, at the Council of Rheims in 1049, to reform the Breton Church and bring it into line with Rome, the Bretons drove him out. By the end of the 12th Century, succumbing to Papal pressures, the Breton Church had virtually accepted the Roman Order and the jurisdiction of Tours. On June 7th, 1199, Pope Innocent III issued a Bull requiring the bishop of Dol to renounce the title 'archbishop' and the rights of the primacy of the Breton Church. Henceforth, the Bretons would be governed from Tours in all ecclestiastical matters. At the end of the 13th Century, the Bretons, so far as the Church was concerned, were firmly in the hands of the French.

Ironically, it was from the Breton clergy that the Breton language began to assume its modern shape. This was the period of Middle Breton among whose 15th Century classics are *An Dialog etre Arzur Roe d'an Bretounet ha Guynglaff* (The Dialogue of Arthur, King of the Bretons, and Gwenc'hlan), and the more famous *Buez Santes Nonn hag he map Deuy* (The Life of St Nonn, son of Devy). It was Father Jehan Lagadeuc, Rector of Plougonven, who gave a boost to Breton literature with the production of his Breton, French and Latin dictionary, *Catholicon*, dated 1465 but first printed in 1499 at Tréguier. A series of miracle plays formed the corpus of Breton literature at this time, such as *Burzu bras Jean* (1530) and *Buhez santes Barba* (1557). Significant poetical works were also produced such as *Tremenvan an itron gwerches Maria* (The passing of the Virgin Mary), *Pemzec levenez Maria* (The fifteen joys of Maria), and *Buhez Mabden* (Life of Man). To this period also belongs another classic *Mellezour an Mary* (The Mirror of Death) composed in 1519 and printed in 1575. Breton literature, within this period, had become a printed literature. The Breton literary form achieved a standard with the publication in 1616 of a Breton dictionary compiled by Guillaume Quicquer of

Roscoff. Another dictionary and a grammar were produced by Julien Maunoir in 1659.

As the imperial power of the French increased, so Breton independence became more and more fragile and, at last, the French armies were strong enough to attempt a conquest. In 1488 the Breton army was defeated at St. Aubin du Cromier and the Breton ruler Francis II was thereby compelled to accept a treaty at Le Verger which recognized the French King's suzereign right over Brittany. Soon after Francis II died and his daughter Anne succeeded him, and tried to resume the fight against the French but she, too, was obliged to submit to avoid a protracted war and disastrous occupation. A condition of her surrender was that she was compelled to marry the King of France, Charles VIII. By this method, the French rulers sought to eliminate the Breton ruling family by incorporation into the French royal family. After the death of Charles VIII, Anne had to marry Louis XII but sought to secure in her marriage settlement, the independence of her country. She went so far as to betroth her daughter Claude, heiress to the duchy, as Brittany now was, to Charles V, heir of the traditional enemy of France, the house of Austria. But after Anne died, on January 9th, 1514, Claude was betrothed to Francois I of France and so the 'union of crowns' was complete.

Breton determination for independence was strong, however. The Breton parliament, Etats de Bretagne, forced a treaty with France which was signed in 1532. Under the provisions of the treaty, the kings of France and their successors became dukes of Brittany. On the other hand, the French crown pledged to respect the political and administrative rights of the Bretons and the French monarchs agreed not to levy taxes in Brittany without the consent of the Breton Parliament. Only Bretons were allowed to be appointed to public office in Brittany, and Bretons were not to be forced to serve as soldiers outside Brittany which in fact, had now become an autonomous state within the French kingdom.

As the rule of the French Kings became more absolute so, too, did their centralist policies. Several times the Bretons were forced to take up arms to defend their rights under the Treaty of 1532. In 1601, came De Mercour's revolt. When Louis XIV tried to levy new taxes in Brittany, in spite of the refusal of the Breton Parliament to approve, a popular uprising took place in 1675 which was ruthlessly suppressed. An attempt to restore Breton independence in 1720 was similarly crushed and its leaders, Pontcallec, Montlouis, Talhouet and Couedic, were beheaded in Nantes. The French Crown and Breton Parliament continued to fight each other. At the end of the reign of Louis XV, it was the Breton Procurer Général La Chalotais, who was the leader of Breton resistance to French centralism. In 1772, a 25-page pamphlet against French centralism was published under the title *Manifesto Aux Bretons*. In 1788, the Breton Parliament issued a declaration denouncing French centralism. One of the signatories was the famous Lafayette, a descendent of the counts of Kernev (Cornouaille), who won fame in the American War of Independence. Extracts of the debate were published in the *Journel de Parlement de Bretagne*, May 31-June 6, 1788, and re-issued in pamphlet form.

It was in Brittany, particularly in the ancient cities of Nantes and Rennes, that the seeds of republicanism found fertile ground. Brittany, long opposed to the abuses of the French monarchy on national as well as on social grounds, was foremost among the revolutionary movement. But the revolutionary assembly in Paris began to prove more centralist than the monarchy it had replaced. At the end of 1789, a 16-page *Address to the Breton People* warned them of the damage to Brittany of the increasing power exercised by the French National Assembly. The warning was prophetic for the French National Assembly decided to abolish the Breton Parliament, repudiate the Treaty of 1532 AD and forcibly annex the country. All Frenchmen were declared equal and the entire territory of France was to be unified with the same laws. The injustice of this was that Brittany was not French, it had a different language and had an entirely different culture and social system.

The Breton supporters of the revolution were appalled. On January 18th, 1790, de la Houssaye, the President of the Breton Parliament, protested at the bar of the National Assembly. Rebuking the French for calling Breton independence and establishment of privileges he cried: *'Les Corps out des privileges. Les nations out des droits!'* (Parliament has privileges. Nations have rights!) On February 13th, the Breton Procurer Général, La Chalotais, raised the same protest in a manifesto and he repeated the protest each year until his death in exile in 1805.

For the next three years, the Breton republicans, who were on the Girondist side of the revolution, tried to convince the French of their mistake. But now the once solidly pro-revolutionary country had split asunder. People with short memories were supporting the royalists who were trying to build up a counter-revolutionary army in the Vendée. In 1793, Georges Cadoudal and Armand de la Rouerie declared a general uprising against the French. De la Rouerie was a committed republican and had commanded a brigade of cavalry in the American War of Independence. He was to die while 'on the run' later, in 1793. Armed resistance mainly took the form of a guerilla warfare and the Breton guerillas became known as the *'chouannerie'*, a name derived from the Breton word *chuin*, a screech owl, because the guerillas would signal to each other in this form. This warfare lasted until 1804, when Cadoudal was finally caught and beheaded in Paris.

This was a period of great confusion in Brittany. There were three armies. The Breton royalists, the Breton republicans and the French republicans. The French troops were able to seize most of the Breton towns, from which the Breton republicans drew their support; and the Breton republicans, faced with the hostility of a mainly royalist rural population, had to be disbanded into guerilla groups. Only in Finisterre did the Breton republicans field an army for a while. All the Finisterre Breton republican deputies of the National Assembly were beheaded in Brest by the French. This confusing state of affairs (and a lack of understanding of it), caused England to land its French émigré royalist army on the shores of Quiberon Bay in 1795, where it was annihilated. The royalists had been led to believe that Brittany was solidly royalist. Instead, they found Breton republicans and French republicans and had to fight both. French historians, not wishing to examine the complexity of the *national* situation in Brittany, have been inclined to dismiss the period of 1793-1804 as a royalist counter-revolutionary war.

Even after the execution of Cadoudal, the *chouans* fought sporadically, suffering heavy losses. With Napoleon's eventual defeat, the French monarchy was more than pleased to inherit the unifying results of the revolution and its aftermath, which now successfully crowned their own three centuries of attempts at abolishing Breton independence.

The French annexation, however, produced one happy result for the Bretons. In order to foster French unity, the French Government had resolved to extirpate the Breton language but, at the same time, an enthusiastic offensive was launched on the refractory clergy, with the consequence that all popular teaching, previously a monopoly of the church, was abolished and not resumed until the end of the revolutionary turmoil. Since 1532, the clergy had been teaching through the medium of French and thus had reduced the Breton-speaking population within the towns and cities. With the abolition of priests as teachers and the growth of a more common awareness of Breton nationality, a new generation of Breton monoglots arose, so that in 1914 it was assessed that there were 1½ million Breton-speakers.

During the 19th Century, a Breton revival began through the works of poets, historians and philologists and inter-Celtic relations were fostered, especially with the Welsh. In 1838, two Breton scholars, La Villemarqué and Ar Gonidec attended a meeting of the Welsh organization Cymdeithas y Cymreigyddion in Abergavenny. In 1843, an Association Bretonne was formed, the first organization of what was to become the modern Breton Movement. This was suppressed by the French Government in 1858 but it continued as an underground movement and organized the first Inter-Celtic Congress in Saint Brieuc in 1867. Petitions to allow the teaching of Breton in Breton schools met with no response from the French. One such petition was presented by a leading Breton poet named Charles de Gaulle, an uncle of General Charles de Gaulle who was to become one of the most virulent anti-Breton Presidents of France. During the Franco-Prussian War of 1870, the French Government cynically allowed the Breton regiments to be decimated at the Battle of Le Mans (1871), fearing that they might become a threat against French unity. These regiments were not reconstituted.

In spite of this, Breton culture was flourishing, partially bolstered by the Celtic Renaissance which had emanated from Ireland. A Comité De Preservation du Breton was formed in 1896. A Union Régionaliste Bretonne was formed in 1898 and one of its leaders, R. de L'Estourbeillon, was elected deputy for Morbihan. A numerous Breton delegation appeared in Cardiff in

1900 to take part in the Welsh National Eisteddfod. A Gorsedd of Brittany was founded in 1901 and Breton delegations became regular attenders at the Celtic Congress formed the same year. There were rapid developments in the early years of the 20th Century. Many Breton cultural groups and societies were formed and numerous newspapers and magazines, devoted to the defence of Breton culture and political aspirations were published, both in Breton and French. Three monthly magazines achieved a wide readership: *Fez ha Breiz* (1899) *Ar Vro*, founded by the poet Fanch Jaffrennou (Taldir) in 1903, and *D'hunamb*, founded in 1905. In 1904, *Ar Bobl* (The People) became the first weekly Breton newspaper published at Carhaix and this soon had a rival in another weekly *Kroaz ar Vretoned*, edited by F.Vallée at St. Brieuc. As the French made no effort to take any census of the Breton-speaking population of Brittany, a private census was conducted showing that, in Lower Brittany alone, out of a population of 1,360,000 in 1910-11, 1,250,000 spoke Breton of which roughly 50 per cent were monoglots.

The French Government were anxious about the strength of the Breton language and, in 1902, even went so far as to try to prohibit its use in churches. The Bretons simply refused to obey this edict. Attempts to enlist support for the teaching of Breton in schools, in 1905 and 1911, fell on unsympathetic ears. It was in 1911 that a Fédération Régionaliste de Bretagne and a Breton National Party were formed.

The Bretons fought in the French Army in World War I, proportionately losing almost double the numbers of French soldiers killed. Some 240,000 Bretons were killed—almost a third of the entire French Republic's death toll! Among these dead was Yann Per Kalloc'h, regarded as one of the greatest Breton poets. The Breton Movement had mistakenly thought that their contribution would entitle them to a hearing at the Peace Conference. After all, the War was supposedly for the freedom of small countries! A petition bearing the signatures of all prominent Bretons asking for the recognition of their national and cultural rights was presented. France vetoed any discussion on the petition. Ruinous centralist economic policies had caused a further loss of 250,000 Bretons by emigration within a decade of the ending of the War.

However, after World War I, there came a great literary outflow with a more diverse literature centred round *Gwalarn*, a magazine founded by Roparz Hemon. In spite of the laws against teaching Breton, some independent schools, under the influence of Bleun-Brug, a movement formed in 1905 by Father Yann Perrot, began to devote one hour a week to teaching the language. In 1934, Yann Fouéré formed Ar Brezoneg er Skol, to campaign for the teaching of the language in schools. Fouéré was successful in getting support. By 1937, more than four hundred municipal councils and three general councils had adopted a motion demanding that the French Government allow the teaching of Breton. On June 30th, 1937, in the face of such support, the Commission for Education in the French Chamber of Deputies unanimously recommended that the French Government accede to this demand. The French Government simply ignored it.

At the outbreak of Word War II, the Breton Movement was split into two camps. There were the regionalists, those who did not oppose French sovereignty but who advocated administrative reform which would give Brittany cultural autonomy. At the General Election of 1936, one third of the Breton deputies had pledged themselves to support 'devolution' in a programme published by a Comité du Ront Breton. On the other hand, a new Breton National Party, formed in 1919 by M.Marchal, O.Mordrel and F.Debauvais, held that the Breton nation must become complete master of its own destiny. Its publication *Breiz Atao* became the organ of a young, radical opposition.

Early in 1938, the French Government moved against the BNP and members were sentenced to terms of imprisonment for illegal propaganda 'likely to endanger the unity of France'. Mordrel and Debauvais were sentenced to twelve months and *Breiz Atao* was suppressed. After their release, Mordrel and Devauvais returned to advocate that Brittany should adopt a pacifist and neutral attitude in the coming conflict with Germany. They pointed to the Breton sacrifice in World War I and the way in which France had repaid Brittany for its allegiance. With their arrest imminent, they fled to Belgium and thence to Germany.

It was during the 1930's that the first armed Breton opposition since the days of Cadoudal manifested itself. A movement named after the Breton flag 'Gwenn ha Du' (White and Black) emerged. Its leader was a chemical engineer and mathematician named

Celestin Lainé-Kerjean who later adopted the Breton form Neven Henaff. A graduate of Rennes and the prestigious École Centrale in Paris, he was the author of a geometry textbook in Breton, *Mentoniezh*, published in the late 1920's. Henaff was to have a profound effect on the Breton Movement. He argued that France had not shown itself disposed to respect the constitutional, democratic or moral demands of the Breton people. The answer, therefore, could only lie in the continuation of the example set by de la Rouerie and Cadoudal. Bretons had to organize into a national force and learn the use of arms to fight for independence. The first impressive accomplishment was the blowing up of the monument at Rennes, the symbol of France's annexation of Brittany, on August 7th, 1932, the very day when President Herriot was solemnly celebrating the 400th anniversary of the union in Vannes. 'Gwenn ha Du' was sporadically active over the next seven years and, thanks to Henaff's careful organizing, when it was dismantled, it had not lost a single activist nor was any member identified by the authorities.

With the French declaration of war on Germany, the French authorities moved to suppress the Breton Movement with raids on the homes of Breton nationalists, and the suppression of newspapers and magazines. Even 'Ker Vreizh', the Paris reception centre for Breton soldiers (equivalent to the London Welsh Services Club) was ransacked and closed down by the police. The French authorities were determined to use the war as an excuse to crush the Breton Movement.

Mordrel and Debauvais, who had fled to Germany, decided to make advances to the Nazi regime, judging France's difficulty to be Brittany's opportunity. They tried to persuade the Germans, in the case of a French defeat, to estabish a Breton state. This was promised according to Marshal Hermann Göring at his trial in Nuremberg. On May 20th, 1940, both Mordrel and Debauvais were condemned to death *in absentia*. At the same time, Germany launched its offensive against France and, by June, the War was over. An Armistice was signed with Marshal Pétain's Government in Vichy. The Franco-German armistice was a blow to the policy advocated by Mordrel and Devauvais. The Germans were no longer interested as all France was now under their suzereignty. It should be pointed out clearly that the vast majority of Bretons, including members of Mordrel's own BNP, repudiated their leader's policies with regard to dealing with the Nazis.

Mordrel and Debauvais founded a Conseil National Breton on July 4th, 1940, in Pontivy, with a weekly newspaper *L'Heure Bretonne*. They were now an embarrassment to the Germans and the Vichy French Government were demanding their arrest. At the end of 1940 both Mordrel and Debauvais fled from Rennes in order to avoid arrest and went into exile.

The BNP chose a new leader, Remont Delaporte. He advocated that while Brittany should remain part of the French empire. it should be given the status enjoyed by a dominion of the British empire. The regionalists, among whom was Yann Fouéré, felt this was asking too much and advocated a regional form of independence within the French state. A new daily devoted to these ideals was launched called *La Bretagne*. The first issue appeared on March 21st, 1941. Soon Fouéré had control of the powerful newspaper *La Dépêche*. A strong Breton-orientated press was changing the attitudes of the Breton people. *Arvor*, a weekly Breton language newspaper, edited by Roparz Hemon, was launched in 1941, followed by another weekly for younger readers. Hemon was elected president of the Celtic Institute and subsequently appointed director of Breton broadcasting...for the first time in its history, the Breton language was heard on radio for one hour's broadcast a week.

A new concession was wrung from the Vichy Government in 1941. The teaching of the Breton language and history was allowed in schools. In October, 1942, a Comité Consultatif de Bretagne was set up by the Préfet Régional as an advisory body in the governing of Brittany. The Comité held a plenary session every three months with a permanent commission of seven members meeting once a month. Yann Fouéré was the second general secretary of the Comité, elected in 1944.

The French were angered by these 'advances' made by the Bretons and many saw the Bretons in simplicist terms as reaping the rewards for being pro-Nazi. Apart from the questionable policies of Mordrel and Debauvais, the Breton Movement was not pro-Nazi. Many prominent members of the BNP, which had disclaimed the attitudes of Mordrel and Debauvais, were active in the Resistance. Major Thomas, a member of the BNP supreme council, was killed in action against the Germans and local party leaders, Dr Leclaire of St Pol de Léon, M.Dieulesaint of Montcontour, and M.Malard of Questembert, were executed by the Germans for their Resistance activities. Nevertheless, ignorance and fear caused certain members of the French Maquis to start an anti-Breton campaign.

Yann Bricler of Quimper, a cousin of O.Mordrel, was the first to be assassinated. Then M.Kerhoas of Plonevez-du-Faou, a leading nationalist, was gunned down. On December 12th, 1943, Father Yann Perrot, the aging parish priest of Scrignac, was shot dead on the steps of his church. Father Perrot, now in his seventies, had been the founder of Bluen-Brug, the organization pressing for the teaching of Breton in 1905.

There followed a meeting of the BNP soon afterwards, when the Bretons realized that the Maquis had declared war on all nationalists of whatever political persuasion. Delaporte, the President of BNP, tried to maintain his neutral line, warning dissidents that the Maquis was trying to provoke Bretons into adopting a pro-German stance. The dissidents had two strong leaders in Marcel Guieysse and Lainé-Kerjean (Neven Henaff). Guieysse was a respected 'elder statesman', born in Kervelean, near Lorient, in 1881. His father, Paul, had been a socialist member of the French Parliament, serving twenty years as Minister for the Colonies and was a supporter of the campaign to allow Breton to be taught in schools. Guieysse himself was a graduate of Celtic Studies under Professor H.Gaidoz. He became a *sous-prefet*, resigning after a duel with a French Minister. He stood for Parliament as a Breton language campaigner. In Paris, he taught literature and wrote *La Langue Bretonne*, becoming chairman of the Paris branch of the BNP in 1936. He was a founder member of the Conseil National Bretonne. Neven Henaff had been arrested in 1939 for advising a friend not to help in the French war effort. Sentenced to four years' imprisonment, he was released in 1940 and devoted himself to building up a nucleus of trained Bretons who would renew the tradition of armed resistance to France. He still believed the day would come when Brittany would have to fight for her independence. Both Guieysse and Henaff argued that Bretons should not sit back calmly and allow the Maquis to gun down nationalists indiscriminately. In fact, Henaff had already received tacit approval of the German authorities to establish a Breton combat unit. Delaporte remained firm in his neutralist line but Guieysse and Henaff left the meeting and went to see the German Commandant in Rennes. The result was that a military unit of young Bretons was formed called the Formation Yann Perrot (Bezen Perrot), taking their name from the murdered priest. Some 200 Bretons aged between 18 and 25 joined and were issued with German uniforms "in order not to impair the good relations existing between the Vichy Government and Germany." It was "a Breton unit, to be engaged in Brittany in conjunction with the German forces, against the common enemies of Brittany and Germany".

In the Spring of 1944, the Bezen Perrot began its first military operations against the Maquis of central Brittany. To the Maquis, they neither gave nor asked for quarter. But there were a number of occasions when they helped Allied officers escaping from the Germans. Major J.D.MacLeod of the USAF was captured by the unit after an attack on a Resistance camp. They helped him on his way to the Spanish border. He tried to give evidence on their behalf after the War. Bezen Perrot made it clear that its only enemy was the French Maquis. In their turn, the Maquis execution squads were active. During the same Spring, the poet Barz Ar Yeodet and his young brother, the historian Madame du Gerny, journalists Louis Stephen and Yves de Cambourg, Christian le Part, Paul Gaic of Plessala and the brothers Tattevin (one aged only sixteen) were all gunned down. Also, a young artist named Philiponn and Father Lec'hvien, the parish priest of Quemper-Guezennec were shot dead.

In July, 1944, the Allies broke through in Brittany and the Bezen Perrot were forced to withdraw with the retreating Germans to St Nazaire. The Maquis was now in power and Le Gorgeu, a former mayor of Brest and a hater of everything Breton, became civil governor aided by General Allard as military governor. By September, a thousand prominent Breton men and women, as well as children, were rounded up and placed in concentration camps. The list included thirty priests and even those who had fought in the Resistance. Mass protests started and angry Bretons surrounded a *sous-préfecture* at Lesneven. Local troops refused to fire on the crowd and General Allard had to send to

Rennes for non-Breton troops. A mass slaughter was only just prevented by the intervention of the Bishop of Quimper.

Soon, French courts were dealing with the Bretons. Marcel Guieysse, then 65-years old, took upon himself full responsibility for Bezen Perrot. He came to trial in June, 1946, partially blind since his imprisonment. He declared his faith in a free Brittany for which he was ready to die. "When one is fighting for an ideal one hopes for a lot but one expects nothing. And while we did not achieve all our aims, those who will follow us will achieve them." The court hesitated before this willing martyr and, giving health as a reason, sentenced him to five years' penal servitude. He was released from jail for an eye-operation in 1948 but was totally blind. In jail, he became 'father' to the political prisoners and a source of inspiration to fellow Bretons. He died in exile in Paris on February 8th, 1967, aged 86 years.

Neven Henaff was tried *in absentia*. He eventually received political asylum in Ireland and took Irish citizenship. On learning of his death sentence, passed in his absence, he said: "We fought the Maquis only after they declared war on Bretons and murdered Father Perrot and many other patriots. To us, France is the only enemy as long as she refuses the right of Brittany to live her own national life." Henaff remained firmly committed to the cause of Breton independence and of the wider Celtic perspective. He was an early supporter of the Celtic League and a contributor to various journals on aspects of Celtic culture and politics. He died in his adopted country in October, 1983.

Ill-treatment before trial was common. James Bouille, a member of the Comité Consultatif de Bretagne, died due to maltreatment as did Father Guivarc'h. The Breton novelist Colonel Charles was so badly knocked about the head that he suffered brain damage and was committed to an asylum. Hundreds of Bretons, passing through Rennes Central Jail, appeared before examining magistrates with broken limbs and bruised bodies.

Many others, including O.Mordrel, H.le Helloco, J.de Quelen, Remont Delaporte, and Y.Delaporte heard their death sentences stoically. Dr Hervé Delaporte, the brother of Remont, received a lengthy prison sentence even though he had been doctor to the Chateauneuf du Faou Maquis. Vissault de Coetlogon thanked the court for the honour they were doing him before he was taken out to be executed. Botros and Kergoat fell before firing squads in Quimper shouting *'Breiz Atao!'* (Long live free Brittany!). In Rennes, Geoffroy and Jasson, identified by Major MacLeod as the men who had helped him escape from the Germans, marched to their death singing the Breton national anthem—*'Bro Goz va Zadou'*. Sixty death sentences were carried out.

Now, for the first time, the French authorities admitted that their campaign was not against alleged Breton collaboration but against Breton nationalism. It was an attempt at a 'final solution' of the Breton problem. Even members of the Free French Forces suspected of sympathies towards Breton nationalism, yet who had not even been in Brittany during the war years, were arrested. One 80-year-old, bed-ridden invalid, Francis Vallée, was dragged out of bed to be gaoled. The repression was the most ruthless since the days of the French Revolution.

What the French were actually doing was revealed by Dewi Powell of the Welsh newspaper *Baner ac Amserau Cymru*, which started a campaign to draw the attention of the world to the plight of the Bretons. It was thanks to Dewi Powell that the French were forced to release Roparz Hemon after a year in gaol. Hemon was a popularly known Celtic scholar and propagandist but the French not only claimed that he was a Gestapo agent but that he was the secret leader of 'Gwenn ha Du'. Many Bretons followed the example of Neven Henaff and sought political asylum in Ireland. Yann Fouéré, imprisoned for a year and then released preparatory to his trial, fled on the advice of friends and was sentenced to penal servitude *in absentia*. The Breton intelligentsia was especially singled out. Professor Eliès, translator of the *Mabinogion* into Breton and author of many books on both Welsh and Breton, was jailed for fourteen months without trial, dismissed from his teaching post, forbidden to teach in public or private, or to publish any work. His case was typical.

The BNP and all other Breton movements were banned by edict in October, 1944. Early in 1947, the French Government formally banned the teaching of the Breton language, literature, history, folklore or, in fact, anything which could be construed as regionalist or nationalist. The Breton repression was complete. The French Government had clearly not deviated from their traditional policy which had been summed up by the French

Minister of Education, Anatole de Monzie, in 1925, when he said: "For the sake of the unity of France, the Breton language must disappear". For the sake of that unity, the Breton nation would be destroyed.

Yet the Bretons were resilient. In October, 1950, the remnants of the Breton Movement gathered together and formed a group called Kendalc'h—a cultural movement. Moving slowly and hesitantly against the anti-Breton attitudes of the French, the Bretons began to rebuild their shattered societies and cultural groups. In November, 1957, L'Mouvement pour l'Organisation de la Bretagne (MOB) was formed as a constitutional party seeking domestic self-government within the French state. Its main political philosophy of moderate 'home rule' was derived from Yann Fouéré in exile in Ireland. Fouéré wrote several books in exile, most notably *De la Bretagne à la France et à l'Europe* (1957), *La Bretagne écartelée* (1962) and *L'Europe aux cent Drapeaux* (1968). The MOB soon had its own newspaper, *L'Avenir de la Bretagne*. In 1963, a Union Democratic Bretonne (UDB) came into existence seeking Breton independence on socialist lines within a federal Europe.

Kendalc'h had succeeded in getting the French Assembly to adopt a more liberal policy with a bill allowing the instruction of 'dialects' in schools in 1959. Thus the Breton language could be represented as a 'regional dialect' and taught. However, the coming to power of Charles de Gaulle stopped even this concession. Although a nephew of a Breton writer and nationalist, De Gaulle was virulently anti-Breton. It was de Gaulle's famous *Vive Quebec Libre!* speech in Montréal, when on a visit to Canada in 1967, that provoked the Bretons to turn away from Fouéré's moderation to the philosophies of Neven Henaff.

During the early 1960's, the Front for the Liberation of Brittany (FLB) became sporadically active with bomb attacks on tax offices, police barracks, the national grid system and other targets. Acts of violence increased so that during the two years ending in December, 1968, there were thirty such attacks. During the course of this campaign, the FLB issued a manifesto which stated:

> We denounce the colonialist and imperialist rule which deprives our people, a distinct entity, of the political power to manage their own affairs.

Here is a case of aggression by a majority ethnical group which is driving a minority group to cultural, socio-economic and demographic extermination.

Exploited as we are by a foreign capitalist state, our struggle for independence must adopt the methods which have proved their worth in the anti-colonialist struggle throughout the world.

It is inconceivable that an impoverished and despoiled people could be really free while tied in the same political system as a rich and powerful neighbour. It would immediately be brought back into subjection by its capital.

Our struggle must, then, conform with the general principles of socialism. But we want nothing to do with bureaucratic, authoritarian, imperialistic state-socialism.

The recent events in central Europe show that genuine socialism must be particular to, and independent for, each people.

Our socialism will be adapted to the needs of the Breton people, based on humanism, co-operation, and the human liberties inspired by the traditions of freedom and the spirit of our Celtic civilization.

The National Political Council of the FLB had decided to continue the struggle for liberation. It will compel the French State either to act according to the principles it proclaims (for Quebec and Biafra, for example) or cynically to reveal its true face to the world.

We Bretons gave hundreds and thousands of lives to causes which did not concern us. We shall now put our courage at the service of the liberation of our own nation, and by implication, of all oppressed peoples.

In January and February, 1969, the French authorities reacted; some sixty Bretons were arrested as alleged members of the FLB. They came from a surprising cross-section of society: doctors, students, factory workers, farmers, school teachers, an architect and four priests. They were immediately taken out of Brittany to the Prison de la Santé in Paris where 'questioning' took place. After such interrogation, Father Antoine Le Bars, a 37-year-old priest, had to be admitted to a Rennes mental hospital. It was later discovered that drugs had been used to force a confession. A 45-year-old architect and town councillor, Pierre Lemoine, had to be transferred to the Hospital Claude Bernard and a student, Ronan Tremel, was released with damaged kidneys. The prisoners were not allowed legal representation until they forced the issue by a three-day hunger strike. A second hunger strike took place in March, 1969, to obtain the right to receive visitors and to receive books in Breton. These 'privileges' were conceded after a seven-day hunger strike. By July, however, only sixteen out of the original sixty were still in prison.

It was later discovered that the French authorities had a list of between 5,000 and 10,000 Breton nationalists. The arrest of the sixty had been a 'sampling' and had there been no reaction outside Brittany, the authorities were due to embark on a repetition of the years 1944-46, in an attempt to smash the new generation of Breton activists. The world media and press were alerted when Plaid Cymru MP, Gwynfor Evans, asked a question in the British Parliament and demanded an international commission to be allowed to investigate the charges of brutality against the Breton prisoners. Prompt inter-Celtic action and the interest of the media stopped this new persecution.

The Bretons, too, laid a new challenge before the French authorities by declaring the FLB to be an open mass movement and by holding a public meeting of the FLB in Paris—the French capital being used so as to gain maximum media coverage. Breton branches of trade unions, student bodies, local branches of the Socialist and Communist Parties, as well as various other Breton groups subscribed openly to the FLB. The meeting drew an attendance of more than 2,000 people. No further action was taken by the French authorities and all charges were dropped against those arrested.

A new energy seized the Breton political scene; several new parties were formed, all vying with each other to lead the Breton people to independence. The problem was that, under French law, the Bretons cannot 'constitutionally' advocate their independence from France. Since June 4th, 1960, anyone who advocates, by any means, the severance of 'French territory' can receive perpetual imprisonment or lesser terms from 10 to 20 years. This did not stop the rise of Sav Breizh (Arise Brittany) in 1969, nor of the Breton Communist Party in 1970. The MOB, now fairly moribund, gave way to Strollad ar Vro (SAV) in 1971 under the leadership of Yann Fouéré. Internal problems caused SAV's collapse, after it had fielded 27 candidates in the 1973 elections and received a respectable vote. Later, another party, Strollad Pobl Vreizh, formed in 1981, appeared, demanding a Breton republic while Parti Pour l'Organisation de la Bretagne Libre (POBL) appeared in 1983, with policies that were reminiscent of the federalist ideas of MOB and SAV. In recent years, it is Strollad Pobl Vreizh which has emerged as the party advocating complete independence from France, but, primarily devoting itself to the task of educating Bretons to think of themselves as a nation whose interests cannot be served by participating in an electoral system geared to serve French interests. Union Democratique Bretonne (UDB), formed in 1963, the oldest Breton nationalist party participating in elections, became a political force to be reckoned with and a member of the L'Alliance de la Gauche (The French Left Alliance), by which means it exerts quite an influence on local councils. In 1977, it managed to get 40 candidates elected at local-government level, and this was increased to 60 candidates in the 1983 elections, including a mayor. In national politics, its voting power at that time was 5 per cent, increasing to 12 per cent in local elections. UDB, in certain areas, has been instrumental in getting bilingual road signs erected. The UDB presence is felt strongly throughout Brittany in the fields of social, economic and cultural life.

The intransigence of the French authorities towards Brittany and the lack of swift progress made by the Breton political parties, caused the reappearence of the FLB in October, 1973. About a dozen bomb attacks were carried out on police stations, tax offices and military installations within a few months. In January, 1974, some 20 Bretons were arrested but only four were transferred to Paris to appear before a State Security Court. Censorship of an item about popular support for the four men, and the formation of support committees in many Breton towns, in an item in the 90-second Breton language TV broadcast on February 12th, caused the producer of the news programme, Charles ar Gall, to resign. Next day, the FLB blew up the 213-metre high TV aerial on Roc'h Tredudon. The FLB has continued as a shadowy force in Breton politics. In 1978 came the spectacular bombing at the Palace of Versailles. By 1980, 21 Bretons were in French prisons serving sentences ranging up to 30 years in the case of Charles Grall. The KAD, a Breton Amnesty group, had become active in support of the Breton political prisoners.

One conflict which did resolve itself in the Bretons' favour was the resistance of the people of Cap Sizhun against the French Government's plan to build a nuclear power station in Plogoff. From January to March, 1980, clashes between riot police and demonstrators were a daily occurrence. In spite of airborne gendarmes and CRS troops, the authorities found the opposition of the people so strong that the power station's plans were shelved.

Just after the Second World War, it was estimated that one million, out of a total population of three million in Brittany, spoke Breton. As there is no linguistic census in the France state, a private census has to be carried out. It is currently estimated that there are about 700,000 Breton speakers (16.6 per cent of the population). As most people are illiterate in the language, thanks to the years of French intransigence against teaching it in schools, the decline is fairly rapid. In 1966, yet another petition asking that Breton be taught in schools was handed to the French Government. It had 250,000 signatures. This was ignored. The growth of political nationalism has also seen the extension of cultural awareness. In the late 1960's, GALV, a militant language movement, seeking status for Breton through a campaign of civil disobedience, was started. It disappeared soon after 1970 but, from 1969, several Breton-speaking school teachers decided to spend their time voluntarily teaching the language to those pupils who wished to learn it, outside normal class times.

Three leading language movements emerged: Skol an Emsav, Kuzul ar Brezhoneg and Emgleo Breiz. It was Skol an Emsav who stressed that Bretons ought to create the structure of their own society and not continue to beg for the recognition of their rights from France.

> Let us ask nothing from the oppressors of Brittany but strive to carry our struggle into everyday life and build structures which will be independent of the French State. The first task is to restore the national consciousness and impart to the people the will to take their own destiny in hand.
>
> It is no business of officials and politicians in Paris or Marseille to say what we should do with our language. Their refusal is, however, a tacit recognition of our existence as a national community. Remember Premier Doumergue, in 1909, opposing the teaching of Breton for fear it would boost the demand of self-government?
>
> The myth of the French 'nation' must be destroyed if we are to be free. We must carry further the work of our writers and linguists who, by developing our language's ability to express modern ideas and feelings, assert independence.
>
> Today the Bretons are rising against subjection and beginning to see the Breton problem in its totality. For us, Breton is not a small language fit for preservation only as a means of expression for a rural society and subor-

dinated to a major language. We reject the French language claim to universality as a disguise for imperialism. The Breton language alone will enable us to establish the link with our history and to express our personality, to create a new cultural medium instead of depending on intellectual productions 'made in Paris'. Our first victory in this struggle is learning Breton and transmitting it to our children. Our second; helping others to learn it. This is the task of Skol an Emsav.

We look upon the French structure, radio, TV, newspapers, administration, as the front on which to carry the fight; they are instruments of alienation.

These were the fighting words of T.Louarn of Skol an Emsav speaking at a meeting of 1500 language enthusiasts at Pondivi on November 26th, 1972. The growth of interest in Breton since then has produced many publications, ranging from books to magazines and comics. The amount of time allowed Breton broadcasts on radio and television has slowly increased. In 1977, president Giscard d'Estaing made a pronouncement which left the Breton people gasping. Speaking on February 8th at Ploermel, he promised the introduction of a 'Cultural Charter' within a year which would allow the Bretons to maintain their language and culture. The first drafts caused speculation: there would be bilingual road signs, proper training for teachers, subsidies for nursery schools, students would be allowed to take a degree in Breton studies and the 'regional languages and cultures' would be taught in schools. When the much heralded 'Cultural Charter' finally made its appearance, it fell far short of those expectations and the French bureaucracy has steadfastly refused to allow a proper implementation of any of the ideas behind it.

Diwan, an organization to run nursery schools in Breton, started in 1977 with one class of five pupils. By 1983, it was covering 20 schools with 28 classes, as well as six primary school classes and continued to expand, employing three full-time administrators and 39 full-time teachers. It had managed to get a small subsidy from state funds but still had to rely for more than 80 per cent of its financial support on voluntary sources. With the theoretical recognition by the French state of the principle of allowing Breton to be taught in schools, a new Union of Teachers of Breton was formed to ensure proper standards and a supporting organisation.

In June, 1982, the French Minister of Education gave his directive on the teaching of 'regional languages and cultures'. It was discovered that, if the schools obeyed the directive, Breton pupils would be worse off than before. For secondary schools, the Minister proposed that one hour a week of *optional* teaching of the language and culture could be given to pupils in the first to fourth grades. Previously, two hours for the language alone had been allowed with attendant culture as an additional subject. Earlier, ten students had been required before a class was constituted, but now the Minister ordered that the figure should be increased to fifteen pupils. The Minister also introduced a *Catch-22* situation in that only qualified teachers would be allowed to teach these classes. To be qualified a teacher had to have a *Certificate d'Aptitude Pédagogique à l'Engseignement Secondaire* (CAPES), but the Minister refused to institute the qualification for Breton, arguing that it would amount to having a competition for the purpose of recruiting teachers specially in Brittany, and that it would be a breach of the principle of French unity.

Another example of French state 'double-talk' occurred at the Celtic Department of the Rennes-Villejean University where in 1983, 550 students were studying first year Breton/Celtic studies; 210 students were taking their Licence (degree) and forty-five were studying for an Master of Arts degree. To cater for this, the largest department in the university, there was only one professor, paid by the state. There were two lecturers and three assistant lecturers. The Lecturer in Welsh was paid by the British Council. The Lecturer in Irish sometimes received no pay at all and the students had to make collections to obtain money for the three assistants.

Skol an Emsav, having been at the forefront of the fight to save the Breton language from the continued French pressures, achieving some notable successes during the 1970's and early 1980's, had joined a 'Cultural Progressive Front' which was pursuing more or less the same policies as Giscard d'Estaing's promised 'Cultural Charter'. In the early part of 1984, many members of Skol an Emsav were unhappy at this association, its growing lack of militancy and of clear-cut aims. The dissidents decided to break away from Skol an Emsav and form a new movement Stourm ar Brezhoneg with the aims of winning official status for Breton, as well as independence for Brittany. Yann Per Delisle was appointed secretary and stated his movement wanted to free itself from any deference towards French political parties which were allowing the extirpation of the Breton language and culture to continue. He rejected the 'begging attitude' of other groups and said his movement saw Breton as a national language not, as others, a 'regional' language or *'une des langues de France'*. Stourm ar Brezhoneg would demand that Breton be recognized as an official language in Brittany, that it be taught in all schools as part of the curriculum and not just as an optional subject. It also announced that to achieve these aims, it would not be adverse to defying the law when the occasion demanded.

With the coming of Francois Mitterand's Socialist Government in Paris, a plan of 'devolution' was put forward and an appointed Breton Assembly was allowed to meet in Rennes with the promise that this assembly would become elected by 1986. But the Bretons have a long way to go before they can expect any reasonable degree of autonomy on a political or cultural level. The French State may no longer openly proclaim its aim to eradicate the Breton language but it continues to stubbornly obstruct every effort to put the theoretical reforms into practice.

Brittany has never surrendered her right to exist as a nation. She was forced to submit to French rule by force of arms. From the French annexation, French policy has been to destroy all the national characteristics of the Breton people, firstly, through the control of the Breton economy, thus weakening Breton national cohesion and inducing emigrations of Bretons on a large scale and, secondly, through the control of the education system and the media—destroying, through these means, the Breton language and culture. Attempts to reverse this policy of assimilation have been consistently and oppressively opposed by the French regime in Brittany. In spite of this, the Bretons have survived and still fight on.

Chapter Four
Cymru (Wales)

By the 7th Century AD, the English had established the basic extent of their western borders, enclosing the British Celts in the western peninsula which they were to designate 'the land of foreigners' or the land of the *'weahlas'*—Wales. During the 8th Century, Offa, the powerful ruler of the Mercian kingdom (747-796 AD) decided to build a dyke which was to mark the border of the two countries from the River Severn to the River Dee. Any Welshman found with a weapon on the Mercian side of the dyke was to have his "right hand forthwith cut off". During the following centuries, Wales—or Cymru, 'the land of comrades' as the Welsh called it, began to emerge as a political and cultural entity, fighting off all attacks from the English and the Norse. Literature flourished and the country was ruled by a sophisticated set of laws whose first known codification was made under Hywel ap Cadell (known after his death as Hywel Dda—The Good) between 910-950. It is from the 9th Century that the first surviving manuscripts date, although Welsh literature can be identified as early as the 6th Century.

During the early 11th Century, Wales was not only able to contain English threats but, under the leadership of Gruffydd ap Llywelyn ap Seisyll, made punitive raids into the English territory forcing Edward the Confessor to accept a peace treaty at a meeting on the banks of the Severn. After the Norman invasion of England, many independent Norman knights set out to carve themselves petty kingdoms among the Welsh and, during the years 1093-99, tried to take the country by storm. By the year 1100, they had only managed to secure a foothold on the south-eastern tip of Wales and, for the next few centuries, a continued warfare took place with Wales managing to retain her independence, her rich cultural life and literary attainments.

It was in 1246 that Dafydd ap Llywelyn died and the succession passed to Llywelyn ap Gruffydd, his nephew. During this time, the old Celtic ideas of succession and land holding were passing into disuse as the concepts of Norman feudal holding and primogeniture were taking root. Llywelyn was able to keep Welsh independence intact due to a civil war sweeping England which ended in 1267 with a victory for Henry III. On September 25th, 1267, Llywelyn and Henry signed the Treaty of Montgomery in which the English King agreed to recognize the national territory of Wales with Llywelyn and his heirs as its rulers. But when Henry died, his son Edward decided on a conquest and in 1277 began to implement his amibition. After a number of battles, Llywelyn was forced to sign a treaty at Conway which gave him four years of peace to reorganize the country. Then he rose against the English. On December 11th, 1282, hastening to rejoin his troops, the man know as "the last prince of Wales" was caught and slain by the English. Gruffydd ab yr Ynad Coch expressed the desperate feeling of the Welsh:

> Oh God! that the sea might engulf the land!
> Why are we left to long-drawn weariness?

Llywelyn's brother, Dafydd ap Gruffydd, was accepted as Llywelyn's heir and tried to continue the struggle but he was caught and beheaded. By the Statute of Rhuddlan in 1284, Llywelyn's principality was formally annexed to the English crown and its dominions. Yet the Welsh fought on. Rhys ap Meredith gathered an army but was soon defeated. Madog, in 1294, achieved several successes but was defeated in 1295 at Cefn Digoll. Edward tried diplomacy to pacify the country by declaring his son as 'Prince of Wales' and establishing the tradition of the English monarchy for the Heir Apparent to take the title. But the Welsh refused to be pacified and Llywelyn Bren tried in 1315 to restore Welsh independence. After the suppression of this rising, Wales was comparatively quiet for eighty years.

Then, in 1400, came an uprising led by Owain ap Gruffydd—Owain Glyndŵr—who, in a quick campaign, drove out the English and united all Wales under his rule. At his crowning, envoys from several European countries attended. His parliaments met at Machynlleth and Harlech, the Welsh Church was declared free of the dictates of Canterbury with the ancient primacy of St. David's being reinstated, and Owain planned the establishment of two universities in Wales. But, by 1408 AD, Wales began to suffer military set-backs and, by 1410, it could no longer claim to be an independent state.

Then came the rise of the Tudor monarchy.

Sir Owain Tewdur (or Tudor) claimed an unbroken descent from the 7th Century Welsh ruler, Cadwaldwr the Blessed, and secured the fortune of his house by marrying the widow of Henry V, Catherine of France. His two sons Jasper and Edmund became Earls of Pembroke and Richmond and supporters of the House of Lancaster. Edmund Tudor had a son, Henry, who became Earl of Richmond after him. Henry Tudor spent some time in exile in Brittany while attempts were being made to topple the despotic English ruler, Richard III. On August 8th, 1485, Henry landed at Milford Haven in Wales and, by cynically playing on his Welsh ancestry, appealed to Welshmen to join him. On the morning of August 21st, 1485, Henry's army, flying the red dragon banner of Wales, came upon Richard III's army at the market town of Bosworth and defeated him. Henry Tudor was King of England...a 'Welsh prince' but of a family three generations Anglicized. The house of Tudor was to enact the most repressive laws of any English monarchy in an effort to eradicate the Welsh nation.

Initially, Henry (Tudor) VII appealed to Welsh sentiment, even calling his eldest son Arthur. London became a focal point for Welshmen. Yet it soon became obvious that the Welsh nation could expect nothing from the Tudors. In September, 1531, Rhys ap Gruffydd was sent to the Tower of London for seeking to create an insurrection in Wales. He was executed on Tower Hill on December 4th, 1531. In the wake of this, Henry VIII, now on the throne, agreed to an Act of Annexation, with thirty-nine sections aimed at making Wales an integral part of England and declaring the intent "utterly to extirpe alle and singular the sinister usages and customs differing from the laws of this Realm". No persons who used the Welsh language were to hold any office nor could they be landowners unless they spoke English. A further Act, in 1542, tidied up the workings of the previous Act. It was not until the 19th Century that these Acts of Annexation were renamed 'Acts of Union' as a sop to Welsh national feeling.

In spite of this, Welsh literature began to flourish. The first known book to be published in Welsh was printed in 1546—a volume by John ap Rhys known by its opening words *'Yn y Lhywyr Hwnn'*. In 1548 William Salesbury produced his Welsh-English dictionary and, two years later, he wrote *How to Learn Welsh*. Griffith Roberts, while in Milan in 1567, published a *Welsh Grammar*. Between 1546 and 1644, some 41 books were printed in Welsh. Most important, and in spite of the Acts of Annexation, came the Act for Translating the Bible and Divine Service into Welsh in 1563, with the proviso that they be placed with English versions, so that the two languages could be compared and people might learn English. The Protestant proselytizing zeal had overcome imperial scruples. In 1567, the New Testament and Prayer Book appeared in Welsh and, in 1588, Bishop William Morgan's translation of the Bible was published.

The year 1568 saw the birth of the Caerwys Eisteddfod, a gathering of Welsh poets and singers, which gave birth to the modern Eisteddfodau. Throughout the next century, the language, as a literary medium, achieved widespread popularity so that an English commentator could remark, in *Wallography*, 1684, "their native gibberish is usually prattled throughout the whole of Taphydom..."

An Act of Uniformity in 1662 made a further attempt to incorporate Wales into England. In reaction, in 1674, a Welsh Trust was established, its foundation inspired by an Englishman named Thomas Gouge, to give status to the Welsh language in education. Gouge wanted to spread literacy among the ordinary people and he financed new editions of the Bible and other works in Welsh from his own pocket. In the 18th Century, Griffith Jones of Carmarthen established a school in his parish to teach people to read the language. By the time he died in 1761, some 3,395 schools had been established based on his first model, teaching 158,000 pupils throughout Wales. Griffith Jones was savagely criticized for propagating Welsh. He replied: "To be able to read one language does not increase the difficulty of learning another, but always renders it easier. It is common for all nations to learn their own tongue first; and it is the most natural method to begin with the easiest and then to proceed to the hardest thing." His literacy campaign increased the demand for Welsh books. From 1721 until 1800, some 1,156 new titles in Welsh were published. To this period belongs Elis Wyn o Lasynys (1671-1734) described as the "greatest of all Welsh prose writers".

In 1746, the English Parliament by enactment reiterated that the name 'England' was to be understood as including Wales. Therefore, the Anglican Church's policy was that English-speaking ministers could enjoy livings in Wales. A Dr Bowles was given a parish in Ynys Môn (Anglesey) in which only five of his parishioners could understand English. In 1768, a case was brought against him at Canterbury where, it was argued, he should be dismissed from the living on the grounds that he could not communicate with his flock. Bowles defended himself by saying:

> Wales is a conquered country, it is proper to introduce the English language, and it is the duty of the bishops to endeavour to promote English in order to introduce the language...It has always been the policy of the legislature to introduce the English language into Wales.

In London, Cymdeithas y Cymmrodorion was founded in 1751 as the first Welsh society aimed at promoting the language. It subsequently launched two periodicals entirely in Welsh.

The 18th century saw Welsh people stirring into a new national political consciousness. In 1640, John Lewis had argued, in a pamphlet, that the Welsh nation had a destiny to fulfil by preserving its language and achieving independence. With the rise of republicanism, and the activities of republicans in Ireland, Scotland and England, the people of Wales too started to organize. In 1790, Thomas Roberts printed a pamphlet, *Cwyn yn erbyn Gorthrymder*—A Complaint Against Oppression.

The 19th Century started on a note of high optimism with the establishment of many Welsh newspapers such as *Seren Gomer* (1818) and *Y Traethodydd* (1845), and others. A new flood of Welsh literature was being published with over 6,000 new titles in the first half of the century. The Anglican Church, now realizing that its language policy had forced the majority of Welsh people into Nonconformity, began to change that policy, allowing marriages to be performed in Welsh for the first time in 1837, followed by the appointment of Welsh-speaking clergy to Welsh-speaking parishes. In 1843, services in Welsh were allowed, provided they were paid for by the congregations.

There were many skirmishes during the early part of the century which had nationalist overtones. The execution of 31-year-old collier Dic Penderyn for allegedly killing a soldier (to which another later confessed) gave the Welsh a folk-hero martyr in 1831. More nationalist in approach were the Rebecca Riots during 1839, in which the movement stated that "it is a shameful thing for us Welshmen to have the sons of England had (sic) a dominion over us". In 1843, some 3,000 followers of the Rebecca movement, carrying banners saying '*Rhyddid*/Freedom' and 'Liberty and better food', set fire to official buildings in Cardiff.

In 1847, three monoglot Englishmen constituted a Commission of Enquiry into the state of education in Wales and reported: "The Welsh language is a vast drawback to Wales and a manifold barrier to the moral progress and commercial prosperity of the people. It is not easy to over-estimate its evil effects.' The commissioners blamed the language for everything. One commissioner did point out the brutal way in which English was being forced on Welsh children:

> My attention was attracted to a piece of wood suspended by a string round a boy's neck, and on the wood were the words 'Welsh stick'. This, I was told, was a stigma for speaking Welsh. But, in fact, his only alternative was to speak Welsh or say nothing. he did not understand English and there is no system in exercise of interpretation.

The report had the reverse effect of what the commissioners had hoped for. It united the Welsh in national sentiment in spite of *The Times* of London, in 1866, condemning the language as "the curse of Wales".

In 1870, the Education Act made the English language compulsory in all Welsh schools. Welsh opinion was disturbed by the Act which would mean the inevitable destruction of the language. Cymdeithas Cymmrodorion circulated a questionnaire to head teachers asking them if they believed the language should be taught in schools. The majority were in favour and, from this, a Society for Utilizing the Welsh Language was formed "to see established in Wales a sound system of bilingual education..."

By 1901, out of a population of 2,012, 876, some 929,824 people spoke Welsh of which 280,905 were monoglots. There were 25 weekly newspapers, 28 monthly magazines, two bi-monthly magazines and two quarterlies entirely in Welsh. Between 1891 and 1898, some 8,425 new book titles were published. This was also the period of the first great national novelist of Wales—Daniel Owen (1836-1895) who created a new literary era. He was a novelist of the Dickens school which he admired. Novels such as *Rhys Lewis*, *Enoc Huws*, *Gwen Tomos* and *Y Dreflan*, established his reputation and have been translated into several other languages, including Irish.

In the first three-quarters of the 19th Century, there were several attempts to form Welsh-speaking colonies in the New World because Welshmen could no longer envisage Wales as being able to separate itself from its neighbour, then ruling the biggest Empire in the world. One of these colonies still retains a Welsh-speaking population—Patagonia in Argentina.

Michael Jones, who had been foremost in establishing such colonies, subsequently realized that the only way to save the Welsh nation was for Wales itself to achieve independence. In 1885, the Liberal Party had committed itself to federal devolution of the constituent nations of the United Kingdom. With Wales then having only 34 MP's in a Parliament dominated by nearly 600 English MP's, the question was how could the Welsh make any impact. Gwilym Hiraethog, writing in *Yr Amserau*, suggested that they "should resolve themselves into a united Welsh party".

In 1886, Michael Davitt, the former Fenian leader, the victor of Ireland's 'Land War' and then an Irish Party Member of Parliament, was invited to speak at a meeting in Wales on independence. At the end of his speech, a young Criccieth lawyer rose to thank him, lashing out at those who objected to the Irish patriot, speaking as being the same people who, on bended knees, begged English princes, who were no better than German half-breeds, to preside at the Eisteddfodau. The lawyer was David Lloyd George.

Later that year, Thomas E. Ellis won a seat in Parliament saying: "I solicit your suffrage as a Welsh nationalist". Michael Jones, Lloyd George and Ellis decided to join forces to form the first Welsh political independence movement called Cymru Fydd (Future Wales). In 1888, Tom Ellis told the House of Commons:

"Self-government is at once the inspirer and goal of nationhood. Without a National Assembly, her (Wales) position as a nation cannot be assured..." Two years later, Ellis was joined by his Cymru Fydd colleague Lloyd George who won the seat at Caernarfon on April 10th, 1890. In his maiden speech to the House of Commons on June 13th, 1890, Lloyd George said:

> The current of the time is sweeping to nationalism. Wales, in throwing in her lot with Ireland in the self-government struggle, has struck a blow not only for the national rights of another Celtic country, but also for her own.
>
> But over and above that, we shall work for a legislature elected by the manhood and womanhood of Wales and to them responsible. It will be the symbol and cement of our unity as a nation, our instrument in working out our social ideals...the deliverer of our message and example to humanity.

The General Election of 1892 saw the Liberals come to power at Westminster with an official policy of devolution. Tom Ellis was appointed to the Treasury, which caused him to lose sight of his 'national' aims. The idea of the Cymru Fydd group, as a party within the larger Liberal Party, soon faded. Angered by Ellis's desertion, Lloyd George, with other self-government Welsh MP's formed Cynghrair Cenedlaethol Cymru Fydd, attempting to bind all those who wanted separation from England with those who favoured a moderate devolution into one force. The group did not last long and Lloyd George decided to form a Young Wales movement. Lloyd George declared, in the new movement's magazine, that he believed "with the whole soul's passion in the sacredness of Welsh nationalism and in the future of the Welsh nation". In the devolution debate on March 29th, 1895, Lloyd George seconded the Federate Home Rule Bill proposed by Sir Henry Dalziel and, whilst the first reading was carried by 128 votes to 102 votes, it was lost on the next reading.

Cymru Fydd and Young Wales' representatives expressed themselves in the London Parliament through the Liberal Party and, unlike the disciplined Irish Party, seemed to have no cohesive plan of action. With the Liberal victory of 1906, Lloyd George (hailed as 'The Apostle of Welsh Nationalism' in an 1896 edition of *Young Wales*) was appointed to the Cabinet. "The entrance of Mr Lloyd George into the Cabinet dealt a death blow to the dream of an Independent Party for Wales", observed the *Welsh Review*. Lloyd George utterly betrayed the cause he had espoused for so long, becoming Prime Minister of the United Kingdom. From the Irish viewpoint, his sending into Ireland of the 'Black and Tan' terror gangs during the War of Independence (1919-21), his cunning and blackmail which created Partition and which also led to the disastrous Irish Civil War (1922-23) are still remembered. The experience is felt all the more bitterly as Lloyd George was a fellow Celt, whose first language was a Celtic one, and who claimed to believe in self-government.

The newly emerging Labour Party was seeking support in Wales and using the catch-phrase of self-government as a means of doing so. It launched its own newspaper *Y Gwladgarwr Cymreig* (Welsh Patriot). In the General Election of 1918, the Labour Party stated:

> Labour believes in self-government. The Labour Party is pledged to a scheme of statutory legislature for Scotland, Wales and Ireland, as part of the larger plan which will transform the British Empire into a Commonwealth of self-governing nations.

Liberal Party promises of self-government had been demonstrated to be meaningless; Wales swung to labour but during their term of office in 1923/4 and again in 1929/31, they claimed they could do nothing about self-government. The *Welsh Outlook* reported that the Welsh people were "politically and nationally at the ebb of our fortunes". The reaction was to establish Byddin Ymreolwyr Cymru (Home Rule Army of Wales) in 1924. Then in August, 1925, in Pwllheli, representatives of self-government groups came together and formed Plaid Cymru, the Party of Wales.

Its first manifesto was written by John Saunders Lewis, a scholar and rising poet and playright. "We must release Wales from the grip of the English. We can aim at nothing less than to do away with the English language in Wales", wrote Lewis. In June, 1926, a party newspaper *Y Ddraig Goch* (The Red Dragon) was launched, and Saunders Lewis became President of the Party. Dr D.J.Davies, a young economist, worked on an economic plan. In 1929, the Reverend Lewis Valentine stood as the first parliamentary candidate for the party in Caernarfon. The party asserted that its aim was "to secure self-government for Wales, safeguard the culture, language, traditions and economic life". Electorally, the party made little headway as the Labour Party was still maintaining its adherence to self-government and, as late as the 1945 General Election, won 27 out of the 36 Welsh seats on the issue.

In 1936, the Air Ministry decided to establish an RAF bombing school at Penrhos on the Lleyn peninsula in the heart of a Welsh-speaking area. In spite of a year of protests, appeals about the inevitable destruction of the language which such a military encampment would bring about, the Government stood firm. On September 8th, 1936, three men entered Pwllheli police station to report that they had set fire to Pen-y-berth Aerodrome, the site of the bombing range, as a protest. They were Saunders Lewis, Lewis Valentine and D.J.Williams. (Williams was a schoolteacher.) At their trial in Caernarfon, they refused to speak in any other language but Welsh. The judge, with surprising candour, told them "...the case in this court is to be decided by the law of England!"

The jury could not agree and the case was referred to the Old Bailey in London, under a storm of protest. The defendants continued to speak in Welsh only and, ironically D.J.Williams (who taught English) was allowed an interpreter because no one could give evidence as to whether he spoke any English. Williams, on behalf of the prisoners, stated: "With every respect to this jury, I say they cannot do justice to our cause. Nor could any jury but a jury of our own nation'. They were found guilty and sentenced to nine months' imprisonment. They became known as *'Y tri'*— 'The Three'. It was the first time since the Rebecca riots that the Welsh had resorted to force in defence of their homeland.

In 1939, Saunders Lewis resigned as President of Plaid Cymru and Professor J.E.Daniel was elected. Plaid Cymru embarked on the unpopular policy of neutrality during World War II, with members refusing military service on the grounds that "England has no right to compel the youth of Wales to fight for her". This caused the Party to become subject to attack as being pro-Nazi and Fascist.

In 1939, the first Welsh medium primary school was established in Aberystwyth under the auspices of Urdd Gobaith Cymru (the Welsh League of Youth). A Committee to Defend Welsh Culture was formed which, after the War, merged with the Union of Welsh Societies to form Undeb Cymru Fydd. There was a struggle during the war years to gain some form of 'official recognition' for the language. One instance, where an elderly non-English speaking couple were trying to send a telegram to their son at the war front and were refused by the Post Office, swung sympathy towards the language. In the face of mounting public opinion, the Home Secretary, Herbert Morrison, introduced a Welsh Courts Act on October 14th, 1942, which, while not conferring full entitlement on the language, at least enacted '...the Welsh language may be used in any court in Wales by any party or witness who considers that he would otherwise be at any disadvantage by reason of his natural language of communication being Welsh."

In the General Election of 1945, the Labour Party issued the following election manifesto:

> Wales is a small nation which, through immense difficulties, has preserved her language and cultural life through the centuries.
>
> The true freedom of Wales depends not only on political control of her own life, but on economic control as well.
>
> True freedom for Wales would be the result and product of a Socialist Britain and only under such conditions could self-government in Wales be an effective and secure guardian of the life of the nation.

As soon as the Labour Party won the election, R.A.Butler, in the House of Commons, stated: 'I must say that we cannot accept any suggestion for a system of a Welsh Parliament to run Welsh affairs". Apologetically, James Griffith, one of the keenest of the Labour Party advocates for self-government, said, lamely: "Circumstances have changed greatly. My advice is that Wales should remain a unit with England". John Taylor, secretary of the Scottish Labour Party, was perhaps more candid than his colleagues, when he told them in December, 1947: "I, myself, ceased to desire self-government as soon as we secured a Socialist Government for Britain". Herbert Morrison remarked with self-satisfaction: "The device of political expediency has served the Labour Party well in Wales".

In the sentiments created by this 'socialist' betrayal, a Welsh Republican Movement was formed and published a manifesto declaring "that Wales must be a sovereign democratic republic, subject only to such authority as it may accept or subscribe to as a member of the community of free nations". Their 12-point manifesto was a socialist document which also recognized "the Welsh language as the native language of the Welsh people shall be the first and official language of the Republic of Wales". It also declared that "the Republic of Wales shall live in close association with all the other Celtic peoples". The movement appeared at the end of the 1940's and seemed short-lived although from the 1950's a republican and socialist political tradition began to emerge more clearly in Welsh political life.

Plaid Cymru was now led by an energetic lawyer, Gwynfor Evans. The Party were achieving successes in local government elections and, in 1949, Gwynfor Evans won a seat on Carmarthenshire County Council, eventually becoming an alderman. Faced with the utter betrayal of the Labour Party, Plaid Cymru launched a campaign for a 'Parliament for Wales in Five Years' on October 1st, 1949. By 1953, only three Labour MP's had deserted their party's new policy to stand for self-government. The Conservatives. observing the strength of the Welsh campaign, created the post of a Minister for Welsh Affairs in 1951. The campaign culminated in the presentation of a petition bearing 250,00 signatures to Parliament on April 24th, 1956. Goronwy Roberts MP said: "Self-government within the framework of the United Kingdom should be conducive to the good government of Wales."

At the same time as the campaign was running, the local councils began to develop a network of bilingual schools and, by 1953, there were fifteen such schools. By the end of the 1950's some 43 primary schools were using a bilingual policy, although it was not until 1957 that the first bilingual secondary school was opened at Rhyl. Others were to follow. In 1957, a Minister of State for Wales was created, again by the Conservatives as a sop to Welsh national sentiment. On November 3rd, 1958, Gwynfor Evans delivered a memorandum to the United Nations on the Welsh case for independence.

Now began a new departure in Welsh thinking. The first manifestation of 20th Century 'direct action' had taken place in 1936. In 1952, a small Welsh republican group called Y Gweriniaethwyr made an attempt to blow up a pipeline taking water from the new Claerwen reservoir to Birmingham. Then, on October 19th, 1954, an attempt was made to blow up the Fron

Aqueduct, carrying water from the Elan Valley to Birmingham. In 1957, Liverpool City Council decided to flood the Welsh-speaking Tryweryn Valley to create a new reservoir for the City. Opposition to the scheme received the backing of the vast majority of Welsh people, 27 out of the 36 Welsh MP's being totally opposed to the scheme as well as 125 local authorities, trade unionists and cultural and religious groups. Yet, on July 31st, 1957, Westminster passed the Tryweryn Reservoir Bill.

On Saturday, September 22nd, 1962, two men were arrested attempting to destroy the site at Tryweryn. On February 10th, 1963, an explosion took place at the site. It was the first action of Mudiad Amddiffyn Cymru—Movement for the Defence of Wales. MAC, as it became known, had been the inspiration of Owain Williams, the son of a tenant farmer in Nefyn, who had worked in the tough logging camps of British Columbia. He had joined forces with Emyr Llewelyn Jones, a student at the University of Wales, and the son of a well-known bard of the Welsh Gorsedd. Others were recruited. Jones was soon arrested and sentenced to a year's imprisonment in March, 1963. MAC blew up a power cable carrying pylon in reprisal. Owain Williams was eventually arrested with other members of MAC and, for a while, the movement became moribund.

When, on Thursday, October 21st, 1965, the Lord Mayor of Liverpool came to open Tryweryn dam, he was met by a vast crowd of protesters. Among the crowd was a small uniformed unit with green forage caps bearing the symbol of the Eagle of Snowdonia. Their leader carried the Welsh flag. He was Julian Cayo Evans, a former member of the South Wales Borderers and a horse-breeder from Lampeter. In the 1960's, the Free Wales Army, as it became known, kept the media busy with its uniformed publicity seeking activities, drilling, demonstrating and holding training camps. It generally attracted the attention of the police. The FWA marched down O'Connell Street, Dublin, in the parade to mark the 50th Anniversary of the 1916 Rising in Ireland. But entirely separate from the FWA were the activities of the MAC. A series of bombs began to explode throughout Wales, aimed at the pipelines sending Welsh water to Liverpool and Birmingham. On March 7th, 1966, came the explosion at Clywedog, followed by attacks on the Elan Valley pipeline, the Lake Vyrnwy reservoir,

Stourbridge and Hapsford, and even the Welsh Office and Tax Offices in Cardiff were bombed. It was soon clear that the MAC was highly organized and had trained explosives' experts in their midst.

At the same time, an intensified struggle took place to secure status for the Welsh language.

In 1961, out of a population of 2,518,711 people, some 656,-002 spoke Welsh and, of this number, 26,223 could speak no English. The lack of status and the hostility towards the language by officialdom caused Saunders Lewis to emerge from a self-imposed seclusion to deliver a hard-hitting lecture on BBC Radio Wales on February 13th, 1962, entitled *Tynged yr Iaith*—The Fate of the Language. He told his listeners that the language was more important than self-government for, if self-government came before status for the language, then its death would be that much quicker. He foresaw that, unless determined action was taken to save the language, there would be no Welsh language by the end of the century. That same year, Cymdeithas yr Iaith Gymraeg, The Welsh Language Society, was formed under the secretaryship of Geraint Jones.

The first campaigns were a simple matter of demanding status for the language in particular places—in the Post Office, courts of law, in local-government notices and so forth. A significant turning point was the February, 1963, demonstration by Cymdeithas at the bridge at Trefechan, Aberystwyth, in which demonstrators were attacked by pro-English toughs. It attracted great publicity towards the inferior status of the language and on July 31st, 1963, Sir David Hughes-Parry QC was commissioned to look into "the legal status of the Welsh language". He reported in October, 1965, and recommended that the Welsh language should enjoy equal validity with English in Wales.

Cymdeithas's campaign continued, with Welshmen and women being sent to jail rather than fill in official forms in English, or be forced to speak English to officials.

Then came Plaid Cymru's election breakthrough on July 14th, 1966, when Gwynfor Evans became the Party's first Member of Parliament for Carmarthen. Although there were massive swings to Plaid Cymru during the late 1960's, the Party failed to gain another seat in Parliament until 1974, when the Party won three seats. They were reduced to two seats in the 1979 General Election but held on to them in the 1983 General Election, coming extremely close to winning a third seat in Ynys Môn and narrowly losing in Carmarthen. Dafydd Wigley held the Caernarfon seat with Dafydd Elis Thomas holding the seat for Meirionnydd.

The Government reacted to the rise of Welsh nationalism by first adopting a Welsh Language Bill in 1967 which fell far short of the Hughes Parry recommendations of "equal validity". It also introduced a new plan for local government in Wales, replacing the 164 local authorities with 36, and set up an advisory Welsh Council. Lastly, with Prince Charles as the Heir Apparent being, by English tradition, Prince of Wales, the prince was rushed through a quick six-week language course in Welsh at the University College of Wales in Aberystwyth, while plans to hold an investiture ceremony at Caernarfon were made. On July 1st, 1969, the investiture, known as *Y Pantomeim* or *Dathliadau Buddugoliaeth* (the pantomime or the conquest ceremony) took place.

The continued activities of the FWA and the MAC caused the Government to flood the area with police, troops and back-up units of the Royal Navy and the Royal Air Force. In spite of this blanket security, the MAC laid several bombs, one of which exploded on the railway tracks ten minutes before the Royal train was due to pass. Two members of the MAC were killed on the morning of the investiture, while a soldier was killed when his truck exploded under the very walls of Caernarfon Castle. As the 21-gun salute sounded, one television commentator counted them...and made it 22! MAC had exploded another bomb, as their tribute to the re-enactment of their nation's subjection. Eggs and rotten fruit were thrown at the Royal family as they came into Caernarfon, an apple just missing the Queen as her landau passed in. The British Government had counted on 250,000 tourists and spectators but only 90,000 attended.

At the end of November, 1969, John Barnard Jenkins, a warrant officer in the Army, was arrested. He was one of the main strategists behind the MAC. Throughout his trial and subsequent imprisonment, having been sentenced to ten years' on April 20th, 1970, he refused to name or implicate any other members of the MAC. His *Prison Letters*, published by Y Lolfa in 1981, show an exceptional political awareness. After his release in 1976, having obtained a degree in sociology while in prison, he was refused admission to do a post-graduate course at Swansea University College, and was continually harassed by the police. In 1983, he was arrested and charged with sheltering Dafydd Ladd who was found guilty of possessing explosives. Jenkins was sentenced to two years' imprisonment and Ladd received nine years.

Plaid Cymru blamed their failure to make a significant electoral breakthrough in 1970 on the activities of the FWA and, more particularly, the MAC. Gwynfor Evans was a declared pacifist and lost no opportunity to denounce violence. However, Jenkins believed that something was needed to raise the political consciousness of the Welsh people which would force them to think seriously about their conditions. It was never the aim of MAC to win any concrete concessions. Its purpose was achieved. The bombings, and the subsequent campaign of arson in 1979 and the early 1980's, in which English-owned, second homes in Wales were burnt, and the Workers' Army of the Welsh Republic bombings, raised not only Welsh national consciousness but exerted an influence on Government attitudes. In the 1979 General Election campaign, the Conservative Party, led by Mrs Margaret Thatcher, announced its support for the establishment of a Welsh television channel—Sianel Pedwar Cymru (S4C). Having won the election, Mrs Thatcher changed her mind. Gwynfor Evans then announced that he would go on hunger strike if the Government did not keep their word. S4C came into being.

A year later, Mrs Thatcher's intransigence allowed ten Irish political prisoners, including Bobby Sands MP and Kieran Doherty TD (member of the Irish Parliament), die on a hunger strike to obtain political status. But she knew, however, that if Gwynfor Evans died, it would lead to a campaign of violence in Wales when her energies needed to be directed to Ireland. Violence had now become part of the objective reality of Welsh politics.

The existence in Welsh-speaking areas of 30,000 holiday homes, owned mainly by English families, had been identified by Cymdeithas yr Iaith Gymraeg as early as 1972 as a contributing factor to the decay of the language. By comparison the areas had a council house waiting list of 50,000. The first attacks on these holiday homes occurred on December 12th, 1979. During that winter, some 30 houses were burnt down and, by early 1984, there had been nearly 100 such attacks causing an estimated half-million pounds worth of damage. It was alleged that the MAC was behind the arson attacks. The police reacted quickly and over the Palm Sunday weekend in March, 1980, they carried out an 'Operation Fire' in which the four Welsh police forces detained, sometimes illegally, 52 people.

On March 19th, 1980, an incendiary device was left at Porthmadog Railway Station in Gwynedd. Two similar devices were placed at the Conservative Party's offices in Cardiff and at Shotton a week later. In May, a Conservative Club was also attacked and, in July, the home of Nicholas Edwards MP, Secretary of State for Wales, was attacked. This campaign of incendiary devices continued into 1981 but in October that year, an explosive device was planted at the Army Careers Office in Pontypridd. A group calling itself WAWR (Workers' Army of the Welsh Republic), and which is also the Welsh word for 'dawn', claimed responsibility. Various suspects were detained by the police but no charges were brought. Some of the early incendiary devices of 1981 had been claimed by a group calling itself Meibion Glyndŵr (Sons of Glyndŵr). More explosive devices were planted in October and November, and the campaign culminated with an explosion at the Welsh Office in Cardiff, following which WAWR sent a manifesto to BBC Wales.

Between April 29 and July 3, 1982 eight people were arrested and spent, in some cases, as long as 17 months in jail before bail was granted, having been charged with responsibility for the WAWR campaign. They were Adrian Stone, Nicholas Hodges, Gareth Westacott, David Burns. Jennifer Smith, Dafydd Ladd, Brian Rees and Robert Griffiths. John Jenkins was later charged with helping Ladd avoid arrest. The charges against Jennifer Smith, a nurse, and Ladd's girlfriend, were dropped at an early stage when Ladd agreed to plead guilty to the possession of explosives. He was sentenced to nine years'. John Jenkins pleaded guilty and received two years' imprisonment. Gareth Westacott, who had spent nine months in jail awaiting trial, disappeared while on bail.

This left five defendants who pleaded 'not guilty' and the trial was held from September 13th through November, 1982, at Cardiff Crown Court. There was a great deal of police 'evidence' but the jury found four of the defendants not guilty of conspiracy and the possession of explosives and found only one man, Brian Roberts, guilty of possessing explosives but not guilty of conspiracy. He received three years' in jail. The Court findings left a number of pertinent questions awaiting an answer. It was clear that the jury had accepted that here was a case of a police conspiracy against the defendants, most of whom were members of the Welsh Socialist Republican Movement which had been formed in January, 1980. Robert Griffiths was secretary of the movement. The claims of planted evidence, false statements and maltreatment during interrogation were accepted by the jury. Also there was evidence that the police tried to induce one defendant to implicate the Meirionnydd Plaid Cymru MP, Dafydd Elis Thomas, in the alleged conspiracy to cause explosions. Those found not guilty had also been held in jail for excessively long periods before being allowed bail. Public opinion forced an internal police enquiry led by Peter Rawlinson, Assistant Chief Constable of Merseyside. However, an unofficial enquiry organized by the Welsh Campaign for Civil and Political Liberties, under Lord Gifford QC, Dr John Davies and Tony Richards (chairperson of Cardiff City Labour Party) did hold a public enquiry and issued a book on their findings entitled *Political Policing in Wales*, published in June, 1984. An account of the background to the trial and the questions it raised was published at the same time by Y Lolfa, the work of television journalist, John Osmond.

The new militant direction of Welsh nationalism from the 1960's had the effect of developing a 'political police force' in Wales whose arrests, surveillance and frequent intimidation of suspects received little publicity outside of Wales. It seemed that, with the Conspiracy Trial, the police had over-reached themselves and were pushed into bringing an ill-prepared case which cost £500,000 to the taxpayers. However, one of the lessons that moderate nationalists learnt from the Conspiracy Trial was that a police force, sworn to maintaining the *status quo* in a colonial country seeking independence, inevitably becomes a political police force doing everything in its power to destroy the national movement. The police force in a colonial country is irrevocably the main weapon of the imperial power which employs it. The 'politicizing' of the Welsh police was in no way astonishing.

During the 1970's, Plaid Cymru continued to make voting gains in all the Welsh parliamentary constituencies but never getting the overnight swings necessary to gain a substantial number of seats. However, the increase in support, coupled with a new radical socialist programme, began to worry the Labour Government. As in Scotland, they proposed an Assembly, an elected body which would have control over some local affairs but not fiscal ones. It was decided to hold a referendum on the matter on March 1st, 1979, with the proviso that two-thirds of the electorate would have to vote in favour of the assembly for it to be established. Only 59.1 p.c. of the electorate voted and only 242,-048 (11.9 p.c.) voted for the assembly. The 'no' vote was 956.330 (47 p.c.). This was seen in London as a vote against self-government rather than a vote against the specific assembly proposals which had been criticised in detail by the nationalists.

The Welsh republican tradition has been a small but significant one and manifestations of republicanism have emerged in the 1940's, 1950's and in the 1960's, when Plaid Gwerin Cymru (Welsh Socialist Republican Party) emerged briefly and a Socialist Nationalist Republican Movement was founded in Bridgend, which gave birth to Cymdeithas Owain Lawgoch, publishing *Ein Llais* (Our Voice).

(Owain Lawgoch—Owain Red Hand—was Owain ap Thomas ap Rhodri, born circa 1330, who claimed descent from Llywelyn of Wales. He won fame serving as a military commander for Philip VI of France and commanded a unit of Welsh exiles. In 1372, he led an expedition to secure an independent Wales which was turned back before he reached Welsh soil. The English feared Owain Lawgoch's reputation and the potential support he had in Wales and therefore employed an agent, John Lamb, to assassinate Owain. Lamb carried out the deed in 1378 during the siege of Mortagne-sur-Mer. From the Celtic viewpoint, the worst aspect of this was that Lamb was a Scottish mercenary!)

In January, 1980, a Welsh Socialist Republican Movement was formed after a former Plaid Cymru research officer, Robert Griffiths, and the organizer of the Welsh school-teachers' union UCAC—Gareth Miles—had published *Sosialaeth i'r Cymry*

(Socialism for the Welsh People) in July, 1979. Griffiths became secretary of the WSRM which soon had 12 active branches and commenced publication of *Y Faner Goch* (The Red Flag), subtitled *The Welsh Socialist*. In 1981, *Y Faner Goch*, another journal *Welsh Republic* and an internal bulletin *Y Fflam*, were being produced. The movement achieved a high profile at numerous demonstrations. One demonstration in support of the hunger striking Irish political prisoners in May, 1982, was broken up by the police. The support and the high profile achieved by the WSRM caused the South Wales Police to single out the movement for special attention resulting in the 'Conspiracy' trial.

Cymdeithas yr Iaith Gymraeg, the Welsh Language Society, had not been content with the passing of the 1967 Welsh Language Act which had, at least, recognized the principle of equal validity between Welsh and English in Wales under English law. By the 1970's, the Society had developed, and continues to develop, policies and strategies based on a broader perception of the language's situation. They claim two fundamental principles: firstly, the right of Welsh-speakers to live their lives fully through the medium of their own language; and, secondly, the necessity of ensuring that Welsh survives as a living language, through the creation of economic and social conditions favourable to its continuation. This involved the maintenance of Welsh-speaking communities where they still existed; the counter-action of Anglicizing influences and the winning of more Welsh-speakers from English. Cymdeithas has its own monthly journal, *Tafod y Ddraig* (The Dragon's Tongue).

Cymdeithas believes in a combination of constitutional methods and 'direct action' to achieve its aims.

> In the first instance, Cymdeithas yr Iaith Gymraeg has always made, and always makes, use of the so-called constitutional methods, i.e. letters, petitions, lobbying, legal demonstrations, discussions with relevant authorities, to try to achieve our aims. This makes clear our demands to the body concerned and, gives opportunities for reasonably detailed and accurate publicity, to the public. Sometimes our requests are fulfilled at this stage. If, however, this fails, we resort to direct action, including action which contravenes the law. Where the law is broken, either the individual members directly involved, or the Society as a whole, accept the responsibility for any action.
>
> One very important point to be made is that, although we are very often

accused by critics of being a 'violent' organisation, the Society is avowedly non-violent. This is stated in our manifesto and is the principle applied in considering any action. Any damage we cause is to property alone and, because of the indirect risk of injury to persons, we do not make use of fire or any kind of explosive.

The 1981 Census showed a further decrease in the number of Welsh speakers to 503,549 (18.9 per cent of the population) of which 21,283 were monoglots. The only comfort in these figures was in the fact that they revealed a strong increase in the number of Welsh-speaking children and this could hold out a promise for the future. However, there still remains the problem of emigration caused by lack of jobs. In addition, comes the purchase of leisure homes by English families, or English investment in shops or other businesses in Wales; migrants following their manufacturing companies, offices or other businesses into Wales; English-speaking immigrants following large-scale development projects to Wales, and also speculative housing.

These waves of English-speaking immigrants into Wales do not make any attempt in general to become part of Welsh life: There is profound ignorance among English people about Welsh culture; the Welsh language does not possess status as a main primary and secondary education medium, nor is there special provision for the absorption of immigrants in a Welsh education system. There is lack of adequate social pressure by Welsh people to compel immigrants to accept and learn Welsh, and also protect to their own Welshness. For these reasons, the immigrants settle in Wales as if it were simply another area of England. This attitude is a reflection of a complex amalgam of educational, economic and historical factors, as well as being due to the influence of the mass media and the political system. These are the pressures against which Cymdeithas yr Iaith Gymraeg and the other sections of the Welsh national movement have to fight. There has been a tendency in the Celtic world to acclaim Wales as a model of successful achievement but Cymdeithas, so far, has only slowed down the rate of the language's decline. The increasing influx of English-speaking families into Welsh-speaking areas is now transforming the linguistic state of the nation and, in 1983, Cymdeithas launched a campaign for the establishment of a Welsh Language Development Body, with the positive function and sufficient budget to ensure that all the children in Wales who wished to do so could receive their education through the medium of Welsh. To safeguard the Welsh language in the future will necessitate Welsh control over Welsh economic, political and cultural life. This, of course, is what the Welsh struggle is all about.

Chapter Five
Éire (Ireland)

During the mediaeval period, Ireland exerted a surprising influence in helping Europe emerge from the Dark Ages. It was a centre of learning and literacy. Some of the Anglo-Saxon kings were sent to Ireland for education, rulers such as Aldfrith of Northumbria in the 7th Century. A few of Aldfrith's poems in Irish are still extant and some scholars look upon him as the 'begetter' of the *Beowulf* saga, for the Northumbrian classic shows many parallels to the Irish *Táin Bó Fráich*. Students from all over Europe attended Ireland's famous medical schools. The country was renowned for her geographers like Diciul; her philosophers like Eriugena (acclaimed the most considerable philosopher in the western world between Augustine of Hippo and Aquinas); her poets like Sedulius Scottus; and her Christian missionaries such as Columbanus. Irish monks and scholars journeyed throughout Europe, re-kindling literacy and learning, in a world recovering from centuries of pagan ravages. They established monastic and church settlements as far east as Kiev, in the Ukraine; as far south as Taranto at the foot of Italy; and as far north as the Faroes and Iceland. Some scholars even maintain that they reached the New World to the west, in the person of Brendan the Voyager, centuries before Columbus.

It was in 1167 that Dermot Mac Murrough, the former king of Leinster, arrived back from exile with a mercenary force of Normans to recover his kingdom. Mac Murrough had been deposed. It must be remembered that under the Brehon Laws, whose first known codification was in the 5th Century, all public offices, including chieftains, provincial kings and even the High King of Ireland, were elected. There was no such concept as primogeniture. Such officials remained in office unless they abused their power or acted against the commonweal. Mac Murrough had fallen from office and, like many other disgruntled deposed Celtic rulers before him, enlisted support from people to whom the concept of elected kingship was so alien that they could not conceive of it. Mac Murrough had gone to Henry II of the Angevin empire who was not particularly interested in Ireland. However, one of Henry's knights—Richard, Earl of Pembroke, who became known as Strongbow—formed an alliance with Mac Murrough, who promised him the hand of his daughter, Dervogilla, in marriage. From Strongbow's cultural viewpoint, as Mac Murrough did not have a son, marriage to Dervogilla would make him heir to Mac Murrough's kingdom.

In 1169, Strongbow and his main Anglo-Norman army arrived, re-instated Mac Murrough and was followed by Henry II in 1171, when the astute king decided to claim his share of the spoils. When Mac Murrough died and Strongbow claimed the kingdom as 'heir', he was perplexed when the claim was rejected and a nephew of Mac Murrough, Murrough Mac Donnchadha, was elected. These initial invasions were not so much a conquest as a settlement, for Norman married Irish and those who followed were swiftly incorporated into the Irish national ethos, adopting its language and culture. As late as 1541, the Irish Parliament was addressed by a visiting English official whose speech had to be translated into Irish by the Earl of Ormond, so that the Anglo-Norman barons of Ireland could understand it.

From the political viewpoint, Ruaidhri Ó Conchobhair (d. 1198) was the last clearly acknowledged High King of Ireland; and it was in October, 1175, that Ruaidhri signed the Treaty of Windsor in which Henry II was recognized as suzereign lord of the country. This established the English claim over Ireland. It was not until the 17th Century that the provincial kings of Ireland, from whom the High King had been chosen, were to fade away concurrently with a series of vicious attempts to destroy the Irish identity and culture and impose the English language in the country.

The idea of colonization, the removal of the Irish from their lands and the settlement of English colonists, was first approved by England's Catholic Queen Mary Tudor (1553-58). The Tudor attempts were met with a strong resilience by the Irish. For example, the poet Edmund Spenser (famous author of ***The Faerie***

Queene) was an early colonist in Munster and one of the most virulently anti-Irish. Yet, less than one hundred years later, his grandson William Spenser, was ordered to remove himself on pain of death to Connacht, during the Cromwellian confiscations, because he was deemed to be an 'Irish Papist' by the new English colonists.

After the conclusion of the brutal Elizabethan Wars, there was an uneasy peace until the major Irish uprising against the colonists in 1641, and the establishment of an Irish government in Kilkenny. The country was devastated by warfare for the next eight years but the coming of Cromwell made such warfare pale into insignificance, as death by the sword, pestilence and famine swept the country. In September, 1653, Cromwell's plans for the colonization became law. Irish estates were confiscated and landowners, tenants and peasants were banished to Connacht and Co. Clare, west of the River Shannon, on pain of death. It was the period in which 'Hell or Connacht!' became the choice for the Irish. There followed a relentless persecution of the Irish people and the elimination of the educated classes by trial, execution, imprisonment, exile, and mass transportations to the West Indies. Irish people who were found on the east bank of the River Shannon were liable, under law, to instant execution. English soldiers bringing in the head of an Irish 'rebel' could receive a reward of £5. No one bothered about identifying 'rebels' too precisely.

After the Cromwellian period, the restored Stuart monarchy was not too concerned with rectifying the situation that they found although, once again, the Irish showed a strong resilience and began to absorb the Cromwellian colonists. The final 'conquest' came during the Williamite Wars at the end of the 17th Century.

During the 18th Century, Irish culture was forced underground but it survived. Agrarian unrest became a feature of life but any action as a cohesive Irish national unit was lacking until 1798, when Protestants and Catholics united in the new creed of republicanism in one of the most formidable uprisings which England had to face. This uprising forced the English to abolish the Irish Parliament which had sat in Dublin, representing the interests of the various colonial settlers.

Ireland was to be an integral part of the United Kingdom. The proposal for union was put to the Irish Parliament in 1799 and defeated. The English Government then used the same tactics which had been used to bring about the union of the Scottish and English Parliaments in 1707. Out of the 300 members of the Irish Parliament, 28 members were given peerages, pressure was brought to bear on 72 members holding positions controlled by the English Parliament, and 84 'rotten borough' members were paid off. As a result of this, the Act of Union was finally passed on June 7th, 1800 by 158 votes with 115 opposing. It cost England £1 million in bribes. One hundred Irish members were admitted to Westminster. As Under Secretary Edward Cooke, writing to William Pitt in 1799, explained: "By giving the Irish a hundred members in an assembly of six hundred and fifty, they will be impotent to operate on that Assembly, but it will be invested with Irish assent to its authority." The same tactic had been applied with success to the Scots and the Welsh.

Insurrection followed insurrection: in 1803 came Emmet's poorly conceived attempt, to be followed by the Young Ireland uprising of 1848 and the Fenian uprising of 1867. The Catholic Emancipation Act of 1829 allowed Irish Catholics to express their wishes 'democratically'. In 1870, Isaac Butt had formed a Home Rule movement which became the Irish Party and won a majority of Irish seats. Butt's policy, however, was the amelioration of the English House of Commons, trying to plead Ireland's moral right to self-government. His successor Parnell made no such compromise. By 1885, the Irish Party held 85 seats out of the 105 Irish seats, including 17 out of the 33 seats which represented the province of Ulster. No effort was spared in attempts to discredit Parnell and to split the Irish Party. Nevertheless, they held the majority of seats until 1918. In 1910, as they had in 1885, the Irish Party held the balance of power in the House of Commons. Needing their support, the Liberal Party agreed on a Home Rule Bill which, in 1914, was immediately shelved because of the War.

The Easter 1916 uprising, in which an Irish Republic was proclaimed, was mainly confined to Dublin but 1,351 people were killed or wounded. The slow, systematic, execution of the leaders caused a wave of revulsion to sweep the country, imbuing the population with a sense of national identity which England had never thought possible. At the General Election of 1918, out of 105 seats at Westminster, Sinn Féin (the Republican Party) won 73 seats; the Irish Party was reduced to six seats (they also won an extra seat in a Liverpool-Irish constituency), and the Unionists won 26 seats.

In accordance with their Election Manifesto, Sinn Féin invited all elected Irish representatives to the establishment of an Irish Parliament, Dáil Éireann, on January 21st, 1919. The Dáil ratified the 1916 proclamation of a Republic and issued a Declaration of Independence. The English administration reacted by an attempt to arrest all Sinn Féin members of the Parliament not already imprisoned and, on September 11th, 1919, Dáil Éireann was declared an illegal assembly. The Irish Volunteers and Irish Citizen Army, reformed as the Army of the Irish Republic (IRA) in 1916, began the War of Independence which was to last two years.

It was on June 24th, 1921, that Prime Minister Lloyd George finally opened negotiations with the leaders of the Irish Government. On December 26th, 1921, a fateful document known as the Articles of Agreement was signed by the Irish delegation, without reference to Dáil Éireann, which gave 26 counties of Ireland independence as a dominion within the British Commonwealth as Saorstát Éireann (Irish Free State), while the Six Counties of North East Ulster would be partitioned and remain within the United Kingdom with a local parliament. The agreement was accepted only under severe pressure.

Dáil Éireann, asked to ratify the document, which was already a *fait accompli*, split. On January 7th, 1922, after heated debating, the Treaty, as it became known, was ratified by 64 votes in favour against 57 votes. By March, 1922, the IRA's 19 army divisions had split with eleven divisions against the Treaty and eight for the new Free State. Several times a seemingly inevitable civil war was narrowly averted by the statesmanship of Eamonn De Valera and Michael Collins. Then Winston Churchill, on behalf of the English Government, threatened the return of English troops if the Provisional Government, now led by Collins, did not take action against the Republican dissidents. Thus, at England's bidding, on July 28th, 1922, the newly constituted Free State Army, with borrowed English field artillery, opened fire on Republican positions. Ireland was plunged into a civil war which lasted until 1923 and whose divisions and effects are still felt today.

After the war, Eamonn De Valera led a split from Sinn Féin, which still adhered to the proclamations of 1916 and 1919, refusing to enter the Free State Parliament. He formed a new republican party, Fianna Fáil, which eventually entered the Dáil. It was in 1932 that Fianna Fáil became the new government of the Free State and De Valera's first act was to draw up a new constitution, removing the oath of Allegiance to the English monarchy. The new constitution was enacted on July 1st, 1937, which made the 26 Counties a republic in all but name. This provoked an economic war from England and even threats of invasion from Churchill, when the Free State announced its policy of neutrality during World War II. Only American pressure stopped Churchill pursuing his disastrous policy to send an army into Ireland. De Valera remained *Taoiseach* (Prime Minister) of the 'dictionary republic' until February, 1948. John A.Costello of Fine Gael (the re-named pro-Treaty party) managed to form a coalition which tidied up the 1937 constitution and declared the 26 Counties the 'Republic of Ireland' on April 18th, 1949. In retaliation, the English Labour Government deemed the 26 Counties to have left the British Commonwealth and declared that "in no event will Northern Irlend or any part thereof cease to be part of the United Kingdom without consent of the Parliament of Northern Ireland".

The Irish people have two major problems: the reunification of the country and the restoration of the Irish language. I must reiterate my introduction to this volume by saying that I can offer no more than a simple primer on these very complex subjects. As, at the time of writing, the war continues in the north of Ireland, it is only possible to present a brief background sketch to the problem.

North East Ulster

It was during the reign of Mary Tudor that England devised its policy of colonization, in an effort to change the Irish "course of government, apparel, manner of holding land, language and habit of life". An experiment was tried in Leinster to establish a 'New England'. Then came the colonization of Munster and Connacht. By the end of the 16th Century, the province of Ulster, in the north, was the heartland of the old Irish social system and national opposition to English conquest. In 1595, the chieftains of Tyrone and Tyrconnell led a grand alliance of the northern clans against the English. The Earl of Essex was sent to Ireland as Lord Lieutenant but found it impossible to win a victory. He was recalled in disgrace and his successor, Lord Mountjoy, engaged in a policy of frightful devastation, destroying all the food, houses, cattle, men, women and children until starvation, coupled with military defeats, led the Irish to submit, as Queen Elizabeth lay dying in 1603. The resulting depopulation of Ulster made its colonization more feasible.

James I (formerly James VI of Scotland) was enthusiastic about the idea of colonization and, in 1603, allowed two Scottish lairds, Hugh Montgomery and James Hamilton, to form a settlement in Counties Down and Antrim. The Brehon Law system was formally abolished in the area during 1605. Sir Arthur Chichester, Lord Deputy of Ireland, created another colony in the same area. Soon the areas of Donegal, Derry (then Coleraine), Tyrone, Armagh, Cavan and Fermanagh were also escheated and colonists were encouraged to settle there.

They came mainly from Scotland and from areas such as Galloway which, as we have already seen from Chapter Two, were then still Scottish Gaelic-speaking. Apart from their Dissenter Presbyterian religion, the new colonists had little difference in language or cultural background from the native Irish. A great deal of intermingling took place which forced the English administration to enact a ban on marriages between colonists and natives. It was immediately shown to be unworkable and was lifted in 1610, to "the great joy of all parties".

It is significant that a large proportion of Protestant Ulstermen bear Irish (Gaelic) names, while strenuously maintaining that they are 'ethnically different' from the Catholic Irish and that many Catholic Irish bear English names. Thus, in July, 1972, at the famous confrontation at Lenadoon Avenue, Belfast (which broke a truce between the IRA and the British Government), an IRA officer could be named Bell while a UDA leader could bear the name of Murphy. The 1812 *Statistical Survey* showed that, in Co. Antrim, the descendants of the Scottish settlers were still speaking Scottish Gaelic rather than the Ulster Irish dialect. In the Census of 1851, it was shown that more people spoke Irish in Ulster than in Leinster, with many speakers of being of settler-origin.

In 1638, the Scottish National Convention had rebelled against the episcopalian (Anglican Church) ordinances. Lord Stafford, the new Lord Deputy of Ireland, tried to force all Presbyterian Ulstermen to declare their disapproval of the rebellion which caused a mass exodus of colonists in search of religious freedom. On Octobrt 23rd, 1641, the Irish rose under Phelim O'Neill in order to regain their confiscated clan lands and reinstate the Brehon Law system. According to a contemporary account, *The Irish Rebellion, or a History of the Beginning and First Progress of the General Rebellion*, 1641, many Ulster colonists had "degenerated into Irish affections and customs" and now sided with the natives against the English administration.

In 1649, when Oliver Cromwell arrived, the opposition of the Irish and the colonial families was crushed in one dreadful campaign. Sir William Petty, writing in his *Political Anatomy of Ireland*, estimated that, out of a total population of 1,448,000, some 616,000 had perished by sword, famine and plague. Of this number, 504,000 were natives and 112,000 were colonists. During the Cromwellian administration a further 100,000 were sold as labour to the West Indies, and 40,000 were allowed to go into exile to enlist in the military service of other European nations. The 'final solution'—the 'Hell or Connaught' order—to the Irish problem was enacted on September 23rd, 1653, which was nothing less than an attempt at the total extirpation of the Irish people.

Nevertheless, at the end of the Cromwellian period (1659), a survey and census showed the population of Ulster as 103,923 of which 63,272 were natives and 40,651 were of settler families. In every county of Ulster, the natives outnumbered the colonists, and Irish was still the general language spoken by both communities. That resilience which had been displayed during the preceding centuries, the ability to absorb newcomers into Irish nationality, caused Robert Molesworth, an Englishman, to observe: "We cannot so much wonder at this, when we consider how many there are of Oliver's (Cromwell) soldiers in Ireland who cannot speak one word of English". (*A True Way to Render Ireland Happy and Secure*, 1697).

Charles II believed in moderation and both Catholics and Presbyterians were allowed comparatively free practice of their religion. The rebellion against his successor, James II, in England was a blow to hopes of developing a 'liberal' regime in Ireland. James II's Parliament, sitting in Dublin in 1689, had tried to abolish all religious discrimination by passing Acts XIII and XV, in which all religions were declared equal under the law; and that each priest or minister should be supported by his own congregation; and that no tithes should be levied upon any person for the support of a church to which they did not belong.

Today, there is the Ulster Unionist myth that the victory of William of Orange brought about a 'new era of religious freedom' in Ireland. It is a central catechism of the Unionist faith. Yet exactly the reverse happened. After William's victory, only the Anglican religion was recognized by law. This was the minority sect in Ireland. The majority of colonists in Ulster were Presbyterian as their descendants are. Presbyterian ministers were liable to three months in jail for delivering a sermon and fined £100 (a staggering sum for the day when one considers that one could live in comfort on £40 a year) for celebrating the Lord's Supper. Presbyterians were punished if they were discovered to have been married by a Presbyterian minister. An Act in 1704 excluded all Presbyterians from holding office in the law, army, navy, customs and excise, or in municipal employment. In 1715, a further Parliamentary Act made it an offence for Presbyterian ministers to teach children. The punishment was three months in jail. Intermarriages between Presbyterians and Anglicans were declared illegal. As late as 1772, it was confirmed by law that jail sentences would be meted out to Presbyterians holding religious services. Thus did William of Orange's 'religious freedom' apply to those Ulstermen who so enthusiastically celebrate his victories today.

William's religious laws caused some 250,000 Protestant Ulstermen to migrate to America between the years 1717 and 1776 alone, in order to seek freedom of religious worship. It was these Ulstermen and their children who were to play a prominent part in the American War of Independence. Ulster Protestants provided 19 American revolutionary generals while five signed the Declaration of Independence, four served in Washington's first cabinet and one was chairman of the committee which drafted the American Constitution. The first governors of South Carolina, Pennsylvania and New Jersey were Ulster Protestants, and the children of Ulster Protestants provided no less than ten American presidents.

It was these same Ulster Protestant Dissenters who, through their acceptance of the republican creed in America, transported it to Ireland. The United Irishmen, formed in Belfast in 1791, became the first major Irish radical and anti-imperialist movement under the leadership of the Protestant lawyer, Theobald Wolfe Tone. Their *Secret manifesto to the Friends of Freedom in Ireland* was avowedly democratic, urging universal suffrage and total religious freedom. Tone's famous *An Address to the Irish People*, published in Belfast in 1796, declared the intention of the movement to establish an Irish Republic "on the broad firm basis of equal rights, liberties and laws", declaring that "the doctrine of republicanism will finally subvert that of monarchy and establish a system of justice and rational liberty on the ruins of the thrones of the despots of Europe".

In 1794, a United Irishmen document declared that the Ulster Protestants "were the most enlightened body of the nation...the dissenters are enemies to English Power from reason and reflection, the Catholics from hatred of the English name". Of Ulster Protestants it comments: "They are steady republicans, devoted to liberty and through all the stages of the French Revolution have been enthusiastically attached to it".

The unity of the Dissenters and Catholics into the widespread United Irishmen movement, which attempted its revolution in 1798, was a severe shock to the English administration. Commenting on republican ideology, Hugh Boulter, Anglican Archbishop of Armagh, wrote to Prime Minister William Pitt, that "the worst of this is that it stands to unite Protestant and Papist and whenever that happens, goodbye to the English interest in Ireland forever". After the suppression of the 1798 uprising, and the union of Parliaments in 1800, steps were considered on how to create a division between the two communities, especially when Protestants were in the forefront of the attempted uprising of 1803. Obviously, Catholics were a majority, so the Penal Laws enacted by William against them remained. It was the

Presbyterians who were singled out for special treatment. The first step was the declaration of a *Regium Donum* of £75 to all Presbyterian ministers who declared their 'loyalty'. By March 30th, 1805, the Government learnt that only two ministers had refused to take the bribe. The restrictions on the Presbyterians began to be lifted, although it was not until 1834 that the Anglican Orange Order opened its ranks to Dissenters and the Presbyterians were able to swamp the Order. The former anti-Unionists had been bribed, cajoled and propagandized into the most strongly Unionist element in the country. Even so, many Protestants, with a clear awareness of their history, still featured prominently in the leadership of subsequent Irish Republican movements.

During the 19th Century, something else was happening which was to play an important part in the subsequent division of Ireland. The industries of Ulster had developed their markets in the English imperial one, so that the capitalists there, through economics, were firmly behind the union. The southern industries relied on the home market and, in order to protect this market, wanted national tariff boundaries and so supported home rule. It was from this diametrical conflict of interests that the partition of Ireland resulted; this was the *cause* whilst religion became a *sympton*.

After forty years of representing the majority of Irish seats, the Irish Party found themselves (with 80 seats out of 105) holding the balance of power in Westminster in 1910. Self-government seemed inevitable in spite of the threats of the Dublin Unionist leader, Sir Edward Carson, who warned that Unionists would set up a provisional Irish government in Belfast. The House of Lords managed to delay the legislation until 1914, when it was shelved for the duration of the European War. This allowed the northern industrialists to begin stirring up sectarian hatreds. 'Home Rule is Rome Rule' became a catchphrase. A series of sectarian demonstrations resulted in attacks on Catholics. By January, 1913, an illegal army called the Ulster Volunteers had been formed to use "all means necessary to defeat Home Rule". The Ulster Volunteers were commanded by a notable soldier, General Sir George Richardson, with many other famous serving generals offering their expertise. Among nationalists there was a reaction and, in Dublin, in November of the same year, the Irish Volunteers were established to defend Ireland.

To the Unionists, however, it seemed inevitable that the Liberal Party in England, to safeguard their position as the governing party in the House of Commons, would inevitably enact the Home Rule Bill. The industrialists, anxious to secure their wealth, sought alternative imperial markets. As early as 1910, the Ulster Unionist Council had warned: "If we are deserted by Great Britain, we would rather be governed by Germany". In 1911, James Craig, a Unionist leader, had emphasized: "Germany and the German Emperor would be preferred to the rule of John Redmond" (the leader of the Irish Party). In August, 1913, Sir Edward Carson lunched with the Kaiser in Hamburg where tentative discussions on German aid to Ulster took place. The *Irish Churchman* declared exuberantly: "We have the offer of aid from a powerful continental monarch, who, if Home Rule is forced on the Protestants of Ireland, is prepared to send an army sufficient to release England of any further trouble in Ireland by attaching it to his dominion..."

The shelving of the Home Rule Bill was a triumph for the Ulster Unionists. Yet it strengthened the position of the Irish Republican Brotherhood which was laying plans for an uprising and led inevitably to the 1916 rising, the election success of the republicans in 1918, the declaration of the Republic, establishment of Dáil Éireann, and the consequent War of independence of 1919-21.

One of the basic problems of Lloyd George's Treaty with the Irish revolutionary government in 1921 was the *fait accompli* of Partition, which had also been part of the Home Rule Bill. The original plan was the separation of the nine counties of the province of Ulster from the rest of Ireland. But only four out of the nine counties had clear Unionist majorities—Counties Antrim, Armagh, Down and Derry. Fermanagh, Tyrone, Cavan, Monaghan and Donegal had nationalist majorities. It would therefore be impossible for the Unionists to rule the entire province. Therefore, Fermanagh and Tyrone were placed with Antrim, Armagh, Down and Derry to form a new statelet, 'Northern Ireland', and the remaining three counties of Ulster were allowed to form part of the 'southern' state. This would give the Unionists a permanent majority in the region of 60 to 40 per cent, by virtue of the fact that one hundred years of successful propaganda had made the word Unionist and Protestant synonymous. Thus the word 'democracy', applied in a Northern Ireland context, left a bitter taste in the mouths of the majority of the Irish people.

The Northern Ireland Parliament came into being in May, 1920, and of the 52 seats in the new assembly at Stormont, 40 went to Unionists and 12 to Republicans. This opened the way for sectarian violence in an effort by Unionist leaders to strengthen their positions by driving Catholics out of the new statelet. On May 31st, over 80 Catholic families were rendered homeless, eight were killed and thousands began to flee for safety to the south. By June 18th, some 428 Catholics had been killed, 1,766 wounded and 8,750 driven from their jobs, while 23,000 were homeless. The pogroms were led by the new Ulster B Special constabulary. English regular troops were ordered not to interfere.

The Unionist Government knew its survival depended on a strengthening of its grip on the machinery of government, on law and security. It consolidated itself by the establishment of ward-rigging and voting qualifications designed to exclude as many Catholics from the vote as possible. In 1929, proportional representation was abolished. Sir James Craig, now Premier of the statelet, saw Stormont as "a Protestant Parliament for a Protestant people". In 1925, an Amending Act of the Education Act ensured sectarian 'apartheid' in schools by insisting that Protestant children could only be taught by Protestant teachers in Protestant schools. In fairness, it must be added that the Catholic Hierarchy was happy to accept this state of affairs, as it meant Catholic management over Catholic schools.

During the 1930's, the years of severe economic depression, there was a hopeful sign when Protestant trade unionists allied themselves with the IRA and left-wing activists, in a campaign of agitation to achieve social reforms. In 1934, the Council of Civil Liberties sent a Commission of Inquiry to Northern Ireland which confirmed that "the Northern Ireland Government has used Special powers towards securing the domination of one particular political faction, and, at the same time, towards curtailing the lawful activities of its opponents".

It was obvious that the undemocratic foundation of the

Northern Ireland statelet, with its various laws designed to keep its rulers in power in perpetuity, precluded the use of 'constitutional means' allowed elsewhere in the United Kingdom for political opposition. As Sir Edward Carson once smugly announced, force had created Northern Ireland and only force would destroy it. The IRA had conducted campaigns against Partition during the 1920's and late 1930's into the 1940's. In 1954, the 'Border War' began which lasted until 1962, leaving six members of the Royal Ulster Constabulary dead and 37 regular soldiers wounded; eight IRA dead, two Saor Ulaidh (Free Ulster) dead, and two civilians dead. There were 200 in jail convicted of IRA 'crimes' and hundreds more interned. During this period, both Saor Ulaidh and Sinn Féin won seats to the Westminster Parliament, the Dáil and the Irish Senate. Republicans refused to recognize elections for the Northern Ireland Parliament. When the campaign ended in 1962, the IRA went into a period of self-examination—even selling some of its weapons to Welsh militants.

The discrimination against Catholics in the Northern Ireland statelet continued with ward-rigging, voting qualifications, gerrymandering, disenfranchizing—with the most blatant religious discrimination in local government, housing, policing and employment. A Unionist employer was able to think nothing of writing 'religion' on a Ministry of Labour introduction card as a reason for rejecting a prospective employee. In a city like Derry, where the nationalist vote was 36,000 compared to a Unionist 18,000 vote, the Unionists could gain control with 12 seats on the 20 seat council.

Early in the 1960's, the capitalists of the north had discovered that Partition was no longer an economic necessity, for capitalism in the Irish Republic had become an adjunct to Anglo-American capital. As it was no longer economic to have a border, it was therefore no longer politically necessary. In 1965, the Northern Ireland premier, Captain Terence O'Neill, held the first meeting with the *Taoiseach* of the Irish Republic (Seán Lemass), as the first step in a north-south dialogue. The sectarian machine developed by the northern ruling class to defend their economic interests took on a life of its own. A century of tireless sectarian propaganda, plus a half century of living in a ruthless 'apartheid' state, had worked only too well: the sectarian forces could no longer be cynically used by the ruling classes. A new period of sectarian violence against Catholics began. In February, 1967, a Campaign for Social Justice in Northern Ireland was established, uniting Catholics with the more liberally minded Protestants and, in the Spring of 1968, the Campaign gave way to the formation of the Northern Ireland Civil Rights Association (NICRA), which took its inspiration from the American Civil Rights movement and began a series of protest marches across the country. Its aims were:

(1) A universal franchise in local government elections, in line with the franchise in the rest of the United Kingdom, abandoning Ulster's proprietorial voting qualification.
(2) The redrawing of electoral boundaries by an impartial commission, to ensure fair representations, e.g. to eliminate situations where Protestants could command disproportionate influence on councils.
(3) Legislation against discrimination in employment at local government level and the creation of machinery to remedy local government grievances.
(4) A compulsory points system for housing to ensure fair allocation.
(5) Repeal of the Special Powers Act.
(6) The disbandment of the 'B' Special Police Force.
(7) The withdrawal of the Public Order Bill.

The Unionists and the sectarian 'B' Special Constabulary reacted with paranoid terror towards the civil rights movement. The RUC already had a formidable armoury of machine guns, water cannons, CS gas, and armoured vehicles, in addition to their ordinary side-arms and carbines, as weapons by which to combat 'civil unrest'. Systematic attacks on civil rights marches culminated in the notorious Burntollet attack in January, 1969, when civil rights demonstrators were led into an ambush by the RUC, who then stood by while known members of the 'B' Specials and off-duty RUC men, wearing armbands to distinguish themselves from the marchers, waded into the attack with a formidable array of weapons. The Unionist 'security forces' were entirely out of control. RUC men fired on unarmed crowds in Derry in July and in August, and 600 fully armed police spearheaded hundreds of armed civilians in an onslaught on the Catholic ghetto of the Bogside in Derry. Thousands of Catholic families were fleeing in the biggest pogrom since the 1920's. The feared 'B' Specials were also mobilized with submachine guns and rifles.

After accepting the Fascist conditions of Northern Ireland without protest for fifty years, on August 14th, 1969, the United Kingdom's Labour Government, pressured by world political opinion, sent regular troops into Derry and Belfast, in order to protect the Catholics against the sectarian ravages of the Unionists. O'Neill's premiership had ended in chaos and now his cousin, James Chichester-Clarke, became Premier. At this time, the IRA and Sinn Féin were almost moribund. The IRA was particularly criticized for its failure to protect the nationalist population in the north. "IRA—I Ran Away" was scrawled on many walls. The IRA held an extraordinary Army Convention in December, 1969, which voted in favour of forming a National Liberation Front (which the media promptly tagged the 'Official' IRA). It also voted in favour of accepting the institution of Partition and to end a policy of abstention from Stormont, Westminster and Dublin. A group of delegates walked out and formed a 'Provisional Army' Council and thus the 'Provisional IRA' came into being. On January 10/17th, 1970, the annual conference of Sinn Féin failed to get a two-thirds majority to support the NLF (Official) line. However, a small majority was in favour and the 'Provisional' supporters left the meeting to establish their own Sinn Féin group.

In the meantime, Unionist extremists started a series of bombings which were promptly blamed on the IRA, and Unionists finally entered into a gun battle with English troops in which an RUC man was killed and some English soldiers were wounded. Significantly, after the June, 1970, General Election, in which the Conservatives came to power as the UK Government, 'security troops' turned on the nationalist population. Chichester-Clarke followed O'Neill into retirement and an extreme sectarian, Brian Faulkner, became Premier. On Monday, August 9th, 1971, against a growing urban guerilla war, he persuaded the Tories to approve the reintroduction of the Civil Authorities (Special Powers) Acts of 1922 and introduce internment without trial. Within two days of internment, 25 people were shot dead, many seriously wounded and 8,000 Catholics had fled to the safety of the 26 Counties. On August 13th, Brigadier Marston Tickell smugly announced that 70 per cent of the IRA leadership had been imprisoned and the movement had suffered heavy losses. He was whistling in the dark.

By the end of December, 1983, the Northern Ireland Office admitted to 507 regular solders and members of the Ulster Defence Regiment (which had replaced the 'B' Specials) killed, 190 members of the Royal Ulster Constabulary and its Reserve killed, and 1,648 civilians killed. Some 3,309 soldiers had been wounded and 3,310 policemen. Also, 17,497 civilians had been injured. And, at the time of writing, the war still continues with an increasing toll of dead and wounded. These figures also pertain to Northern Ireland itself and not to the soldiers and civilians killed in incidents in the 26 Counties or in England. The IRA has persued a policy of excluding any action in other Celtic countries. In terms of financial cost, by that date, the United Kingdom Government had paid £4,507 million in compensation for deaths, injuries, damage to property and additional security. In terms of indirect money lost, some £3,278 million was estimated as the cost of depressed investment and the collapse of the Northern Ireland economy. The 26 County State's equivalent losses were £901 million and £983 million.

The violence unleashed by Faulkner caused the United Kingdom Government to suspend the Stormont Parliament on March 30th, 1972, and to rule the Six Counties directly from Westminster, with a Secretary of State as 'supremo'. In 1972, secret negotiations between the UK Government and the IRA leadership took place which led to a short truce. A similar truce and negotiations took place in 1975/6. The will to arrive at the inevitable political solution to the problem has been lacking from all the English political parties which has allowed one of the world's most immoral conflicts to continue.

The record of Army and police brutality is truly frightening and, whilst the UK has been found guilty of using "inhuman and degrading treatment" in the questioning of suspects, by the European Court of Human Rights, the use of torture, sensory deprivation, electrical-shock treatment, beatings and other techniques continues. Some times the 'cover-ups' have not been successful and, during the period 1974-84, some 87 regular soldiers and nearly 100 members of the UDR were jailed for murder, armed robbery, rape, sectarian arson and other crimes. It is a record which no other European 'security force' can approach.

One of the most dramatic crimes of the UK 'security forces' took place in Derry on January 30th, 1972, when Lt.Colonel Derek Wilford's 1st Battalion of the Parachute Regiment opened fire on a civil rights demonstration and killed 13 people (another was to die of wounds later) and wounded 17 others. Five Irish political prisoners have met their deaths in English jails to date, and the world stood by shocked when the United Kingdom allowed 10 hunger strikers (in Long Kesh, an internment camp in Northern Ireland) to die, in an attempt to gain recognition as political prisoners—a status granted to Irish prisoners before 1976. Of these ten, Bobby Sands had been elected a Member of Parliament for Fermanagh and South Tyrone, and Kieran Doherty was an elected member of Dáil Éireann for the Cavan/Monaghan constituencey.

The Westminster propaganda machine has been very successful in distorting the truth of what is happening in Northern Ireland. Liz Curtis's astonishing book *Ireland: The Propaganda War* (1984) has done much to demonstrate the distortions, censorship and falsifications. Nevertheless, the general attitude of the English people towards the war is one of ignorance and apathy. While the United Kingdom military leadership no longer talks of a military victory, the phrase 'acceptable levels of violence' has become part of the political vocabulary. The average Englishman and woman seem to accept the Government propaganda that the IRA, Sinn Féin, the Irish National Liberation Army (created in 1974 by a further split from the 'Officials') and the Irish Socialist Republican Party, had no popular support and were just a 'criminal minority', in spite of the fact that they have, over the past decade and a half, kept one of the world's most sophisticated and well-trained armies, with its auxiliary forces—the RUC and UDR—in a war situation.

Supporters of the 'criminal minority' propaganda were shocked when Sinn Féin entered the political arena, standing for the Northern Ireland Assembly elections of October, 1982, and winning five out of the 12 seats they contested. Then in the June, 1983, General Election, Sinn Féin won a seat in West Belfast, overturning Gerry Fitt's majority and ousting him from a seat he had held for more than twenty years. Another Sinn Féin candidate came within 78 votes of winning the Mid-Ulster seat. In all, Sinn Féin polled 40 per cent of the nationalist vote in the north. Westminster remains intransigent, even ignoring the moderation of three middle-of-the-road solutions to the problem presented in a New Ireland Forum Report in May, 1984, proposed by a combination of Fine Gael, Fianna Fáil, the Irish Labour and Social Democratic and Labour Parties.

Since 1971, there has raged a ruthless war in northern Ireland; a war of terror, counter-terror and attrition. The policy of Westminster has never apparently deviated from 'military containment'. There is, it seems, no lesson for the English politicians to learn from history. Westminster MP's seem too immersed in their own propaganda, and ingrained in their own rhetoric, to find a way out of the situation that they have created. The UK cannot hope to bludgeon the IRA and INLA out of existence. The only solution now lies, as it has always done, in a phased withdrawal, both militarily and politically from Ireland. This would be the first step along the road towards a reunification of the island; the first step in bringing back the Protestant people of Ulster to their proper historic tradition.

The Irish Language

The second national question which the Irish people are faced with is one they share in common with their fellow Celts—language restoration. By the 16th Century, the Irish language contained one of Europe's oldest and most diverse literatures. Ironically, the first printing of books in the language arose from a desire by England to proselytize the Irish. It was Elizabeth I who ordered that a Protestant Bible be made available in Irish and she had an Irish phrase book printed for her own use. It was that doughty English Queen who had the first fount of what is known as 'Gaelic type' struck. Seán Ó Ceannaigh translated the Protestant Catechism, publishing it in Dublin in 1571. Uilliam Ó Domhnaill translated the New Testament which appeared in 1603 and then a Book of Common Prayer in 1608. Bishop William Bedell, from Essex, becoming provost of Trinity College in 1627, encouraged his clergy to use and study Irish and organized the translation of the Old Testament which finally appeared in 1685.

With the publication of Protestant works in Irish, the need for a Catholic counterblast became obvious. *An Teagasg Criosdaidhe*, a book of Catholic doctrine by Bonaventura Ó hEodhasa, was published in Antwerp in 1611, becoming the first of countless Irish volumes published in Europe. The most important publication for the advancement of the language was that of the first Irish dictionary, Micheál Ó Cleirigh's *Foclóir no Sanasan Nua*, published in Louvain in 1643.

The ruthless conquests and colonizations of Ireland during the 17th Century, the executions, enforced exiles and selling of the Irish to Barbados, caused the destruction of the educated classes and intelligentsia. Irish literature managed to survive and went underground, achieving a new impetus in poetic saga and song. Even under such harsh conditions as the 'Penal Years' of the 18th Century, such a masterpiece as *Cúirt an Mheán Oíche* (The Midnight Court) could be produced by Brian Merriman, a mathematics teacher of Co. Clare, which is a daring piece of writing for its day and an evocation of the vivacity of the natural life. Since its rediscovery, it has had three different English translations as well as translations into German and other European languages.

It was estimated that in the mid-18th Century, two-thirds of the population of Ireland used Irish as their everyday language. In 1799, however, Dr Whitley Stokes (1763-1845)—not to be confused with the great philologist of the same name (1830-1909)—estimated that, out of a population of 4,750,000, some 2,400,000 spoke Irish of which 800,000 were monoglots. In 1812, Dr Daniel Dewar believed that between 1,500,000 and 2,000,000 people in Ireland were "incapable of understanding a continued discourse in English". When the first Government language census was held in 1851, the Irish-speaking population had been savagely depleted. The Census was held after the terrible devastation of the sadly 'artificial' famine in which 1.5 million died of starvation and the diseases that accompany malnutrition, and a further 1.0 million were forced to emigrate. The bulk of deaths and migration occurred among the Irish-speaking population. The 1851 census, therefore, gives a figure of 1,524,286 speakers of Irish (23.3 per cent of the population) of which 319,602 were monoglots.

During the 18th Century, the Government attitude had been to ignore the existence of the Irish language. It is not insignificant that the beginnings of an attempt to prevent the decline of the language occurred among the Protestants of Northern Ireland; and it was in Belfast that the first-ever Irish language periodical *Bolg an tSolthâir* (Miscellany) was published in 1795 "to recommend the Irish language to the notice of Irishmen". The Ulster Gaelic Society, founded not long afterwards, began to produce a number of contemporary works in Irish, including translations of two novels by Maria Edgeworth, whose works such as *Castle Rackrent* (1801) and *The Absentee* (1812) are classics of Anglo-Irish literature.

When a 'national' system of education was introduced into Ireland in 1831, the presumption that Irish did not exist resulted in there being no place for the language in Irish schools, either as a subject or as a medium for teaching. The 'national' system of education therefore became the most important cause for the acceleration of the decline of the language. From 23.3 per cent of the population in 1851, speakers declined to 14.4 per cent of the population by 1901 with only 0.5 per cent (20,953) remaining monoglots. Rightly did the poet-revolutionary Pádraic Pearse, leader of the 1916 uprising in Dublin, call it 'The Murder Machine'.

To counteract the 'national' school system, Philip Barron founded an Irish College near Bonmahon, Co. Waterford, in 1835, in order to promote the study of the language. He announced his intention to agitate for the teaching of Irish in every school, and the teaching of other subjects through the medium of Irish to Irish speakers. Richard D'Alton launched his newspaper *An Fíor-Eireannach* (The True Irishman) in Co. Tipperary in 1862, declaring that Irish language societies ought to be established all over the country. Both Barron and D'Alton lacked financial backing.

In 1878, after a great deal of agitation, Irish was recognized for the first time as a subject of academic value to be taught in Intermediate Schools as an optional subject only. A Society for the Preservation of the Irish Language had been formed in 1876, to be replaced in 1879 by a movement called the Gaelic Union which interested itself in the complexities of encouraging teachers as well as publishing books in Irish at cheap rates.

In 1892, Dr Douglas Hyde delivered a lecture on 'The

Necessity for De-Anglicizing Ireland' to the Irish National Literary Society and, early in 1893, Professor Eoin Mac Neill, editor of *The Gaelic Journal* (founded in 1882) suggested that a new, popular movement ought to be formed to save the language. The result was the formation on July 31st, 1893, of *Conradh na Gaeilge* (The Gaelic League) which had the specific aims of saving Irish from destruction in Irish-speaking areas, and restoring it to those areas from which it had dissappeared. Branches began to be formed. In 1894, the League took over publication of *The Gaelic Journal* and launched new Irish language periodicals such as *Fáinne an Lae* (Dawn) and *An Claidheamh Soluis* (Sword of Light). In 1897, Tomás Ó Concheanainn was appointed the League's first full time organizer and teacher. By 1904, the League had 150 full-time travelling teachers and 593 active branches.

In 1899, a Government Commission was set up to enquire into Secondary Education and an attempt was made to oust Irish entirely from the school system into which it had crept as an optional subject from 1878. The League, backed by all the leading Celtic scholars of Europe, so effectively answered this attack that, in 1901, the language was given a new improved status in the Intermediate Schools. New grammar books, teaching manuals and other literature, were published by the League which also established a summer training college, Coláiste na Mmhan, in Ballingeary, in 1904. From 1900, the League was also publishing fiction, including comtemporary novels such as *Cormac Ua Conaill* by Pádraig Ó Duinnín, regarded as the first modern Irish novel. At the same time, *Tadh Saor* by Peadar Ó Laoghaire, staged in Macroom, Co. Cork, was the forerunner of a new Irish theatre.

Acceptance of the Gaelic League's bilingual education policy in primary schools in the Irish-speaking areas was made in 1906. Following this victory, the language was allowed as a teaching medium in Irish-speaking areas although, by 1921, only half the schools were using it. Fierce resistance to the language from Government sources continued and, in 1905, the Post Office insisted that all letters and packets should be addressed in English only—a challenge which was so effectively answered by the Gaelic League that the ruling was rendered inoperative and withdrawn.

In 1909, the University Commission accepted Irish as a subject for matriculation.

The language was, naturally, an integral part of the Irish independence movement and, during the period of the 'revolutionary Dáil' (1919-21), a Ministry of the Irish Language was established with Dr Douglas Hyde at its head. To those who accept the Unionist/Protestant myths of the north, it has to be pointed out that Dr Hyde was a Protestant. He was to become President of Ireland in 1938, in accordance with the revised 1937 constitution. From the outset, the Irish State proclaimed that Irish was the first official language and that the intention of an independent Irish State was to restore the language throughout the country in every walk of life. The last census before independence had shown that Irish speakers (553,717) constituted only 14 per cent of the population.

With the restoration of the language as state policy and the enthusiasm of an emergent nation behind it, it might be supposed that Ireland would swiftly achieve her linguistic goals. Language restoration has worked in many other countries. The commonly quoted example is that of Hebrew in Israel, although better examples as parallels to the Celtic experience can be found in Europe. Ireland remains the only example of a nation, with the protection of a political state, which has embarked on a linguistic revival and failed to achieve its aims. There will be some who will disagree and point to the census figures which are indicative of some success. From the 1911 figure of 553,717, we find an increase by the 1946 census to 588,725, some 21.2 per cent of the population. There was a further increase by the time of the 1961 census to 27.2 per cent (716,420 speakers) and again in the 1971 census to 28.3 per cent (789,429 speakers). The figures for the 1981 census demonstrated a further increase to 31.6 per cent (1,018,312 speakers), but the figures leave no room for complacency. Merely increasing the number of people *able* to speak Irish does not create an Irish-speaking society *per se*, nor has it strengthened the Irish-speaking communities.

On careful examination, one finds a declining trend among the population who live in Irish-speaking areas and therefore among those who use Irish as their everyday means of communication. In fact, the Irish-speaking areas show a population which is only one per cent of the total. For example, in 1961, only 64,272 speakers were to be found in the Irish-speaking areas (Gaeltachtaí), and these constituted 86.6 per cent of the population of the area. In 1971 there was an abrupt decline to 54,940 speakers with a corresponding percentage drop to 83.3 per cent. The severe decline was shown in all the Irish-speaking areas except in An Rinn, Co. Waterford, where, although there was a small increase in Irish-speakers, there was a similar increase in English-speakers, so that the actual percentage dropped from 93.4 to 91.1 per cent of the population. This percentage fell again, in 1981, to 84.5 per cent and, indeed, the 1981 figures revealed that Irish-speakers in the Gaeltachtaí—while increasing to 58,026 on a head count—had suffered a further sharp decline to 77.4 per cent of the area population.

What, then, is the problem? The attitude of early Irish Governments to the language revival was more or less simplistic, that, by getting Irish taught in schools at all levels, the restoration would come about naturally. Therefore, the restoration was made into a *voluntary* policy. One of the basic lessons that has been learnt from language restoration in other countries is that a degree of compulsion from the state has to be made. Compulsion is a necessary factor in language destruction, therefore compulsion is a vital factor in language rehabiliation.

The only compulsion of the Irish state was the introduction of Irish to the state schools' curricula, so that it could be used as a medium of instruction in Irish-speaking areas and as a subject in English-speaking areas, until a generation with sufficient fluency made it possible to change it to a medium in these areas too. After nearly fifty years of this policy, by 1966/7, out of 4,685 state schools, only 222 in Irish-speaking areas and 74 in English-speaking areas were able to teach through the medium of Irish.

No thought was given by Government to the creation of Irish-speaking environments outside of the Gaeltachtaí in which children from English-speaking schools could exercise their knowledge. Lack of use of the language in the media, in public administration and assembly, and in the workplace, led children to be instilled with the idea that they were being taught some dead, irrelevant subject, which had to be endured to get through matriculation and then dropped. By pursuing a half-hearted attitude, teaching the language without providing uses for it, generations of people hostile to the language were growing up. The following statistics (showing percentages of the Irish-speaking population) demonstrate that, at any given period, the highest number of Irish-speakers are to be found among children at school and that, after they have left school, knowledge of the language is immediately in decline through lack of use.

	3-4 yrs	4-9	10-14	15-19	20-24	24-35	35-44
1946	4.1	21.6	47.5	43.4	32.2	20.8	11.2
1961	5.9	28.5	52.0	50.5	38.0	31.1	26.2
1971	5.5	27.6	50.5	51.5	29.4	27.2	14.7
1981	4.9	27.8	50.8	51.0	40.0	32.8	30.0

With such a rich reservoir of Irish-speakers among school children, the examples of other linguistic revivals has shown that, given the will, Ireland could become Irish-speaking within two generations. Due to lack of political will, the non-provision of an Irish environment outside school, the term 'compulsory Irish' has become a catchphrase, something to complain about, whereas 'compulsory arithmetic', 'compulsory history', 'compulsory biology' or, indeed, 'compulsory English', are not seen in the same light. The frustration felt among those believing that they were wasting their time, learning a language which was of no use to them, caused many to resent and reject the language and inevitably led to an anti-Irish movement making its appearance in 1966. This 'Language Freedom Movement', as it was called, found a sympathetic audience among the Fine Gael party. Fine Gael flirted with the LFM for a time before public opinion compelled them to desist, although the LFM's influence on the party seems to be emerging in the current Fine-Gael and Labour Coalition Government's new attitude to the language.

One of the LFM's main propaganda arguments was that, by making Irish a matriculation subject for the Intermediate Certificate of Education, many worthy students failed because of their inability to pass the language section. The figures produced at the time of this argument demonstrated what a nonsense this contention was. The figures for those failing their Irish examination, compared with those failing another randomly chosen 'compulsory' subject, mathematics, is as follows:

	Failure in Irish	Failure in mathematics
1966	9.8 p.c.	19.9 p.c.
1967	8.3 p.c.	22.6 p.c.
1968	7.79 p.c.	19.2 p.c.

Overall, only 0.5 per cent of children failed their Certificate of Education in Irish only, and those who did so were shown to have very poor marks in other subjects. The contention of the LFM was therefore demonstrated to be fallacious, but it is surprising how many of those who argue against 'compulsory' Irish in schools still adhere to the notion.

Although every Irish Government since 1921 has paid lip service to the revival, and has commissioned numerous reports and White Papers, they have failed to take the necessary compulsory measures which would bring about a linguistic change within the state. Only 0.2/0.3 per cent of the National Budget is spent on the Irish language and only 2.0 per cent of debates in the Dáil Éireann are in Irish, and those are mainly concerned with the Irish-speaking areas. No Irish Government since 1921 has demonstrated the will to restore the language because an English-speaking Ireland provides a reservoir of cheap emigrant labour to the English-speaking world. Migration has been an economic safety valve for modern Irish Governments. At the same time, the Irish Governments could not be seen to stand against the national ideal.

In 1926, a test of competence in the language was made a requisite for recruitment into the Irish Government service. The current Irish Government has managed to contract out of this simple requirement in accordance with the ideology expressed by the *Taoiseach*, Garret FitzGerald in his book *Towards a New Ireland*, 1972. In that book, he made it quite clear that he would be willing to remove the language requirement, both in public services and in matriculation, as a means of making the 26-County Irish Republic a more acceptable society in the eyes of Ulster Unionists. Through ignorance or sheer cynicism, Dr Fitzgerald even declared that he recognized that Irish Protestants "do not belong to the native Gaelic tradition". Even before the removal of the test of linguistic competence, none of the Irish civil service departments conducted any degree of their business in Irish.

As an example of changing attitudes, we may take the Gárda Siochána—the Irish Police Force. Until the latest ruling takes effect, every recruited policeman is presumed to have passed a test in the language and, during their initial training in the force, stress is laid on general conversation and a knowledge of legal terms. However, only 10 per cent of the Irish police would be able to carry out their duties in Irish and these, of necessity, would be found in Irish-speaking areas.

In the early years of independence, the Irish police was a mainspring of enthusiasm for the revival. Early police publications—*Guth an Ghárda* (Voice of the Guards) and *Iris an Ghárda* (Gazette of the Guards)—were replaced in December, 1925, with *The Gárda Review* which laid great stress on the language, in spite of its recourse to an English title. During the 1930's, when Colonel Eamonn Broy was Police Commissioner, it was stated that the aim was to make the police entirely Irish-speaking. The force then boasted 58 Irish-speaking stations in Irish-speaking areas. In January, 1936, Broy directed his men: "Irish only is now used by members of the Force of all ranks in giving evidence in the courts and in the Irish-speaking Divisions..."

There was an outcry from a small group of solicitors and those not sympathetic to the language to which Broy replied: "In giving their evidence in Irish, and in Irish only, in preference to a foreign language, the Gárdaí are acting perfectly within their rights—common rights conferred by the Constitution on every citizen..." and he urged his men: "Those members who know Irish must use it and those members who do not, must learn it".

Had this trend continued, the Irish police would have been an effective influence but lack of Government enthusiasm soon made itself known. Officers are still reminded that fluency in Irish is a stipulation for promotion but they are also informed that it is not really necessary because assistance in communicating in Irish can be obtained from the Irish Section at Police Headquarters. Symbolic of the abandonment of its early aims came when the *Gárda Review* was re-launched under a new editor in 1973, with no word of Irish in its columns.

Radio Telefís Éireann, as the State's broadcasting system,

badly lets down the national ideal by broadcasting only 1.6 per cent of its programmes in Irish. The State's airline, Aer Lingus, offered financial incentives for the recruitment of French and German-speaking staff but do not even provide moral encouragement for Irish. As for the 'national' daily newspapers of Ireland, the *Irish Times* appears openly hostile to the language, whilst the 'nationalist' *Irish Press* devotes only one article, about one per cent of its space, to Irish.

On the positive side, modern Irish literature is exceedingly virile, due in no small part to the Government sponsored publishing house, An Gúm (established in 1926). An Gúm has been instrumental in providing a wide variety of translations into Irish from the literature of other nations. Most heartening has been the virile state of native literature which has ranged from the serious work of Máirtín Ó Cadhain (d.1970) who is still acclaimed as the greatest novelist in Irish. His *Cré na Cille* (Dust of the Graveyard), published in 1949, has been compared to James Joyce's *Ulysses.* On the other side of the scale, there is the writing phenomenon of Cathal Ó Sándair, who is most popular for his detective thrillers featuring Réics Carló, but who has also written science fiction and westerns and has now published over 160 novels in Irish. A significant proportion of novels and plays, originally written and published in Irish, have now become bestsellers in English translation. The production of such a thriving literature has been one of the brighter aspects of the revivalist years.

Irish Governments preferred to let voluntary bodies do all the work while giving an occasional, half-hearted cheer from the sidelines. By 1943, there were about 16 such voluntary organizations covering several aspects of the revival and the Government felt obliged to establish Comhchaidreamh na Gaeilge, to co-ordinate the work of these movements. This body was renamed Comhdháil Náisiúnta na Gaeilge and still exists today as the coordinating body, carrying out promotional schemes. It fell to voluntary efforts, however, to establish a body which would make films and records in Irish. In 1953, Gael-linn was set up as a private organization, financing the first feature-film in Irish. From Gael-linn came records, films, television programmes, a new theatre—all of which were funded by private enterprise. Thanks to its efforts, a Glór na Gael award was established in 1962 as an annual award to the town which was deemed to have done the most to promote the language.

Along the west and south coasts of Ireland are scattered the six Irish-speaking areas: Donegal, Mayo, Galway, Kerry, Cork and Waterford. There is also a tiny Irish-speaking community in Meath. These are the places where Irish is still the ordinary, everyday vernacular—the Gaetachtaí. At the time of independence, they were remote and impoverished regions. Since independence, every generation of Gaeltachtaí inhabitants has fallen to half the size of the preceding generation. Independence has not prevented things reaching a position where the Gaeltachtaí is in danger of disappearing. The introduction of industries has led, in many cases, to the influx of English-speaking settlers who have not become Irish-speaking but have exerted a pressure on the natives to change to English. The establishment of the mass media, radio and television, whilst of material benefit, reinforced the position of English in those areas, and precipitated Irish-speakers into a world that was indifferent or hostile to their language.

To the Gaeltacht dweller, the Irish language became associated with penury, drudgery and the harshness of life in the rural community. By contrast, English was associated with wealth, ease and advancement. It became the language of the cities, of officialdom, of the Irish Government and all its services and, moreover, of the affluent tourists who visited the areas. The adoption of English is viewed as a necessary step to a better life. Gaeltacht industries have been no more than a means of training, in order to migrate in search of work in English-speaking areas. The current generation is witnessing the death of the last remaining monoglots and, when a language loses its monoglots, unless there are very special circumstances, it swiftly changes to the more economically viable language.

The process is not all one-sided. We are now witnessing the Gaeltachtaí youth fighting back, a process which began in the 1960's, especially in Conamara, where a Civil Rights for the Gaeltacht Movement was launched, taking as its model Cymdeithas yr Iaith Gymraeg (the Welsh Language Society). *'Bás don Bhéarla!'* (Death to English) was a slogan seen on walls and public monuments. The movement coordinating the campaign was *Misneach* (Courage)—the inspiration of the great Irish writer Máirtín Ó Cadhain. Ó Cadhain (1906-1970) was a teacher who joined the IRA in the 1930's, was interned for five years, became a professor of Irish at Trinity College, elected to the Irish Academy of Letters and is rightly regarded as one of Ireland's greatest writers. He was a devoted pan-Celticist, speaking not only his native Irish but Scots Gaelic, Welsh and Breton. He also spoke and read English, German, Russian, Italian and French. He was much impressed with Saunders Lewis' lecture *Tynged yr Iaith* (The Fate of the Language) which gave birth to Cymdeithas yr Iaith Gymraeg (Welsh Language Society). Ó Cadhain translated it from Welsh into Irish as *Báis nó Beatha* (Death or Life) which provided the inspiration for *Misneach*. A campaign of blacking-out English road signs in the Gaeltachtaí resulted in the Government accepting Irish-only road signs. A pirate station Saor-Raidio Chonamara (Free Radio Conamara) resulted in the Government's approving a state-controlled Raidio Gaeltachta, broadcasting entirely in Irish. The pirate station was part of a concerted campaign in which many people refused to pay radio and television licences, as a protest against the lack of Irish broadcast by the state network RTÉ. A similar campaign to get an Irish television service for the Irish-speaking areas commenced early in 1984. By mid-1984, more than a hundred people have refused to pay for television licences, in protest at the 1.6 per cent Irish programming on RTÉ.

RTÉ has shown no compromise or concern at their lack of Irish programmes, not even in view of the 1981 census showing the 31.6 per cent of the 26-County state was a potential audience for such programming. RTÉ went so far as to prosecute Mrs Cáit Uí Chadhain, a relative of the famous writer, who was also a widow with nine children, for refusal to pay her licence. RTÉ succeeded in having Mrs Uí Chadhain imprisoned in November 1983. The case had initially been heard by a sympathetic District Judge but the High Court overturned his probation order in favour of jailing, arguing that RTÉ had no legal case to answer in relation to its relegation of the language. What was more significant was a case in February, 1984, in which Mr Justice Ryan could dismiss the request of an Irish-speaking defendant for his trial to be held in Irish as an 'impertinence', and the Irish Supreme Court to make a ruling that judges did not have to hear cases in Irish, even within Irish-speaking areas of the country.

Yet, over and above the various Human Rights charters and agreements which such a ruling contradicts, Article 8 of the Constitution of the Irish Republic clearly states:

> (1) The Irish language, as the national language, is the first official language.
> (2) The English language is recognized as a second official language.
> (3) Provision may, however, be made by law for the exclusive use of either of the said languages for any one or more official purposes, either throughout the State or in any part thereof.

Even before the State's blatant ignoring of Article 8, Irish-speakers had great difficulty in doing business in Irish with the Irish State. There is an appalling lack of bilingual forms, and of forms in Irish only, which should be available under the Constitution. The lack of facilities for Irish medium schools and the weak position of the language in education generally are also causes for concern.

In February, 1984, it was announced that the Irish Government's meagre subsidy to the Irish weekly newspaper *Inniu* (Today), the only national newspaper entirely in Irish, founded in 1943, would be withdrawn. The paper ceased publication in August, 1984. There was talk of merging *Inniu* with the Gaeltacht weekly *Amárach* (Tomorrow) which closed down in 1983, and which, of course, catered for a different audience. At the same time as withdrawing its subsidy from the Irish national weekly, the Minister for the Gaeltacht announced that the Government would be prepared to subsidize a new Sunday newspaper to be called *Anois* (Now) which was launched in September, 1984. This is a sort of curious, sideways and backwards shuffle. In language terms, *Taoiseach* FitzGerald talks of a new 'pluralist' society in Ireland, by which he apparently means the abandonment of the national ideal of language restoration and the confinement of Irish to the Gaeltacht regions. The *New Ireland Forum Report*, published in May, 1984, states: "The Irish language and culture would continue to be fostered by the state, and would be made more accessible to everyone in Ireland *without any compulsion or imposition on any section*". This indicates a clear abandonment of revivalism.

Reactions to the Government's change of attitude towards Irish have been immediate. In 1983, the Gaelic League called for a Bill of Rights for the Irish language, in view of the necessity to clarify its status, since Article 8 of the Constitution apparently no longer applied. Support was gathered and a draft of proposals was prepared. (Many other countries, such as Canada, for example, have a Bill of Rights on their statute book for the protection of minority languages.) This Bill of Rights has received widespread support.

The revival has also received a new impetus from developments in Northern Ireland. In the latest language census which applied to Ulster before Partition, it was revealed that some 67,711 inhabitants spoke Irish (which ironically compared to 40,225 in Leinster). In the 6-Counties, Irish speakers constituted 2.3 per cent of the population. On a single-country basis, the percentage figures were:

Antrim	0.4 p.c.	*Down*	0.3 p.c.
Armagh	2.4 p.c.	*Fermanagh*	0.8 p.c.
Derry	1.8 p.c.	*Tyrone*	3.9 p.c.

The City of Belfast returned 0.4 per cent of its population as Irish speaking.

The percentage figures for the three other Ulster counties which form part of the 26-County state were:

Cavan	3.0 p.c.
Donegal	33.4 p.c.
Monaghan	0.4 p.c.

During its fifty years of existence, the Government of the 6-Counties recognized no other language within the Northern Ireland statelet except English. During those years, many Ulstermen have been imprisoned for having the temerity to try to plead in Irish. In spite of this, at the start of the current conflict in 1969, Irish was being taught to 6.36 per cent of the statelet's school children in 156 primary schools (out of a total of 1,332 primary schools). These children were mainly Catholic school-children, although a few schools run by Protestant denominations included Irish in their curricula. There are two all-Irish medium schools: one in Derry and one in Belfast. The most surprising development, in view of the previous official anti-Irish language attitudes, was announced by the Northern Ireland Office in April, 1984.

Formal recognition was given to the Irish medium school, Scoil Ghaelach Bheal Feirste, in Shaw's Road, Andersontown, Belfast. The Minister responsible for Education, Nicholas Scott, said that the school would have recognition within the state system and receive full maintained-status, grant aid for all running costs and 85 per cent of capital costs from September 1st, 1984. This School, which has been in existence for 13 years, has 125 pupils at primary level and 72 pupils at nursery level, and is run by a staff of 12 teachers. Scoil Ghaelach caters for the children of Pobal Feirste, Belfast's small but significant Irish-speaking community. Whilst the decision was immediately attacked in rather hysterical terms by Unionist politicians, Mr Scott felt that the School represented "valid cultural aspirations which the Government had a responsibility to finance".

It will be remembered that the Stormont Government was suspended on March 30th, 1972, and it is one of the ironies of the situation that there have been encouraging signs for the language during this 'direct rule' period from Westminster. October, 1981, saw the first-ever Irish language radio programmes being broadcast on BBC Radio Ulster—although it had a mere 15 minutes at an unpopular time, this has become an established programme, and the BBC has recently appointed a full-time producer for Irish-language programmes. The BBC also announced its intention to increase its output and also broadcast a series of learners' programmes. The same month, October, 1981, also saw the launch of a new all-Irish weekly newspaper in Belfast, *Preas an Phobail* (The People's Press). Since 1972, an annual average of 2,000 pupils take GCE 'O' level examinations in Irish in the 6-Counties, whilst an average of 300 pupils take the 'A' level examinations.

When the Fianna Fáil *Taoiseach* Jack Lynch took the 26-County republic into the European Economic Community in January, 1973, Irish became an official EEC language with the Treaty of Rome and all the ancilliary treaties and agreements translated and signed in Irish. It did not, of course, become one of the seven working languages nor are there facilities for translation within the European Parliament, although some Irish members have spoken the occasional few sentences as a gesture within the debating chamber. There has been much criticism that this outward badge of Irish nationhood is hardly ever used before representatives of the other nations of Europe. Even the most informed Europeans tend to regard Ireland simply as an English-speaking province with self-government. One Greek deputy thought Ireland's connection with England was comparable to Crete's cultural relationship with Greece.

Pressed to use the Irish language on occasion, the Irish Government does so in an embarrassed and half-hearted fashion. Such an example occurred at the EEC signing ceremony in 1973. Jack Lynch began his speech in Irish. The Irish Government, however, had not provided other delegations, with a text, translation or means of translation. While the delegates looked bewildered and hastily scrabbled among their papers, the English media commentator hazarded that the Irish Prime Minister was "saying something in Gaelic". After an embarrassed ten minutes, Mr Lynch plunged into English. When the important *New Ireland Forum* report was published, it was launched in English, with an Irish version not being available for a month afterwards. Such things are typical of the linguistic approach of official Government bodies.

In recent years, the European Parliament has adopted policies to protect and support the least used languages of the EEC and, in 1982, established the European Bureau for Lesser-Used Languages. These languages are spoken by 30 million people—languages other than the seven working languages of the Community. On September 15th, 1983, Ireland became affiliated to this bureau which supports the basic rights for speakers of minority and regional languages in education, public administration and the mass media.

Before Dr FitzGerald's Fine Gael-dominated coalition came to power in 1982, a previous Irish Government had set up Bord na Gaeilge (1975), to make yet another inquiry into the state of the language and deliver a series of recommendations. In mid-1983, its long-awaited report and plan, *Plean Gníomhaioghta don Ghaeilge* 1983-6 (Action Plan for Irish 1983-6), was produced setting out a number of linguistic targets to be achieved, especially in the Gaeltachtaí and in Government service. Initially, it was greeted with guarded approval by the language bodies; but then it was discovered that Dr FitzGerald had changed the position of Bord na Gaeilge from a statutory body to a merely consultative one, and no Government funds were allocated to meet its recommendations.

Whilst Ireland tends to be an example to which the other Celtic nations look, the only lessons to be learned seem to be negative ones. (An honorable exception is the recent launch—on August, 13th, 1984 of the first all-Irish daily newspaper—the first daily in a Celtic language, as far as I am aware. It is called *Lá* (Day) and comes from the publishers of *Preas an Phobail.*) Yet nearly one-third of the population of the 26-County state can speak Irish.

So long as Dr FitzGerald's Government does not tamper with Article 8 of the Constitution, it remains the first official language of the State; it is recognized on the international stage and is an official EEC language. It has considerable goodwill from the people of Ireland: a recent Irish Marketing Survey showed that 76 per cent of the population was in favour of seeing Irish spoken and used as the first language throughout the country. Every Irish Government since independence has paid some degree of lip-service to that national ideal.

In Northern Ireland, in spite of some progressive moves, one still encounters examples of outrageous discrimination against Irish-speakers. For example, in May, 1984, an Irish language teacher, Breandan Ó Fiaich was stopped by an army patrol in Belfast. He gave his name and address in Irish. He was then arrested and taken to an RUC station in Queen Street, where he was beaten up because he refused to speak English. Magistrate Aidan Cullen of Belfast Magistrate's Court dismissed a charge brought against Ó Fiaich, under Section 18 of the Emergency Provisions Act, which lays down that anyone questioned by the security forces must provide his or her name and address. The magistrate pointed out that Ó Fiaich had done so. As Ó Fiaich left the court, the RUC arrested him with two new charges—obstruction and failing to give information. A second magistrate was obviously not bothered by the civil rights' aspects and fined Ó Fiaich a total of £50. This is a more blatant example of a denial of fundamental human rights, and one of the continuing problems that the Irish language faces in Northern Ireland.

In his attempt to placate Unionist attitudes to Irish, Garret FitzGerald has subscribed to Unionist myth-making, as we have noted, and declared that Irish Protestants "do not belong to the native Gaelic tradition". What is particularly cynical about FitzGerald's attitude is the fact that his mother was an Ulster Presbyterian who was very active in the Irish revivalist movement. The real Ulster traditions have been clearly outlined in *Hidden Ulster*, a superb booklet by historian Pádraig Ó Snodaigh, 1973. FitzGerald's new 'pluralism' and his negation of the national aspiration of language revival is already creating a backlash. There is much stronger activity on the part of the language movement. Perhaps the FitzGerald Government will be seen as the catharsis needed to give new impetus to the language struggle. In the meantime, as the only Celtic country with a voice on the world political stage, the 26-County state is hardly an example to her Celtic cousins, for she speaks with an Anglicized voice. In September, 1803, Robert Emmet, the leader of the abortive 1803 uprising, addressed the court which sentenced him to death with these famous words: "When my country takes her place among the nations of the earth, then, and not till then, let my epitaph be written". That epitaph cannot be written yet.

Chapter Six
Kernow (Cornwall)

As the Anglo-Saxons pushed westward, establishing the kingdom of Wessex, they constrained part of the British Celtic population into the south-western peninsula of the island. There arose a short-lived Celtic kingdom called Dumnonia, from which modern Devon takes its name. The Dumnonian kingdom became cut off from the rest of the British Celtic population, when Caewlin and Cutha forced a Saxon wedge as far as the Severn in 577 AD. Dumnonia fell to Wessex in the 8th Century when Geraint, the last king, was slain and the Saxons pushed the Celts as far west as Exeter around 710 AD. Geraint, to whom Adhelm, the first 'English' scholar of distinction, wrote rebuking him for his adherence to Celtic Christianity rather than Roman orthodoxy, is also immortalized in 'A Lament to Geraint', popularly ascribed to Llywarch Hen.

Soon after Geraint's death in battle, the Celts rallied and in 721 AD managed to defeat the Saxons on the banks of the Camel. This battle is traditionally called 'Slaughter Bridge' at Camelford, and is entwined in Arthurian legend. The defeat gave the south-western Celts a further century of freedom from Saxon expansion. Then, in 814 AD, Egbert of Wessex resumed the attack. In 825 AD, the south-western Celts suffered another defeat. It is then that Bishop Kentsec appears as Bishop of Kernow, which the Saxons called the land of the 'Kern-weahlas', or Cornish foreigners and sometimes called the land of the 'West Welsh'. Cornwall, therefore, had begun to emerge as an entity distinct from the larger Dumnonian kingdom, although the River Tamar was not its boundary and the Celts occupied the country as far as Exeter until the 10th Century.

In 838 AD, the Cornish made an alliance with the Norse to expel the English from pressing on their eastern border and a combined army met Egbert at Hingston but were defeated. By a stroke of luck, Egbert died the following year and the Saxons were unable to follow up their advantage. Cornwall had time to consolidate under its native rulers. According to the *Anglo-Saxon Chronicle*, in the year 927 AD, Athelstan, having attempted a conquest of the Cumbrian Celts, received the submissions of certain Celtic kings near Carlisle. Among these was Hywel, king of the 'West Welsh'. It was three years later that Athelstan, the grandson of Alfred, launched his attack on Cornwall and brought it under English control. Athelstan is on record as driving the Celts out of Exeter, and establishing the Tamar as the boundary between England and the 'West Welsh'.

According to William of Malmesbury, Athelstan "...attacked them (the Cornish) with great energy, compelling them to withdraw from Exeter which, until that time they had inhabited on a footing of legal equality with the English. He then fixed the left bank of the Tamar as the shire boundary, just as he has made the Wye the boundary for the North Britons. Having cleansed the city of its defilement by wiping out that filthy race, he fortified it with towers and surrounded it with a wall of square hewn stone". This has given rise to two schools of thought. Firstly, it is argued that the Celts were still living east of the Tamar, as far as the environs of Exeter until this event and that, in 930 AD, Athelstan simply drove them beyond this river. Secondly, orthodox scholarship suggests the Tamar was already a national boundary and that the Cornish lived in Exeter as foreign settlers. Certainly, after Athelstan's victory, we hear no more of kings of Cornwall; but we do find that Cador (sometimes written Condor) was recognized as *eorl* of Cornwall at the time of the Norman Conquest. He was deposed by the Conquest although his son Cadoc was reinstated and, in 1104 AD, the daughter of Cadoc married Reginald, son of Henry I, who then claimed the earldom of Cornwall. Cornwall remained a distinct entity from England. Edmund (939-46 AD) had a charter drawn up two years before his death in which he styled himself 'King of the English and this British Province' (Cornwall). The phrase *in Anglia et Cornubia* occurs many times in the Middle Ages and on maps Cornwall was frequently marked as 'West Wales'.

In 931 AD, the Celtic Church of Cornwall was under Bishop

Conan whose primacy was at St. Germans. Padstow had previously been Cornwall's principal monastic foundation and it was at Padstow that the only surviving Celtic gospel book dating from the period was written—the famous Bodmin Gospels, originally know as St. Petroc's Gospels, written during the 9th and 10th Centuries. After the Conquest, the English forced Roman orthodoxy upon the Cornish, and the monasteries at St. Buryan and St. Michael's Mount were dissolved and reformed as collegiate churches. In the reform of these monastic centres, it is apparent that a wealth of manuscripts in Cornish and Latin was destroyed (the survivals and evidence for which I have already given in *The Cornish Language and its Literature* (1974). In 1050 AD the Cornish diocese was abolished.

However, during the period of Middle Cornish, a flourishing literature began to develop consisting mainly of Miracle Plays. The biggest survival of these works is the *Ordianlia*, a cycle of three religious plays said to have originated from Glasney Priory during the period 1275-1450. But the most interesting surviving drama is *Bewnans Meriasek* (Life of Meriasek), the oldest surviving life of a Celtic saint in drama form in any British Celtic language. In the earliest manuscript of this play, we find the signature of 'Dominus Rad Ton' and the date 1504. He has been identified as the Dominus Ricardus Ton who, in 1537, was parish priest at Crowan near Camborne. Another fascinating work from the period is a versified narrative of the Passion of Christ, *Pascon agan Arluth*. There were other plays which are now lost and, so far, only a fragment of one containing 41 lines, found on the back of an old charter dated 1340, has survived to demonstrate the sophistication of Cornish writing at that time.

The Tudor period began to see the rapid decline of the Cornish language due to Tudor centralism. New laws, taxation and centralism, gave rise to a reaction among Cornish people. William Antron, a Member of Parliament for Helston, denounced this centralism. So did a blacksmith from St. Keverne named Michael Joseph, subsequently called *An Gof*, the Smith. So, too, did a Bodmin lawyer, Thomas Flamank and a peer, Baron Audley. A rebel army of 15,000 Cornishmen was raised and led by these four men. They marched across the Tamar, first taking Bristol, then Salisbury and then Winchester. It was Flamank who tried to make a common cause with the English peasants, suggesting the Cornish army should march to Kent "the classic soil of protests", a reference to the English Peasant Uprising of 1381.

Henry VII was worried by the rapid advance of the Cornish army. His own army, under Lord Daubeny, engaged the Cornish near Guildford and were beaten off with severe losses. On June 16th, 1497, the Cornish encamped on Blackheath in Kent but there was no support from the English. Henry VII led 25,000 veteran troops into the field and the battle began at dawn on June 17th. The odds were against An Gof and his Cornishmen. Having lost 2,000 men, An Gof gave the order to surrender. On June 27th, An Gof and Thomas Flamank were hanged, drawn and quartered at Tyburn. Lord Audley was beheaded the next day at Tower Hill. (On October 22nd, 1966, Mebyon Kernow erected a memorial stone to An Gof and Flamank which was unveiled by Alderman K.G.Foster, Chairman of the Cornwall County Council.)

With the first Act of Uniformity in January, 1549, introducing the English language in all church services, riots took place throughout Cornwall. When it became law on June 9th, 1549, Cornwall once more rose in revolt and the insurrectionary army was led by Humphrey Arundell of Helland and Nicholas Boyer, mayor of Bodmin. The insurgents made their demands clear. Article Eight of those demands stated: "We, the Cornishmen, whereof certain of us understand no English, utterly refuse this new English". After some initial victories, the Cornish insurgents met Lord Bedford's army. There was a vicious battle and a great slaughter. The English army rested for ten days before moving into Cornwall with Sir Anthony Kingston appointed provost marshal. Hangings, burnings, and a ruthless suppression followed as harsh as anything under Cromwell in Ireland, or Cumberland in Scotland.

With Cornwall shocked by this devastation, it was a well-known playright, Nicholas Udall, who wrote a pamphlet suggesting that the new Protestant Service, the Prayer Book and Bible ought to be made available in Cornish. A Conference to study the laws of the new Anglican Church in 1560 passed a resolution "that it may be lawful for such Welsh or Cornish children as can speak no English to learn the Premises in the Welsh tongue or

Cornish language". Unfortunately for Cornish, the resolution was ignored. During that year, however, John Tregear translated into Cornish twelve of Bishop Edmund Bonner's sermons and a thirteenth from an unidentified source which were lost and not rediscovered in manuscript form until April, 1949.

The Reformation not only started the swift decline of the language but it also stopped the age-old intercourse between the Cornish and the Bretons. Between 1540-60, the lay subsidy rolls and parish registers showed large numbers of Bretons living in Cornwall but, following the reforms of the church, the Bretons seemed no longer welcome in Cornwall, although there is evidence that the Cornish still clung to Catholicism for quite a while.

Cornish priests were being trained in Spain and those priests were able to speak Cornish. One such trainee priest, Richard Pentrey actually delivered a lecture in Cornish before the Spanish monarchs in Valladolid on September 7th, 1600.

Towards the end of the 16th Century, there is evidence to show that Cornish was still spoken in east Cornwall. In a case heard before the Bishop's Consistory Court in 1595, a girl gave evidence concerning a conversation in Cornish at the village of St Ewe near St Austell; and a similar case had been heard earlier, in 1572, concerning an incident at Lelant. But during the 17th Century, the language's decline was almost abrupt, in spite of the fact that many Cornish gentlemen became interested in preserving the language and developing its literature. The main inspiration of this school was William Scawen, a vice-warden of the Stannaries, who was the first Cornishman to express a desire to save and restore the language. he prevailed on several of his contemporaries to start writing in Cornish. The most prominent writer of this new school was Nicholas Boson of Newlyn, famous for his *Nebbaz Gerriau Dro Tho Carnoack* (A Few Words About Cornish). Many of Boson's manuscripts have been lost although *Jowan Chy an Hor* (John of Chyanhor) survives. This little Cornish classic, dating back to 1667, was made into a Cornish-language film by Vegville Enterprises as *Jowan Chy an Horth*, an entry for the Fifth Celtic Film and Television Festival in 1984.

Nevertheless, the 17th Century saw the death of the last Cornish monoglots and, with their passing, it became obvious that the language would not long survive. Scawen's immediate hopes were unfulfilled although the interest among antiquarians continued and, among them, William Gwavas of Paul, whose manuscript remains has left us the most important collection of Late Cornish works. Perhaps the most significant development in the study of the Cornish language was the arrival of Edward Lhuyd, Keeper of the Ashmolean Museum in Oxford and, according to Sir John Rhys who became the first professor of Celtic at Oxford in 1876, "the greatest Celtic philologist the world has ever seen". He spent time collecting manuscripts, conversing with Cornish speakers and learning the language well enough to compose a 19-verse elegy on William III in it. His work on the Celts, *Archaeologia Britannica*, was published in 1701 and he printed in this a Cornish grammar and the story of *Jowan Chy an Hor*. A projected vocabulary was not published.

Then occurred the foundation of one of the great historic Cornish myths. The antiquarian Daines Barrington, visiting Cornwall, looked for speakers of Cornish and was introduced to Dolly Pentreath of Mousehole. He wrote an account of their meeting in the Society of Antiquaries' journal, *Archaeologia*, May 6th, 1775. It is clear from his account that Dolly Pentreath was not the last speaker of Cornish, for Barrington mentions two other younger women who interpreted her words during the interview. The result of Barrington's article brought forth a letter written in Cornish, with an English translation, from a Mousehole fisherman named William Bodener, who demonstrated by his letter that he knew the language, was literate in it and mentioned that four or five other people in Mousehole also spoke Cornish. Indeed, when Dolly Pentreath died a man named Thomson of Truro composed an epitaph in Cornish! Yet if Dolly Pentreath was not the last native speaker of Cornish, who was? We shall never know, for a language does not die suddenly, snuffed out with a single 'final' speaker. It lingers on for many years after it has ceased as a form of communication between people. Throughout the 19th Century, the remnants of Cornish lingered on in folk memory and in dialect speech. At the end of the century, John Davey of Boswednack, Zennor, who died in 1891, was also to be claimed as the last native speaker.

By this time, work in the language was becoming more popular.

Robert Williams published a *Lexicon Cornu-Britannicum* in 1865 and Prince Louis Lucien Bonaparte had become fascinated by the language and was busily collecting manuscripts. Edwin Norris published texts and translations of the Middle-Cornish dramas, under the title *The Ancient Cornish Drama* (1959). A German linguist, he had learnt the language well enough to write two poetic epistles in 1859 and 1861, the first Cornish poems composed in a century, which he sent to Norris. Whitley Stokes, one of the most prominent 19th Century Celtic scholars, translated and edited a text of *Pascon agan Arluth*. There was generally a great deal of academic interest now that the language was dead. Such work resulted in Frederick W.P.Jago's *The Ancient Language and Dialect of Cornwall*, followed by an *English-Cornish Dictionary* in 1887 and W.S.Lach-Szyrma's *The Last Lost Language of Europe*, 1890, which contained some primary lessons in Cornish.

In 1901, there was a sufficient number of interested Cornish people to form a movement which aimed to revive the language, to establish a Gorsedd along Welsh lines, and to encourage Cornish sports such as hurling and wrestling. The movement was called Cowethas Kelto-Kernuak (The Celtic Cornish Society) and it was the brainchild of L.C.Duncombe Jewell, who became its secretary with Sir W.L.Salusbury Trelawny as president. Among its three vice-presidents was a scholar named Henry Jenner who had already become a bard of the Breton Gorsedd. In September, 1903, he had tried the experiment of a speech in Cornish on an audience of Bretons and was surprised that they understood almost all of it. Thus encouraged, Jenner launched himself into working on a suitable textbook for learners to use. In 1904, David Nutt of London published Jenner's *Handbook of the Cornish Language*. Jenner declared:

> Why should Cornishmen learn Cornish? There is no money in it, it serves no practical purpose, and the literature is scanty and of no great originality or value. The question is a fair one, the answer is simple. Because they are Cornish.

In 1904, Jenner addressed the Celtic Congress on why Cornwall should be admitted to membership as a Celtic nation and won their approval.

Along with many others in the movement, Jenner started a new school of Cornish poetry but, during World War I, Cowethas

Kelto-Kernuak lapsed. The war saw a journal *An Howlsedhas* (Sunset) produced from a military hospital by one enthusiast. After the War, in 1920, an Old Cornwall Society was formed in St. Ives with the motto: *Cuntelleugh An Brewyn Us Gesy Na Vo Kellys Travyth* (Gather ye the fragments that are left that nothing be lost). The aim of the Society was the preservation of all that was Celtic in Cornwall, especially the language. Jenner became president. By 1924, there were enough societies to form a Federation and, from 1925, a twice yearly journal *Old Cornwall* was published.

Conversational Cornish soon had many adherents and enthusiasts were especially keen on providing easy-to-learn text books. R.Morton Nance produced *Cornish For All* in 1929, in which he introduced a new spelling system which he called Unified Cornish, based on the surviving Middle-Cornish literature. Other text books came spilling forth from A.S.D.Smith (*Lessons in Spoken Cornish*) and W.D.Watson (*First Steps in Cornish*). Poems, plays and short stories were being written and published and a new thriving literature was growing.

Jenner's long-cherished dream of establishing a Cornish Gorsedd on the lines of the Welsh and Breton Gorsedd of Bards became a reality on September 21st, 1928 when, at Boscawen-Un, he became Grand Bard of the first *Gorseth Kernow*. The Gorseth Kernow has been held annually ever since and its history has been recorded in *Gorseth Kernow: The First 50 Years* (1978) by Hugh Miners.

In the early 1930's, there came a new development. With the re-awakening of the Cornish language had come a re-awakening of Cornish nationhood. On December 31st, 1932, the *Western Morning News* published a speech of Henry Jenner in which he used the phrase *'bedheugh byntha Kernewek!'* (Be Forever Cornish!). A group of young men and women, enthused by the language revival, formed what can be described as Cornwall's first national political movement under the name Tyr ha Tavas (Land and Language). They became a pressure group, lobbying Parliament. They were led by Dr E.H.Hambin, C.H.Beer and B.Y.Couch.

Nance, working on his unified Cornish spelling system, published his *English Cornish Dictionary* in 1934 which replaced

Jago's outdated work. The same year saw the launch of an all-Cornish language magazine *Kernow* (April, 1934) as the official journal of Tyr ha Tavas which was edited by A.S.D.Smith. Smith was extremely active in promoting the language and wrote a text-book called *Cornish Simplified* which sold 2,500 copies in a comparatively short time. He was to write a Cornish version of the epic *Trystan hag Ysolt* which was not published until after his death in 1950.

The war years saw Tyr ha Tavas become moribund and replaced, for a short while, with a movement called Young Cornwall. On January 6th, 1951, at Redruth, a group of Cornish men and women met and formed Mebyon Kernow (Sons of Cornwall). Their initial aim was "to maintain the character of Cornwall as a Celtic nation, to promote the interests of Cornwall and the Cornish people and to promote the constitutional advance of Cornwall and its right to self-government in domestic affairs". It was a tentative beginning but, from a ridiculed pressure group, Mebyon Kernow had achieved the position where, by 1966, three of Cornwall's five Members of Parliament openly advocated many of their major policies. Mebyon Kernow originally envisaged a Cuntelles Kernow (Assembly of Cornwall) on the model of the Isle of Mann or the Channel Islands' parliaments.

The language movement continued to progress during the 1950's and in January, 1952, Richard R.M.Gendall launched an all-Cornish magazine called *An Lef* (The Voice) to fill the loss of Smith's *Kernow*. Designed as a monthly, with the tenth issue Gendall passed the editorship to E.G.R.Hooper and it took the new title *An Lef Kernewek*, appearing quarterly until 1984. Gendall, a writer of a great deal of original poetry and plays in Cornish, launched another magazine in May 1956, entitled *Hedhyu* (Today) which ceased publication in 1961 when he launched a mainly English language magazine entitled *New Cornwall*.

In May, 1964, Mebyon Kernow revised its aims. These were now "to maintain the Celtic character of Cornwall and its right to self-government in domestic affairs, to foster the Cornish language, literature, culture and sport, and to demand that Cornish children have the opportunity in school to learn about their own land and culture". From a political pressure group, Mebyon Kernow made the change to a political party with candidates standing, firstly, in local-government elections. In 1967, Colin Murley was elected as Mebyon Kernow's first county councillor for St Day/Lanner on the Cornwall County Council. Election successes followed to district councils. In 1970, Richard Jenkin stood as Mebyon Kernow's first parliamentary candidate for Falmouth-Cambourne and received 960 votes. It was a beginning.

There were many Cornish nationalists who felt that the Mebyon Kernow aim for domestic self-government was not adequate for the needs of Cornwall. A split occurred in Mebyon Kernow ranks and in June, 1969, Leonard C.Trelease, a former national secretary of Mebyon Kernow, established a Cornish National Party which envisaged Commonwealth Status for Cornwall. Robert Holmes, who had won a seat on Liskeard council as a Mebyon Kernow candidate in 1968, became the Party leader. But when the Cornish National Party put forward its first parliamentary candidate in 1979, its aims had been modified to "regional status within the United Kingdom, within Europe".

In 1979, three of the Cornish parliamentary seats were contested by Mebyon Kernow (St. Ives, Falmouth-Cambourne and Bodmin). A fourth was contested by Dr J.Whetter of the Cornish National Party who had stood as a Mebyon Kernow candidate in the 1974 elections. In the 1983 General Election, two constituencies were tackled by Mebyon Kernow and a third by the Cornish National Party. The votes for both parties fell slightly against the 1979 votes but, at local level, both parties continued to have a strong voice. There was now a number of Cornish political journals; Mebyon Kernow published *The Cornish Nation* and, for a while, published *Kernow* for younger readers. The Cornish National party published *The Cornish Banner*. *An Weryn* (The People) was an independent radical journal. *Keveren* (Link) was the journal of a group called Cowethas Flamanck which is a nationalist pressure group. The rise of this political national consciousness had been a remarkable achievement, after it had long been considered that Cornwall had been totally assimilated into the English ethos.

One aspect of this political nationalism was the emergence of a shadowy movement taking their name from the leader of the 1497 Cornish uprising—An Gof. In the winter of 1980/81, An Gof claimed responsibility for bombing a magistrate's court at St.

Austell. The apparent attack on the symbol of a court became confused by the subsequent An Gof statement attacking 'Marxists' in Mebyon Kernow. Fires at a cosmetics factory and at a building society's offices, denied to be arson by the police, were claimed as such by An Gof, much to the delight of the media. An Gof then disappeared until January, 1984, when it claimed responsibility for fires at a bingo hall, a village hall, and for planting broken glass on a beach used by locals rather than tourists. The bizarre nature of these claims caused many commentators to suggest that An Gof was the creation of a police 'dirty tricks squad', of the kind known to operate in other Celtic countries, with the aim of discrediting the Cornish movement. Hoax letter-bombs to Government offices in Plymouth and Exeter, and press releases threatening tourists, were guaranteed to cause widespread 'horror' coverage in the media which would be made to reflect on both Mebyon Kernow and the Cornish National Party. Even if An Gof was an element in a 'dirty tricks' campaign, as seemed likely from its strange actions until 1984, such a militant national group could eventually emerge, as it has, among Cornwall's fellow Celtic national movements.

The continued growth of the revival caused the establishment of *Kesva an Tavas Kernewek* in November, 1967. This 'Cornish Language Board' took over all aspects of the revivalist movement, conducting examinations in the language to GCE level. Kesva an Tavas Kernewek was endorsed both by the Gorseth Kernow and by the Cornwall Education Committee. The first general secretary was P.A.S.Pool whose textbook *Cornish For Beginners* became popular. However, *Kernewek Bew* (Living Cornish), with records and tapes as aids, has since become the 'last word' in teaching manuals. This was compiled by Richard Gendall and remains his greatest contribution to the movement whose basic aims were to promote the study and use of Cornish and publish in the language.

By the end of the 1970's, it was realized that Kesva an Tavas Kernewek was an isolated academic body without the base of a lay membership. Activities in the language tended to be splintered and it was thought the time had come for a grass-roots organization to help the board. During the 1950's, there had been a group called Unyans an Cows Kernewek, a Cornish speaker's union, but this had disappeared. In 1979, Kesva an Tavas Kernewek instigated an associate membership under the title Cowethas an yeth Kernewek (The Cornish Language Fellowship). It took over responsibility for the publication of a monthly magazine *An Gannas*, launched in December, 1976. The magazine, entirely in Cornish has a circulation of more than 300 copies. After the sad demise of *An Lef Kernewek* in 1984, following 32 years of publication, *An Gannas* (The Ambassador) became the premier Cornish language magazine. In 1984, Cowethas an Yeth Kernewek published *Kernewek Hedhya: Deryvas War Stuth an Tavas*, a bilingual report on the state of the language.

Until the end of the 1960's Cornish and Cornish studies in general had been ignored by the academic world as a subject unworthy of separate consideration. In 1969, the University of Exeter put forward the idea of an Institute of Cornish Studies to coordinate and encourage all forms of research in Cornwall. The Institute was founded in 1972, with Professor Charles Thomas as its first director who laid emphasis on the study of the language. One of the problems was the academic world's attacks on Nance's Unified Spelling which had become the standard for the revivalists. These attacks were joined by the younger generation of revivalists, though from an entirely different standpoint.

Tim Saunders, who was to edit *Cornish is Fun*, in 1978, a method of learning Cornish through cartoons, began the attack with an atricle 'Scubyon Lyenegyl' (Literary Garbage) in the 1972 Annual Volume of the Celtic League. He rejected Nance's synthesis and pointed out that Nance's spelling system did not pay sufficient attention to pronounciation. The Unified Cornish system had had its critics for some years. Eventually, unable to deal with the problem, Richard Gendall faded from the revivalist movement. Tim Saunders tried to devise his own spelling whilst others, acknowledging the problem, have simply pressed on with the material to hand. In "Cornish—Symbol and Substance" (*For a Celtic Future*, edited by Cathal Ó Luain, 1984), Tim Saunders felt that 'Nance succeeded in paralyzing Cornish for over forty years'. He wrote:

> People bringing up their children in Cornish are thrilled by the advances in the language made by their children. Sooner or later, however, their joy turns to alarm as the children's competence overtakes their own. To the

> child's constant question *'pyth yu hymma?'* they rarely have an answer. Faced with a plethora of unexplained verbal inflections, they have to abandon most and are reduced to pidginizing two or three of them. With few constant supporters, and no assistance from the education and broadcasting systems, they have an uncertain and lonely road ahead of them. As the task of standardizing spoken Cornish falls increasingly on young speakers, we face the possibility that the slow process of creolization may have to carry out what the Nancean revival could not. But what function of social communication in early twenty-first century Cornwall will require a creolized Cornish?

Yet Saunders is not downhearted: "Indeed a wider public awareness allows for a qualitative change in the character of Cornish activity. The next ten years promise interest and excitement".

Dr Ken George, the secretary of Cowethas an Yeth Kernewek's Education Committee, wrote in *Kernewek Hedhya*:

> This is not a newly discovered matter. People have been troubled by this since the Board's 3rd rule was written. They can behave in three ways, to retire completely and be lost to the movement (like Dick Gendall), or to write a spelling nearer to the pronunciation (like Tim Saunders), or try to carry on with a state of trouble (like us). I have never heard a discussion on this problem in the Board. We cannot do it unless there is one. In my mind, this wise body should grasp the problem and be seen to be doing something about it.

One of the most significant and exciting developments in the revivalist movement was the birth of Dalleth (Beginning). By the end of the 1970's, it was seen that, despite the ever-increasing facilities for the learning, practice and use of Cornish, the activities were organized with adults in mind. To revive a language, one needs young people. In October, 1979, Dalleth was launched with the following aims.

> (1) To raise money to publish childrens' books in Cornish and investigate the feasibility of initiating a printing organization, possibly in conjunction with other organizations.
> (2) To investigate more fully bilingualism through contact with other Celtic countries.
> (3) To promote opportunities for children of all ages to learn Cornish and help to organize social activities and playgroups in Cornish.

Dalleth launched a new monthly *Len ha Lyw* in September, 1981, for the benefit of children and, by 1984, it had a circulation of 120 copies selling mainly in the schools. Booklets, such as *An Dre Noweth*, provided excellent illustrated stories for children.

Originally, Dalleth organized regular play-groups but found them difficult to sustain. Those parents interested in Cornish-speaking, playgroups lived scattered throughout Cornwall and it was found difficult to bring them together on a regular basis. However, playgroups were still organized at Cornish events. It was noticed, however, that one of the problems was that children who learned Cornish at home and in playgroups, tended to reject the language when moving on to primary schools and finding a hostile, English-speaking environment. Dalleth began to concentrate on publications and on encouraging teachers to introduce Cornish culture in its widest sense into schools, producing cassettes of nursery songs and rhymes in the language.

By 1984, seven Cornish schools were teaching the language (five primary and two secondary), and there were 18 evening classes in the language being held in various Cornish centres. Five more evening classes were established outside of Cornwall, from Bristol to London. Also, a 'Cornish by Post' course was attracting learners from many different parts of the world. Kesva an Tavas Kernewek continued to maintain a high standard in their examinations and during 1983, out of 37 candidates entering for the 1st grade only 18 passed; of 12 candidates for the 2nd grade, only eight passed; and out of ten candidates to the 3rd grade, only six passed.

As early as 1560, the newly reformed Anglican Church had recommended the translation of religious works into Cornish but, unlike other Celtic countries, the Bible was never translated into Cornish, although many individual books and excerpts were translated. At its meeting on December 3rd, 1983, Kesva an Tavas Kernewek decided to establish Kescoweth Treloryon Scryptor Sans, which would pursue the translation and publication of a Bible in Cornish. At the beginning of 1984, work began on the project.

At the Fifth Celtic Film and Television Festival, held in Cardiff, Wales, in April, 1984, Cornwall submitted eight films and two of them were in Cornish: *Jowan Chy an Horth*, directed by Sarah Stuart Wood for Vegville Enterprises and *An Canker Seth—An Scath* (The Crab Pot—The Boat), directed by J.Phillips for Television South West Ltd.

Introducing the 1984 report on the state of the Cornish

language, Hugh Miners, the Grand Bard of Cornwall, was able to declare:

> *Marnas y coth neppyth na yller ragweles a wharfo saw a vo an yeth bynytha; byth a whyrfyth arta an ystory morethek a'n 17es ha'n 18es cansbledhynnow. Dyskys ha dyghtys a vyth Kernewek avel yeth vew hedra vo tus ha benenes Kernewek.*
>
> Barring wholly unforeseen circumstances, the language is now safe for all time; never will the history of the 17th and 18th Centuries be repeated. Cornish will be learned and used as a living language for as long as there are Cornish men and women.

Cornwall was the first of the modern Celtic nations to lose its language. Today there are many lessons which the other Celtic nations can learn from the truly astonishing rebirth of this nation. Just as Cornish was disappearing into the English ethos, a few dedicated men and women snatched at the embers, blew on them and fanned them into a flame that grows stronger with each passing year.

Chapter Seven
Mannin (Isle of Mann)

The Manx are the smallest of the modern Celtic nations and, like their cousins the Cornish, they no longer have any nucleus of native speakers of the language. The last acknowledged native speaker was Ned Maddrell who died on December 27th, 1974 and is buried at Rushen. Nevertheless, Mannin is possessed of a virile revivalist movement. They have one distinction from their fellow Celts in that they can claim to be the oldest self-governing Celtic nation, being granted 'home rule during pleasure' in a United Kingdom Government Act of May, 1866. However, the Manx parliament has been an Anglicizing force since that date when 50 per cent of the islanders spoke Manx. Self-government under these circumstances has done little to aid the survival of the Manx nation. The status of the Island was defined in the report of the Royal Commission on the Isle of Mann Constitution, published on March 14th, 1959, which stated that "the Isle of Mann is not part of the United Kingdom" but that "the power of the Imperial Parliament (Westminster) to legislate for the Isle of Mann is supreme".

Little is known about the Island before the 4th Century AD. Popular tradition has it that the Island was named after Manannán Mac Lir, the Celtic ocean god. It is accepted that the original inhabitants were Brythonic Celtic in speech and, in support of this contention, one of the five Ogham inscriptions on the Island is usually cited—that of Knoc y Donee in Andreas. The names on this stone are Irish but are recorded in Brythonic Celtic. A list of the early rulers of the Island show Brythonic names rather than Goidelic. Even as late as 682, it is recorded that Merfyn Mawr ruled the Island. However, Goidelic Celtic was brought to the Island from the 4th Century onwards and the linguistic change was swiftly made. The divergence from a common Gaelic, shared with Ireland and Scotland, did not occur until the 13th to 15th Centuries. Because of this, there is no indentifiable 'Early Manx' literature or literary remains. Old Irish would have been the standard written language and impossible to identify as of Manx provenance. Cormac's Glossary mentions a fascinating visit to the Island by Ireland's chief bard, Senchan Torpeist (649-662 AD). He went there with fifty pupils and found a high degree of literary knowledge among the Manx people. One old fisherwoman entered into a literary contest with him and knew her ancient poetry by oral tradition word perfectly. The epic Irish sagas and poems were known for many years in oral tradition and from folk memory. This was demonstrated by antiquarians in the 17th Century and the Ossian saga was recounted by an old fisherman and written down by the scholar Heywood in 1789. His manuscript is still held by the British Museum.

Christianity was introduced into the Island at an early stage and the Manx were part of the Celtic Church structure. During the 7th Century, the monastery of Maughold, named after a disciple of Patrick, had risen to pre-eminence on the Island. In the 9th Century, the Norse started to raid the Island and they imposed a ruling class upon the Manx. For a while, the island was at the mercy of any powerful Viking lord so that, one year, it might be ruled by a Danish king from Dublin, or the next by the Norwegian kings.

It was not until 1079 that Godred Covan made the Isle of Mann into a self-governing state which had dominion over no less than thirty-two Hebridean islands which became known as 'The Kingdom of Mann and the Islands'. With this Norse conquest, Celtic Christianity received a check. Then, towards the middle of the 10th Century, Christianity was revived as the Norse settlers not only accepted Christian religion but also became absorbed into the Celtic cultural life. Intermarriage and an acceptance of the language took place. One example of this can be seen in a stone cross from the period erected by one Thorleig for his son *Fiac!* Even names of Manx kings now became bilingual such as Mac Ragnall (921-940 AD) who also claimed suzereignty over York. There followed Godred Mac Ragnall (1060), Fingal Mac Godred (1070), Donal Mac Teige (1096-98) and so forth.

Whilst the Celtic language was accepted by the Norse, the old

Celtic social order, the method of holding lands and laws of succession gave way to Norse custom. This included the displacement of the Celtic Church which, under Godred Covan's reign, accepted Roman orthodoxy and the first pro-Roman bishop of the Island—Roolwer, a Manx corruption of the Norse name Hrólfr—began to reform the church. Olaf (1113-53) succeeded his father Godred and continued the reorganization along English lines, introducing a parochial system. The old Celtic monastery of Maughold was replaced by a Cistercian house at Rushen by a group of monks invited to the Island from Furness in 1134 AD. Rushen Abbey became an important centre of Manx learning and it was here that the *Chronicle of Mann and the Isles* was written. The Roman form of ritual and administration now dominated, in spite of protestations from some conservative Celts who argued for the retention of Celtic Church usages as late as 1203.

The Island constituted a diocese of the Roman Church which was entitled *Ecclesia Insularum*, and sometimes *Ecclesia Sodorensis*. This latter name was the Latin form of the Norse *Sudrejoy* or *Sudreys*, meaning 'southern islands'. The Nordreys were the Shetlands and Orkneys. Although political connections between Mannin and the Hebrides ceased in 1266, the ecclesiastical links persisted until the 15th Century, when the Pope established the Western Isles as a separate bishopric with its primacy on Iona. The diocese 'Sodor and Mann' survives in the Anglican Church today, its name having been adopted in the 17th Century in ignorance of the meaning of *Sodorensis'*. The bishopric of Mannin, from 1152 to the 15th Century AD, was actually under the control of the archbishop of Trondhjem in Norway. When the Norse relinquished their claims on the Island, it passed to York and, in 1542, was confirmed part of that English ecclesiastical province.

The last independent king of Mannin was Magnus who died in 1266. On his death, he ceded his kingdom to Alexander III of Scotland. By this time, the Manx had established a tradition of stable democratic government as the kings ruled through a Thingvöllr (Parliament Field)—a name that has come down in the modern Manx Parliament—the Tynwald. An annual Tynwald Day ceremony is held on July 5th each year, when officials of the Government are sworn in and the laws of the Island are read in both Manx and English. The actual executive chamber consists of the House of Keys—from the Manx *kiares-es-feed*, the Twenty-Four, for its members once constituted sixteen elected representatives from Mannin and eight from the islands. After the loss of the Hebrides, the additional eight members came from Mannin itself.

Scotland ruled Mannin for twenty-three years, until Edward I of England annexed the island and installed Walter de Huntrecombe as custodian. Balliol won it back for Scotland but the English took it again. Robert Bruce recovered it for Scotland in 1313 and actually stayed on the Island in Rushen Abbey. In 1346, the English landed a powerful force on the Island and this time they stayed. Henry VII instituted a 'Lordship of Mann' which he granted to Sir John Stanley, afterwards Earl of Derby, for his aid in the defeat of Richard III at Bosworth. The lordship of the Island was taken over by Elizabeth I in 1594, after she had fallen out with the Stanley family. James I restored it to the Stanleys in 1612. In 1736, the lordship passed to James Murray, Duke of Atholl. The Atholls sold it to the English Government for £70,000 in 1764 but, from 1774, the 3rd Duke of Atholl was appointed Governor-General of the Island.

During the whole of this time, the House of Keys, as the Island's Parliament, continued in existence. In the year 1422, the House of Keys had issued a famous Declaration of the Manx Constitution, setting forth the duties and privileges of the Manx Parliament. During the late 17th and 18th Centuries, however, the idea of election to the House of Keys had been corrupted. As early as 1791, a Commission of Enquiry was established to examine the constitution of the Island when Manx people began to protest at the system of self-election to the Parliament which permitted the members of the House of Keys to virtually hold office for life. Although calling themselves the representatives of the people, they were in fact drawn from leading insular families and represented only their own interests, seldom sitting in public. After continued agitation, the House of Keys agreed to the principle of popular elections in 1853.

In May, 1866, in return for financial concessions to the Island's economy, the House of Keys was established as an elected body of twenty-four representatives meeting as a government of the Island. A Lieutenant-Governor, as the representative of the monarch on the Island, was also appointed. The Island, therefore, was recognized as having self-government or, as the Act described it "home rule under pleasure". The new Manx Government was not a national expression of the will of the people. It was an Anglicized body and continued to act as a means of Anglicization. In 1866, more than half the Island was Manx-speaking. The Manx Government presided over the swift decline of the language.

The Reformation was a slow process on the island, although the English Act of 1539, suppressing religious houses, was enacted on the Island. The Manx remained Catholics owing to the barrier of the Manx language and the staunch Catholicism of the 3rd Earl of Derby (1521-1579), the Lord of Mann. Previously, religious publications had been in Latin but the priests were Manx-speaking. The new availability of religious works in English had no effect on the religious views of the islanders. The new Protestant clergy realized that only the promotion of Manx, and literacy in that language, would help the conversion to the new religion. In 1587, John Phillips, a Welshman, became rector of Kirk Andreas and, in 1604, became Bishop of Mann. He set about translating the Book of Common Prayer which, unfortunately, was not published, although the manuscript survived to be published for the first time in 1895. Contemporary commentators not only refer to this translation but to a translation of the Bible itself. If such a translation were made, it has not survived.

Antiquarians were taking an interest in the language and collections of oral traditions, of epic poems and ballads that were being made. In 1656, James Challoner, on a visit to the Island, found that "few speak the English tongue". The landed gentry knew English and Camden, on a visit in 1695 noted: "The gentry are very courteous and affable and are more willing to discourse with one in English than in their own language". Bishop Thomas Wilson's *The Principles and Duties of Christianity* became the first book to be published in Manx in 1699. Wilson was keen that his clergy knew the language and could preach in it "for English is not understood by two-thirds of the island". He founded schools in which Manx people could be taught through the medium of their own language. he also translated the Gospel of Matthew in 1722, although this was not published until 1748. His Gospels of Mark, Luke and John were also published in that year.

It was Bishop Hildesley, appointed Bishop in 1755, who started the movement to have the entire Bible published in Manx. In 1758, he urged his clergy "to use their best endeavours to improve the use and practice of the Manx tongue'. In 1763, the Society for Propagating Christian Knowledge conducted a survey among the islanders and found that, out of the population of 20,000, "the greater number are ignorant of English". Hildesley's project was coming to fruition and, indeed, the biggest monument to the Manx language remains the Bible. The story of its translation by a group of dedicated Manx clergymen, under the direction of a Manx scholar, is an exciting adventure story in itself. At one point, a clergyman taking the precious translation to the printer, was shipwrecked and saved the years of toil by swimming for hours while holding the papers out of the water above his head! The Acts and Gospels were published in 1763; the Bible up to the Book of Job appeared in 1771; and a complete Old Testament and Apocrypha appeared in 1773 and, finally, the new Testament in 1775. Soon after they were combined as *Yn Vible Casherick*. which has been acknowledged a significant piece of literature in itself and not merely a translation.

The production of the Manx Bible presented a sound basis for the literary language. Most of the literature at this time was of a religious nature. The first secular book published in Manx was Milton's *Paradise Lost* (*Pargys Caill*), translated by Thomas Christian of Marown and published in 1796. Of course, there were numerous ballads and folk tales which were popular such as *Baase Uilliam Dhone*, printed in 1781. This was a celebration of the life and death of the famous Manx folk hero Uilliam Dhone (brown haired) Christian, who took possession of the Island for Parliament against the Royalist tyranny of the Stanley family. On the Restoration of Charles II, an amnesty had been declared for those who supported Parliament (except those who had signed the death warrant of Charles I). Charles Stanley, the 8th Lord Derby, returned to the Island and declared as Lord of Mann that the amnesty did not cover Mannin. Uilliam Dhone was seized and brought to trial. Some members of the House of Keys refused to condemn Uilliam Dhone and were replaced. He was condemned to death and shot on Hango Hill. The ballad had been popular for many years before it was finally published.

Scholastic work was now proceeding on Manx philology. As early as 1703/4, the great Celtic scholar Edward Lhuyd, Keeper of the Ashmolean Museum, Oxford, had collected many Manx lexical items but only published a vocabulary of 95 words of Manx in his famous *Archaeologia Britannica* in 1701. The first scientific study of the phonology of Manx was therefore made by Sir John Rhys, the first Professor of Celtic at Oxford, during the course of visits made to the Island between 1866 and 1893. However, Dr John Kelly had been working on a dictionary in the 1780's and 1790's which was published in 1804. This was revised by the Reverend Hugh Stowell and W.Fitzsimmons in 1811-14. Kelly's original dictionary was reprinted in 1859 and again in 1870. A Manx grammar was produced by a German scholar and another Manx-English Dictionary, compiled by Archibald Creegen, appeared in 1835. An English-Manx Dictionary, compiled by Gillmand Clarke, was published in 1866.

The linguistic and literary activity, however, was not a protection against the decline of the language. Writing in 1859, William Gill of Malow stated:

> The language is no longer heard in our courts of law, either from the bench or the bar and seldom from the witness box. The courts are indeed still fenced in Manx according to ancient traditional form, and the island laws are still promulgated in the language on Tynwald Mount...it is rarely now heard in conversation, except among the peasantry. It is a doomed language—an iceberg floating into southern latitudes. Let it not, however, be thought that its end is immediate. Among the peasantry it still retains a strong hold.

The Anglicized Manx Government determined that the 'strong hold' should be broken. In 1872, they passed an Education Act ensuring that English was taught in all the Island's schools and, indeed, forbidding children to speak Manx in school, ordering punishments for any who did so. This became a significant factor in the startling decline of Manx speakers during the last three decades of the 19th Century: a drop, as we shall see, from 12,350 in 1874 to 4,598 in 1901. It also brought Mannin in line with the enforced English-dominated Celtic countries. With the Island's education system totally committed to English, the death of the language seemed inevitable.

In 1858, a Manx Society had been formed "for the publication of national documents" and existed until 1907. The Manx Society was responsible for much work in the language—studies of place-names, personal names, grammars, vocabularies and other works. It was an academic rather than a revivalist movement and was eventually overtaken by Yn Cheshaght Ghailckagh, founded in 1899, which specifically aimed at the preservation and teaching of Manx and of the culture associated with it.

Among the Celtic scholars who visited the Island was Henry Jenner, who was to become 'Father of the Cornish Language Revival'. In November, 1874, he carried out a survey, excluding the capital of Douglas, and found that, out of a total population of 41,084, only 12,350 spoke Manx as their first language and only 190 spoke no English at all. The main Manx-speaking area was in the north of the Island, where twice as many Manx-speakers lived as in the south. However, the major number of Manx monoglots was actually to be found in the south. Of the seventeen Manx parishes, the rector of only one parish, Kirk Lonan, with 1,850 speakers, declared that a knowledge of Manx was necessary to cope with work in the parish. It was not until 1901 that an official Manx Government census of Manx speakers was made and then it was found that 4,598 people spoke both Manx and English and 59 spoke only Manx. This represented 8.1 per cent of the population.

The Island was not by-passed by the Celtic Renaissance which started in Ireland and spread throughout the Celtic world. The Breton secretary of the Celtic Association visited the Island and this resulted in the growth of an awareness of a common Celtic identity among the Manx. On March 22nd, 1899, Yn Cheshaght Ghailckagh (The Manx Gaelic Society) was formed with the motto *'Gyn Chengey, gyn cheer'* (Without language, without country). Mr A.W.Moore, who was to become Speaker of the House of Keys, was its first president. It was at this time that Sophie Morrison emerged as a champion of the language revival movement which Yn Cheshaght Ghailckagh spearheaded. She had persuaded William Cashen of Peel to publish *First Lessons in Manx*, in 1898, as an elementary primer in the language. She was secretary of Yn Cheshaght Ghailckagh and a delegate to the Celtic Congress. The Isle of Mann *Examiner* began to publish a regular column in Manx, and the Manx Government was pressed to allow the language to be adopted in the Island's schools. The Government refused but supported the idea of evening classes.

There was a great deal of feverish scholastic activity in publishing grammars, textbooks and other studies. *Yn Saase Jeeragh* (The Direct Method) by J.J.Kneen, 1911, became a popular learning method. Kneen's *Grammar of the Manx Language* was published by the Oxford University Press in 1931. A new popular literature, translations of English classics, stories, plays and poetry, began to be established. Scholars were anxious to make serious examinations of the language and the first sound recording of spoken Manx were made by Dr Rudolph Trebitsch from the Osterreichische Akademie der Wissenschafen in Vienna during August, 1909, on a series of cylinders. W.H.Gill went to Manx-speakers, recording stories, sayings and songs soon afterwards. Sophie Morrison continued her prodigious production of works in Manx and was instrumental in the establishment of The Peel Players, acclaimed as the Manx equivalent of the Irish Abbey Theatre, performing plays in the Manx language.

Word War I (1914-18) was a tremendous blow for the revivalists and a particular tragedy for the Island. Out of its tiny population, 5 per cent of its young men gave their lives in the War. There was an abrupt decline in native speakers and, in the 1921 census, it was found that only 896 people spoke Manx, with 19 monoglots.

The Celtic Congress was held on the Island, in 1921, when Douglas Hyde of Ireland visited Mannin. It was at this time that another great Manx personality emerged in the person of Mona Douglas, who formed Aeglagh Vannin (Manx Youth) to foster the language among young people. The motto of the movement was: *paitchyn jiu, ashoon mairagh*...children today, a nation tomorrow. Caarjyn Vannin (Friends of Mannin) was also formed to work alongside Yn Cheshaght Ghailckagh for the revival. Yet, in 1931, the census figures showed that only 529 people spoke Manx, with no monoglots being listed. Two years later, Professor Carl J.S.Marstrander of the Department of Celtic, University of Oslo, visited the Island to make the first extensive recordings of Manx in 1933. Surprisingly, in view of the published census figures, he believed that there was only *one native speaker* left. The Welsh scholar, A.S.B.Davies, published a correction to this erroneous concept in the *Bwletin y Gwybodau Celtaidd* (Bulletin of the Board of Celtic Studies), No.XII. Nevertheless, it was true that the figures were still declining owing to lack of Manx Government interest. The number of people returned in the 1951 census as able to speak Manx had dwindled to 355. This was less than 1 per cent of the Island's population. The last Government Census of Manx speakers was in 1971, when 284 people (144 males and 140 females) were returned as being able to speak Manx.

On July 23rd, 1947, Eamon De Valera, then *Taoiseach* of the 26-County Irish state, paid an official visit to the Island and was interested in the position of the language. He met and was able to converse with Ned Maddrell, each man speaking his respective Goidelic language. It was through De Valera's personal intervention that the Irish Folklore Commission sent a sound-recording unit to Mannin to make extensive recordings of the language from the remaining native speakers. But the Anglicized attitude of the Manx Government meant that there was no hope of any survival. Yet, this same attitude started to see the inevitable rise of a political nationalism. The first Manx national, political group was Ny Manninee Dooie (True Manx Folk), founded during World War II, but it lacked support because people saw it as anti-English at a time when the common enemy was regarded as Germany. During the 1940's and 1950's, a magazine *Yn Coraa Ghailckagh* (The Manx Voice) had a degree of success in awakening national consciousness.

Things passed into a moribund state for a while as the Manx Government made the Island a 'tax haven' for countless English families which were now flocking there. The 1981 census revealed that 47 per cent of the Island's population was a 'newcomer' or immigrant population. This migration from England, the growing economic problems, the lack of constitutional clarity over the Island, and the disappearance of the Manx language and culture, caused a group of Manx men and women to form a new political party on Saturday, January 11th, 1964, which they called *Mec Vannin* (Sons of Mannin). Its first president was L.Crellin. The party claimed that the Manx Government was destroying national morale on the Island and that the only answer to the problems was 'full independence'. However, "to assuage the fears of the more timid section of the electorate", Mec Vannin started as a pressure group supporting those independent members of the House of Keys who allied themselves to its policies. One of the leading figures among such members of the House of Keys was a Manx lawyer named Alfred Howard Simcocks of Ballasalla, elected to the House of Keys in 1956, who became the Island's strongest advocate for total independence. Mec Vannin stated that their aims were:

> (1) The furtherance of the interest of the Isle of Mann and the protection of the individual and collective rights and privileges of its people.
> (2) To endeavour to establish and maintain the Isle of Mann as a fully autonomous state having at all times a proper government elected upon and bound to wholly democratic principles and responsible only to the citizens of the Isle of Mann.

The emergence of Mec Vannin also re-awoke enthusiasm for Yn Cheshaght Chailckagh. Mec Vannin played a leading part in bringing about a change of attitude which caused the Manx Government to disagree with several dictates of Westminster. It rejected the bill to outlaw 'pirate' radio stations being pressed on them by Westminster in March, 1967. The 'pirate' station in question, a ship anchored in the waters of Mannin, became Manx Radio. It was the first time that the Manx Government had rejected legislation considered by Westminster as essential. In June, 1967, a seven-man committee of the House of Keys recommended that the Manx Government should stop dealing with the United Kingdom's Home Office, and conduct all further dealings through the Commonwealth Office.

Mec Vannin can be credited with playing a part in initially pointing out the need for a Tenants' Protection Act, a Health and Safety at Work Act, and a Factory Act for the protection of workers, and the need for specific laws to protect building-trade workers. It was Mec Vannin who first proposed the idea of an independent Manx Post Authority which is now a financial success. Mec Vannin stimulated the Manx to assert their identity and shake off the feeling of political apathy.

The new sense of Manx identity resulted in the emergence of a shadowy movement called Fo Halloo (Underground) during the early 1970's which began to wage an active campaign of daubing road signs, Manx slogans, placing posters in prominent positions, and issuing a regular newsheet which made allegations of corruption in the Tynwald and Athol Street (the Manx financial centre in Douglas). An arson campaign was laid at Fo Halloo's door by the authorities but never substantiated. Fo Halloo appeared as a popular movement with popular support, which allowed it to sustain a vigorous campaign of action until the 1976 General Election on the Island. A similar group called Irree-Magh (Insurrection) also made a transitory appearance.

By this time, Mec Vannin had entered the political arena and had already come within 25 votes of winning a seat in the House of Keys. Three Mec Vannin candidates (including party leader, Mrs Annette Bridson) had been elected to the Manx Education Board. Mrs Bridson had come second in a bye-election for the Ramsey and Peel seat in a traditional Manx Labour Party stronghold. In the November, 1976, General Election, Mec Vannin fielded ten candidates among a record 71 candidates for the 24 House of Keys seats. The party polled 13 per cent of the votes cast and one candidate, Peter Craine in South Douglas, became the first Mec Vannin candidate to enter the Manx Parliament. Of the 24 members of the 1976 House of Keys, it was significant that 12 were 'newcomers', the Manx euphemism for English immigrants.

In June 1977, members of the Manx branch of the Celtic League were beginning to be worried at the use of the Island by British armed services. An Anti-Military Alliance was formed between the Manx branch of the Celtic League and the Western branch of Mec Vannin, although ties with Mec Vannin were subsequently loosened. The Manx branch of the Celtic League now publishes *The Celtic League, Mannin, and AMA News*. The aims were for a de-militarization of the Island and the declaration of a nuclear-free zone. More immediately, the Anti-Military Alliance discovered that British regular troops and members of the Ulster Defence Regiment were using Jurby military base for training for the war in Ireland. Jurby had also become a NATO base. Soon afterwards, the executive of Mec Vannin met to discuss the fact that the Western branch had been one of the formulators of AMA. Some members felt that AMA would damage the Party and Peter Craine, the Mec Vannin Member of the House of Keys, threatened resignation if AMA members of Mec Vannin did not resign. A motion called for resignation. The AMA members refused and there was a resignation of some leading members of the party including Peter Craine, party chairman David Keggin, vice-chairman John Garrett, secretary John Wright and Audrey Ainsworth, who had been recently elected on a Mec Vannin ticket to Douglas Corporation.

Those who resigned from Mec Vannin formed a new political party, the Manx National Party of which Peter Craine became a leading member. However, in the General Election of 1981, he lost his seat in the House of Keys. Mec Vannin only contested one seat in this election but received a small vote. The split was obviously still in the minds of the electorate. Disillusionment among radicals led to the appearence of a new political party Pobblaght Soshiallagh Vannin (PSV), a Republican Socialist Party. In their first publication, they issued 'The Manx Republican Socialist Charter'. The immediate aims were:

> (1) We are resolved to assert Mann's independence as a sovereign nation.
> (2) To establish a new society in Mann based on the socialist doctrine.

In its second publication, PSV declared:

> Culture is the accumulated inheritance of a people. The character of a people is determined by its past development.
>
> Culture is the slow growth over thousands of years of intellectual, moral, social and aesthetic endeavours of a race. The inheritances of cultural values are transmitted almost exclusively by means of language; in the case of Mann, Gaelic. A sense of belonging and cultural cohesion gave the Manx people resistance to conquest. Would-be conquerors were assimilated or very soon disappeared. Natural assimilation enriched the cultural heritage of Mann.
>
> Lack of self-esteem did not arrive with the learning of the English language, but with the 'loss' of the Gaelic language. A society that cuts itself off from its cultural past, which is enshrined in the language, ignores not only the most important part of its history but also its mind, personality and the most priceless knowledge of what it is. Language is the life-blood of a nation and if the supply is rudely cut off the nation dies.
>
> Pobblaght Soshiallagh Vannin gives high priority to the tranfusion of a proper and worthy education programme of Manx history, language/culture. This is essential if the patient is to revive.
>
> Pobblaght Soshiallagh Vannin sees no conflict in the establishment of a dual linguistic tradition. Gaelic and English can co-exist as English and other languages do.
>
> Pobblacht Soshiallagh Vannin will not be content to be assimilated into the English-speaking world without retaining Manx individuality and

aspiring to the realization of the worth of our separate ethnic identity.

Pobblaght Soshiallagh Vannin offers honesty! Self-confidence will be restored as the necessary basis for a rewarding future. A consciousness of our past will better enable us to play a fitting role in the community of nations.

A third pamphlet was issued as a Social Economic Programme. So far, the PSV has remained a pressure group.

As enthusiasm for the Manx language revival grew during the 1960's and 1970's from younger Manx people, so did the number of books, journals and other publications. The publication in 1979 of the English-Manx Dictionary of 888 pages, whose chief compiler was Douglas C.Fargher, a founder of Mec Vannin, went into an immediate reprint and was a testimony of the new interest. It is now regarded as the modern definitive work. Membership of Yn Cheshaght Ghailckagh increased to the extent that towards the end of the 1970's, a northern branch, Banglane Twoaie ny Sheshaght Ghailckagh, was formed. Banglane Twoaie took the opportunity of presenting all candidates in the November, 1981, General Election, with a questionnaire about their views on the future of Manx. Only 66 per cent of the candidates bothered to reply and, when the election results were known, this dropped to a 62 per cent response of those elected, some 56 per cent advocating no official support for Manx. Banglane Twoaie reported:

> The survey confirms that whilst the language is not subjected to overt suppression, it remains the victim of ignorance and indifference emanating from the highest level in the community. It is self-evident that the language societies within Mann need not look to their own government for support, either moral or financial, as their ambitions are demonstrably low in the league table of political priorities.
>
> The language movement in Mann must either continue to draw more deeply upon its already depleted reserves of manpower and finance or, alternatively, look further afield for the recognition and encouragement that it deserves and needs to flourish. Until this happens the outlook remains bleak for any positive action and expansion on the language front in Mann.

Nevertheless, a GCE 'O' level in Manx was allowed for the first time in 1982 and was taken by 12 adult students. While Manx is not yet taught in the Island's schools, in a few schools a teacher capable of doing so will take a small class of children for some elementary lessons during the lunch-break. In one primary school, a weekly half-hour lesson has been established during school time. As there is no Manx Government backing, the activities in this field are hampered by a lack of funding.

During the early 1980's a number of bilingual street name-plates were erected by many local authorities—some paid for by Yn Cheshaght Ghailckagh. Some of the Manx towns now have all their streets named bilingually, though the English version appears topmost in larger lettering. A few public buildings also have their titles shown in Manx, notably the Government Offices in Douglas, and the Town Hall and Court House in Ramsey. The language has achieved a physical presence.

There has also been a revival of interest in Manx music, with many young people learning and playing songs and dance tunes. In fact, Manx dancing is now taught to children in a number of the Island's schools. The Island also has its own inter-Celtic cultural festival, Yn Chruinnaght (The Gathering), which was revived after a lapse of many years. It had originally been established in the 1920's. It is now a great success as a week-long festival of music, dancing, arts and crafts, competitions and concerts, in which local and visiting Celtic artists take part.

The year 1983 saw the première of the first film ever made in Manx entitled *Ny Kirree Fo Niaghtey* (The Sheep Under the Snow), directed by Shorys y Creayrie for Foillan Films of Laxey. The film was entered in the Fifth Celtic Film and Television Festival at Cardiff in 1984. More such films are planned.

In December, 1983, the Manx branch of the Celtic League, organized a conference on 'Manx Gaelic Today' at the Prince of Wales Hotel, Ramsey, at which three leading members of the revivalist movement discussed various aspects of the revival, including its future. These were Dr Brian Stowell, Colin Jerry and George Broderick. Dr Stowell told the Conference that it was desirable to establish Manx nursery schools to encourage the spoken language. Parents alone could not create a suitable Celtic-speaking environment. It was necessary to set up a situation in which children communicated amongst themselves in Manx. Asked for suggestions as to ways of improving the language's position, it was George Broderick who summed up the aspiration of the Conference when he replied: *'Loayr Gaelg!'* (Speak Manx!).

As in the rest of the Celtic world, although the problems might seem insurmountable, there is optimism for the future.

Chapter Eight
The Celtic Diaspora

When one speaks of a diaspora, the scattering of a people to the far corners of the world, one tends to think specifically of the Jewish people and, indeed, the word has come to mean the dispersion of the Jews after the Babylonian conquest. Yet the Jews, that singular enclave of one of the larger Semitic peoples, were not the only group to suffer a diaspora of immense proportions. The Celtic peoples have been forced to spread themselves across the world but, unlike the Jews, they did not have a singular religion with sacred texts recorded in their languages, as a badge of identity to keep them as distinct communities in the new lands in which they settled. Only in two places in the world have Celtic-speaking settlements survived with any degree of significance into modern times. Elsewhere, the Celts have tended towards ready assimilation.

Of the modern Celtic nations, it has been the Irish who have suffered a diaspora of most terrifying proportions. Beginning with the Elizabethan conquests, and the colonizations of the 17th Century with brutal plans for the extirpation of the Irish as a national community, emigration has become a way of life. The Penal Years and the awesome period of the Famine Years continued the process. Even successive native governments have never successfully grasped the nettle of migration because it was found to be an economic safety valve. This simplistic economic policy also finds a motivation for the native governments' lack of realism in the task of language revival. English-speaking migrants can more easily find work in the English-speaking world.

In the 17th and 18th Centuries, precluded from using their natural talents in their native community by the Penal Laws, the Irish migrants and their descendants were astonishingly successful in their new homelands. In the political field, they produced a President of France, Prime Minister of Spain, several High Chamberlains of the Austro-Hungarian Empire, President of Argentina, President of Chile, President of Mexico, Prime Minister of New Zealand, Prime Minister of Australia. Although John F.Kennedy is quite rightly regarded as the first Catholic Irish-American to have become president of the United States of America, it should also be remembered that three other presidents had Irish-born parents, and a further eight could have claimed Irish grandparents or great-grandparents. There is, perhaps, an irony in the fact that the current President of Israel, Chaim Hertzog, is an Irish-speaking Irish Jew, born in Belfast and educated in Dublin. While James Callaghan, Prime Minister of the United Kingdom, 1976-79, could claim Irish descent, the Duke of Wellington has been the only Irish-born United Kingdom Prime Minister (1828-30). However, Wellington was quick to echo the old Irish saying: *'An té a rugadh i stábla ní capal é!'* (Everything born in a stable is not a horse!).

Daughters of Irish emigrants have become Queens of Sweden, Spain and a Princess of Monaco.

Irishmen have been acclaimed as 'Fathers' of the navies of America, Russia, Japan, Chile, Argentina, Equador and Venezuela.

The French Kings had an Irish Brigade as part of their standing army (no less than 450,000 Irishmen are said to have given their lives for France in the 17th and 18th Centuries). Disbanded in 1792, the Irish Brigade was reformed by Napoleon in 1803 and, on his fall, became the French 3rd Legion Etrangers. Spain also had an Irish Brigade in its army. An Irish Brigade and an Irish Legion fought in the Federal Army of the USA during the Civil War and the Confederacy had several Irish regiments. Mexico, in 1846-7, had its famous St. Patrick's Battalion, fighting American expansionism. Brazil had its Irish Brigade in the 19th Century. During the Boer War, the Boer Republicans boasted two Irish Brigades and an Irish-American cavalry unit. Irish regiments were recruited in the Swedish Army and the Austrian Army. In the 18th Century, Austria boasted 16 Field Marshals, six Major-Generals and eight Masters of Ordinance who were Irish-born or of Irish parentage. Though the British Army once boasted eight regiments raised from the nationalist population of Ireland, it was never confident of the political consequences of forming an Irish Army Corps or even a division. The Unionists' regiments were brigaded as the 36th (Ulster) Division.

In the 17th and 18th Centuries, Irish migrants did particularly well in France. Families such as the O'Ryans became foremost in perfume manufacture while the Shiels took to banking; the Morgans were goldsmiths and jewellers while the Kirwans, Fitzgeralds and Mac Carthys were renowned in medical and pharmaceutical fields. Today, one can still see the influence of the vineyards founded by Irish families. In Bordeaux, the Lynch family, who provided a mayor of the town, founded a famous vineyard. In 1725, Thomas Barton of Donaghmore and Thomas Dewlap and the Kirwan family also established vineyards. One can still buy Lynch-Barges and Lynch-Moussas; Chateau Kirwan, Chateau Talbot and Leoville-Barton—all excellent Bordeaux wines. There is also a Graves called Haut Brion Blanc (Brion from the O'Brien family) and one of the best-known cognacs is Hennessy.

It is interesting and perhaps a significant observation that during the centuries when Irish was the common language of Ireland, the emigrants tended to settle in Europe, particularly in France, Spain and, to a lesser extent in Italy and Austria. As the linguistic change towards English was made, emigrants tended to drift only towards the English-speaking world. But, wherever they went, they achieved distintion in commerce, science and medicine, in politics and in the arts. Ireland's loss of its talented sons and daughters, prevented by the English conquest and Penal Laws from exercising those talents in their own country, was the gain of other countries.

In this remarkable spread of Irish people across the world, it is surprising that the migrants have nowhere established any defined Irish-speaking settlement, as the Welsh and Scots have done. It can be pointed out that Montserrat, in the Leeward Islands of the West Indies, was reported to have been Irish-speaking until the close of the 18th Century. This came about from the fact that large numbers of Irishmen, women and children, were forcibly transported for labour to the West Indies during the Cromwellian period. Between 1655 and 1660 alone, it was estimated some 50,000 Irish were so transported. Also, in June, 1984, the

National Irish-Canadian Association reported that, in the province of Manitoba, there was an Irish-speaking community of 90,000 people. The Association had bought a 140-acre site to establish a centre for them.

In October, 1984, the Association advertised for Irish teachers to teach at the community schools to keep the language alive. Canada once had several identifiable Irish-speaking communities, such as the towns of Peterborough, Ontario, and Douro, Ontario. A particularly strong community was established in Newfoundland, Talamh an Eisg—The Land of Fish, as the Irish called it. Montreál, Québec, had an Irish-speaking quarter in the suburb of Verdun. The first Irish language periodical to be published in Canada—*An Bád Beag Glas*, The Small Green Boat—was launched in Montreál in 1909 by Cumann Muintearach na hÉireann. Montreál television broadcasts an Irish community programme which has an Irish language section presented by Pádraig Ó Laighne, a former founder of *Misneach* in Ireland. Newfoundland saw the production of the first native New World poetry in Irish during the 18th Century. This was the work of Donnchadh Ruadh Mac Conamara (d.1810) who wrote an account of his Newfoundland wanderings *Eachtra Ghiolla an Amarain*. Irish-speaking communities thrived for a time in the USA, where numerous Irish-language schools were founded. Large numbers of Irish language publications were produced in New York, Boston and Washington and there are still Irish-language periodicals produced in North America today. *An Gael* appears from New York while Keshcarrigan Books of New York launched a new bilingual journal *An Droichead* (The Bridge) in 1985. Books in Irish and dual-language books (Irish/English) are also produced in the USA by publishers such as Stone Street Press of Statten Island.

Ironically, London, with an estimated 30,000 Irish-speakers, has been classed as the third largest 'Irish-speaking city' in the world. Conradh na Gaeilge has had an active London branch since its foundation. It was in London, in 1898, that Cumann na Scribheann nGaedhilge, the Irish Texts Society, was formed for the purpose of publishing texts, accompanied by introductions, glossaries, translations and notes. It remains in existence and is as active as ever. England, and to a lesser extent Scotland and Wales, have thriving Irish emigrant communities among which a number of Irish organizations thrive. Various political and cultural organizations have branches in London and other centres; and there have been some indigenous organizations such as the Connolly Association, perhaps the oldest political association among emigrants, whose *Irish Democrat*, launched during the 1930's, is certainly the oldest surviving emigrant newspaper in England. However, the most successful general newspaper for the Irish emigrant community is Brendan Mac Lua's *Irish Post*, launched in 1970. Because of the current war in Northern Ireland, the Irish emigrant community found itself under increasing police harrassment in England, Scotland and Wales and, under such pressures, emigrants felt particularly oppressed. In the late 1970's, the Irish in Britain Representation Group was established, to put new heart and backbone into the Irish community. One interesting facet of the IBRG's activities is a plan to establish Naíora, an Irish-speaking school, in Lambeth in South London along the lines of the already established, Welsh-speaking school at Willesden in North London.

Outside of the English-speaking world, Argentina holds the biggest Irish migrant community, with an estimated 400,000. The community identifies itself around their own weekly newspaper, founded in 1874 *La Cruz del Sur* (The Southern Cross), and a Federation of Irish Clubs of Argentina. They play Irish sports, have Irish classes and Irish is used in broadcasts on local radio. It must be remembered that William Brown of Co. Mayo is regarded as Father of the Argentine Navy, remaining its head and Admiral until 1845, and E.Farrell was Argentine President in 1944. One of the most famous of all Irish-Argentinians was Doctor Ernesto Guevarra Lynch...better known throughout the world by his nickname 'Che'.

The sadness of the Irish diaspora can be encapsulated in the Falklands/Malvinas War of 1982. The first 'British' casualty was Petty Officer Kevin Casey, RN. The 'Argentinian' officer in charge of security on the Falklands/Malvinas was Major Patrick Dowling. The 'Argentinian' responsible for conducting the surrender negotiations was Captain Melbourne Hussey, aide of General Menendez. However, perhaps the greatest irony of all is that the first person ever to be born on the Falkland Islands was named Sullivan, the child of Irish emigrants.

Although there is no arriving at a proper figure, it has been estimated that there are 24 million persons living outside of Ireland who would be entitled to claim Irish citizenship, under the current nationality laws. Yet, while the Irish diaspora has been individually successful and extrordinary, in terms of the migrants' influence on the situation in their mother country, its influence on bringing about its independence or in trying to maintain its language and culture has been extraordinarily ineffective.

Two years after the Treaty of Union, in which Brittany became an autonomous region of France, Francois I commissioned a Breton from St. Malo to discover a new route to China and Japan. Jacques Cartier set out and reached Labrador, Prince Edward Island, Chaleur Bay and Gaspe in 1534. He formally took possession for his new French monarch. Later, Cartier returned with a second expedition and pushed back the frontiers of his discovery and then returned with a third expedition to colonize the land which was called Canada. During the 17th Century, the Bretons who followed in the footsteps of Cartier, played a prominent part in the colonization of Acadia (Nova Scotia) and, in 1657, a Breton named Le Borgne from Enez ar Gêrveur (South Brittany) governed this area. Settlers were mostly Bretons financed by merchants from Rennes and St Malo whose Breton company was subsequently suppressed as not being in the interests of the French Government.

Some 333 Breton officers took part in the American War of Independence and sixteen warships, commissioned to help the Americans, which left Brest in 1778, were commanded by Count Gwizien (Guichen). Lafayette, much extolled as a 'French' hero of the War of Independence, was in fact a Breton and spoke in the Breton Parliament in 1785, stating that he would always remain attached to Brittany. He signed the protest against the French monarchy's attempt to suppress Breton autonomy. Colonel Armand (Armand Tuffin de la Rouerie), another Breton, was colonel of the First Legion of Partisans fighting for the Americans and became a brigadier of cavalry in 1783. He was a friend of Washington and Jefferson. After the abolition of the Breton parliament and annexation, he was instrumental in organizing for an armed insurrection. He was an unrepentent republican but felt that republicanism meant the liberty of *each* nation. He died of exhaustion in January, 1793, while 'on the run'. Another Breton prominent in the American War of Independence was Kerouarzh, the son of the President of the Breton Parliament.

Breton migration on a mass scale to Canada did not actually begin until 1763. Before this time, due to their autonomous state, the Breton people had little desire to migrate. But the 18th Century saw the start of the centralist policies of the French monarchs which were continued by the abolition of the Breton parliament under the new republic. Bretons did not only migrate to Quebec but formed centres in Manitoba and Saskatchewan where one can see numerous Breton place-names. The Breton language and customs survived for a while in these places and one emigrant, A.Raynal, even thought it possible for 'the Armorican race and language to develop some day at the foot of the Rockies and around the fjords of Columbia...'

However, the Bretons migrated primarily to improve their material status and, if dropping their language and culture were necessary to achieve that improvement, then they did so. Today, the Bretons are strongest in Montreál where thousands work in hotels, the building industry and in factories. They are also to be found in Quebec (City), although it is Port Colborne on Lake Erie which possesses the second largest Breton colony in Canada. The majority of these emigrants use French rather than Breton and become integrated in a French-Canadian ethos, rather than remaining a minority of a minority. There are exceptions to this, though not on a widespread scale. The Unvaniezh Bretoned ar C'hanada in Montreál and a Club Jabadao seek to sustain the Breton identity among migrants.

The island of Laval, near Montreál, contains a Breton speaking pocket and the International Committee for the Defence of the Breton Language has a strong sub-branch in the area which is part of the North American branch whose headquarters is in Plymouth Meeting, Pennsylvania, U.S.A.

Migration from Cornwall only began on a noticeable scale in the 19th Century when young and more enterprising miners, realizing there was no future in the Cornish mines, joined the gold rush for California. It was the copper miners who led the way. During the 1830's Cornwall had been the centre of world copper production, producing 116,000 tons as against 102,000 tons for the rest of the world. But Chile, Australia and the United States' copper mines were being developed and, during the 1850's, the figures fell to 122,000 compared with 384,000. By the 1860's, the figure had fallen even further to 90,000, compared to 810,000 for the rest of the world. Cornish emigrants began to leave Cornwall for California and for Pennsylvania. The Vivian family transferred their entire mining works from Cambourne to Pittsburgh. Others went to seek a living in the newly discovered Australian gold fields.

Then came the rapid decline of tin mining and it was found cheaper by the Westminster Government to extract large quantities of cheap alluvial tin from Malaya. The tin miners began to follow the copper miners. While the population of England grew steadily during this period (at the rate of 13 per cent every ten years), that of Cornwall fell by two per cent in the 1860's, and by nine per cent in the 1870's. Houses became empty, cottages fell into decay and the engine houses at the mine heads, one by one, became silent.

The once large, Cornish fishing fleets also went into decline as trawling fleets from as far afield as Lowestoft and Yarmouth worked their seas. The old Cornish toast of *Puskes, Sten ha Cober!* (Fish, Tin and Copper!) had become ironic. Arthur Quiller-Couch ('Q'), editor of the *Cornish Magazine*, commented in 1898: "I see Cornwall impoverished by the evil days on which mining and (to a lesser degree) agriculture has fallen. I see her population diminishing and her able-bodied sons forced to emigrate by the thousand. The ruined engine-houses, the roofless cottages, the cold hearthstone are not a cheerful sight to one who would fain see a race so passionately attached to home as ours is, still drawing its vigour from its own soil".

Cornish migration to the United States, South America, South Africa and Australia, gave reality to the statement that "where a hole is sunk in the ground, not matter in what corner of the globe, you will be sure to find a Cornishman at the bottom of it, searching for metal". By the time the Cornish began to migrate from their native land, English had totally replaced the Cornish language, and therefore the Cornish migrants took nothing of their native culture except a vague pride of being 'different' and a sentimental attachment to Cornwall.

It was in the 17th Century that the Manx began to make significant migrations, forming a settlement in Barbados while some Manx families settled in Virginia, America. These Virginian Manx, particularly the Christian family, played a prominent part in the American War of Independence. Robert and George Christian were friends of Washington and George served on his staff. A third brother, James, was killed during General Burgoyne's invasion of New York. Christian County, Missouri, was named after another member of the family. In the 18th Century, a considerable trade developed between Mannin and the New World, with Manx merchants establishing themselves in the American colonies and in the West Indies.

In the early years of the 19th Century, the Manx traveller and explorer, Dr Harrison, encouraged Manx people to settle in America. Thomas Quayle established his famous ship building firm in Cleveland at this time. John Gill, whose home was at Port Erin, established a building company. The first school in Cleveland was built by Manx emigrants and was called Manx Street School.

The English language was not known among these early emigrants. Manx was used in several townships in the north part of Ohio. In Cleveland, it is estimated that there are some 30,000 people of Manx origin. One area of Pennsylvania was Manx-speaking until the early part of this century. Manx-Americans still make sentimental trips to Mannin and there is a North American Manx Association which holds bi-annual conventions. The North American Manx Association, founded in 1929, has taken an active part in helping to maintain a knowledge of the language and Manx cultural heritage. It publishes a quarterly journal from its headquarters in Minneapolis, Minnesota.

The first notable migration of the Welsh took place in the aftermath of the victory of Henry Tudor at Bosworth when he became King of England. Many Welshmen followed the 'Welsh' monarch to London and a Welsh community was founded in the City. From that period, there has always been a sizeable Welsh population with, in 1984, an estimated 35,000 Welsh-speakers. London has a Welsh Club, a London-Welsh Rugby team, Welsh chapels and a Welsh-speaking school in Willesden. As early as

1751, Cymdeithas y Cymmrodorion was founded and launched two periodicals exclusively in Welsh—*Trysorfa y Gwybodaeth* in 1770, and *Cylchgrawn Cymraeg* in 1793. The Cymmrodorion Society continues as a movement interested in antiquarian studies, somewhat divorced from modern Welsh life, whose president Ben G.Jones, CBE, could tell a 1984 Symposium on 'The Future of the Celtic Languages', in London's County Hall, that all was now well with the Welsh language. The Cymmrodorion Society publishes and transacts its business mainly in English. Another Welsh society, Cymdeithas y Cymreigyddion, formed in London in 1793, published the famous collection *Myvyrian Archaiologi* between 1801 and 1807.

The Welsh were early settlers in America and the American Declaration of Independence was signed by Francis Williams of Llandaff, Glamorgan, who had started a mercantile business in New York and Philadelphia. Thomas Jefferson is on record as being proud of the fact that his ancestry was from Snowdonia and Dr Richard Price of Llangeinor, Glamorgan, was one of the committee which drew up the Constitution of the USA. The State of Wisconsin had its constitution translated into Welsh because of the predominance of Welsh-speaking settlers in the state. One of the most famous Welsh sons of Wisconsin was the architect, Frank Lloyd Wright. It was also in Wisconsin that the Welsh newspaper *Y Drych* (The Mirror) was launched in 1851 and which has continued publication to this date. *Ninnau (Ourselves)*, is another North American Welsh monthly published from New Jersey. Cymdeithas Madog, the Welsh Studies Institute, was formed in 1977 'to promote and further the Welsh language and culture in America'. It is based at 102 Longwood Road, Baltimore, MD 21210. It organizes numerous language courses.

From an early period, the idea of migration to preserve the Welsh language made Welsh migration different to that of the other Celtic peoples. Morgan John Rhys, a Baptist minister from Glamorgan, was fired to preserve Welsh and migrated in 1794. Two years later, he formed the Cambrian Company which acquired land in western Pennsylvania for a Welsh-speaking community called Cambria, of which Beulah became the chief town. The scheme failed as the community was overwhelmed by English-speakers. A similar scheme to found a Welsh-speaking community in Brazil, in the 1850's, called Nova Cambria, failed. Yet another attempt to create a Welsh-speaking community by Samuel Roberts in Tennessee in 1857 was also doomed to failure. Welsh-speaking communities were established in Canada, in Ponoka, Alberta, and Bangor, Saskatchewan, where it is still possible to find descendants of settlers with a knowledge of the language.

Among the Welshmen who believed in the idea of establishing an independent, Welsh-speaking colony, was Michael D. Jones of Llanuwchllyn, Meirionydd. He had spent some years among the Welsh of Ohio and had married the sister of the State Governor. He returned to Wales in 1853, aged 31 years, and devoted himself to radical, nationalist policies. He saw that Wales was placed next door to the centre of the biggest thalassocratic empire in the world. For him, it was a practical question—could Wales ever hope to achieve her independence while incorporated in such a state, backed with all the imperial resources at her command? Jones saw thousands of his countrymen flooding to American and losing their nationality, as they assimilated into English-speaking states. He also saw the failure of his compatriots to establish Welsh-speaking communities in this area of Englishness. Apart from the community in Brazil, no attempt was being made to establish a Welsh-speaking community in the non-English-speaking world.

Forming a small group of interested people in 1861, Jones chose Patagonia, at that time a no-man's land disputed by Argentina and Chile. The venture was to be called Y Wladfa (The Colony). "Our national weakness at present is our servility," Jones declared in an appeal for settlers, "but in a Welsh Colony we can be imbued with a new spirit!"

Two scouts, Lewis Jones, a type-setter, and Love Jones-Parry of Caernarfon, set out to reconnoitre the area. They consulted with the Argentine Government and Dr William Rawson, the Argentine Minister of the Interior, encouraged the scheme. On May 28th, 1865, 153 Welsh settlers sailed on the *Mimosa* to land at a spot north of the River Chubut, on an empty beach which was to be named Port Madryn. The party then set off towards the mouth of the Chubut where they utilized an old abandoned fort and started to build the nucleus of the new settlement. The fort became known as Caer Antur or Yr Hen Amddiffynfa and became the centre of Trerawson (Rawson's Town) which they named after the Argentine Minister who later helped the colony survive, by giving it a monthly grant of £140 for the purchase of seeds and food.

More settlers from Wales began to arrive and in October, 1865, the first crops were sown. The first two seasons' harvests failed. It was not until November, 1867, that Aaron Jenkins found a way of irrigation which led to the success of the colony. A steady stream of new immigrants reinforced the first arrivals. The colony had its own government, meeting as Y Senedd (The Senate) and flying the red dragon flag of Wales. Welsh was the sole language. Michael D.Jones had achieved his desire:

> ...to plant a free Wales on Patagonian soil; a Wales with its own Senate, with the Red Dragon flying over its tower, and the Welsh language used officially within it; a Wales with her language taught in her schools; a Wales conducting business and commerce in her own language; a Wales maintaining her religion, her culture and her institutions; a country with its own independent judicature and her laws in her own language, a land where her farmers own their land and her workers control their industry.

Michael D.Jones made one mistake. He believed that the Argentines—unlike the English—would allow the Welsh colonists their freedom. As soon as the success of Y Wladfa was known, the military governor of Carmen de Patagones despatched a military force to hoist the Argentine flag at Yr Hen Amddiffynfa and the colony was claimed as an integral part of the Argentine state, governed by its laws and using the Spanish language. Thus the Welsh were deprived of their independence almost immediately. But it was not military force which brough Y Wladfa into Argentina. The Welsh Militia were better disciplined and trained than the Argentine troops sent against them. The Senate of Y Wladfa compromised because the colony was in desperate need of practical assistance.

As more and more colonists arrived from Wales, the Welsh began to push into the Patagonian interior along the Chubut Valley as far as the sub-Andean zone, founding Bro Hyfryd (Pleasant Country) and Cwm Hyfryd (Pleasant Valley). They began to move away from the coastal settlements they had originally made so that today only their names remain, such as Port Madryn, which displays little Welsh except for a monument on the seafront in concrete and bronze which marks its foundation.

As the Welsh moved into the interior, establishing new farms and settlements, they developed good relationships with the native Indians and treated them as equals and brothers. One of the few exceptions, where this relationship broke down, was the massacre of a small exploration party returning from the foothills of the Cordillera to the township of Trevelin in March, 1884. On March 14th, John Evans, with three friends, Hughes, Parry and Davies, were attacked by Indians and only Evans escaped by spectacularly leaping his horse over a precipice. Lewis Jones, the leader of the Trevelin settlement, could not believe that the Indians would attack without reason. It was discovered that an Argentine army partol had trespassed into their territory and attacked them first. A marbel monument now marks the spot where the Welshmen died. It is inscribed: *Biddmyd os syrfeddod*—a line from the Argentine-Welsh poem written by Angela Parry of Trevelin.

Today, the township of Gaimán is the centre of Welsh-speaking Patagonia, with its neighbouring settlements of Trelew and Trevelin. Houses are found here in typical Welsh style, bearing such names as *Nith y dryw* (Wren's Nest) and with a small hotel called *Y Draigoch*. The Brwn-Crwn Chapel, built in 1896, caters for the townships' religious needs.

But it cannot be said that the Welsh language has prospered here as Michael D.Jones hoped it would. Control from Buenos Aires has meant the incursion of Spanish and most of the Patagonian Welsh are bilingual. According to figures given in the London *Times* (September 30th, 1967) it was estimated that there were 75,000 Patagonians of Welsh descent of which only between seven and eight thousand spoke Welsh as a first language. There still remains bilingual Welsh/Spanish schools and a small number of Welsh books and magazines are published in the area. Y Wladfa, therefore, remains a 'Wales beyond the seas', a fact which led to tragedy for the Welsh people during the Falklands/Malvinas war of 1982. Plaid Cymru had raised its voice in protest at the use of Welsh regiments in this war, as they pointed out that it could result in Welsh troops meeting Patagonian Welsh troops in combat. There is evidence that some individual confrontations did take place. Sadly, the Welsh Guards were to suffer the highest casualty rate of any single United Kingdom unit engaged in the war.

Welsh migration to many other areas of the world, even to Russia where mining families established a town called Hughesovka (later renamed Stalino, in the Ukraine) resulted in total assimilation. In the early years, the Welsh clung doggedly to their identity through their chapels, their Eisteddfodau and Cymanfa Ganu, their newspapers and periodicals in Welsh. But gradually, except in the now small Patagonian community, their language and culture has disappeared.

Scottish migration started at a very early stage and Scottish soldiers of fortune were to be found in many armies of Europe in the late Middle Ages, as were their Irish cousins. During the 1420's the Gardes Ecossaises (Scots Guards) became the bodyguard of the French monarch. It was not disbanded until the 1830's which makes its history older than its British counterpart. According to Marshal MacDonald, the son of a Scots emigré who became one of Napoleon's greatest generals, the regiment was using the Scottish Gaelic language as the 'regimental language' until the time of its disbandment. MacDonald himself spoke only Scottish Gaelic and French, a fact which caused the insular English some puzzlement when he paid an official visit to Scotland. Visiting his relatives in the Western Isles in 1825, it was reported that Marshal MacDonald addressed them in Gaelic "for," says the reporter in obvious amazement, "neither they nor the Marshal spoke English!". The Scots also gravitated around a Scots College in Paris and were to be found, like the Irish, involved in French radicalism during the 1780's and 1790's. The famous Thomas Muir of Huntershill, named as president of the Scottish Republic during the abortive 1797 uprising, died in Chantilly in 1799. He was the first non-Frenchman to be made an honarary citizen of the French Republic.

One of the most significant Scottish migrations, of which we still hear much today, was the settlement in Ulster. But the Scots and Irish—sharing the same culture and speaking the same language—had been continually crossing back and forth for many centuries. In the 17th Century, only religious differences marked off the Scots and Irish, as we have seen in the previous chapter on Ireland. The Williamite Conquest, with the enactment of William's Penal Laws against the Presbyterians and other dissenter groups, caused 250,000 Protestant Ulstermen to migrate to America between the years 1717-1776. It was here that they came to be called the 'Scots-Irish' and played a prominent part in the foundation of the United States. The creed of republicanism found a fertile ground amongst them and they transplanted it back to Ireland, uniting both Catholic and Protestant Irish under its banner in the uprising of 1798. No less than 19 Generals in the American War of Independence were Ulster Protestants, and we have already seen how active they were in other fields of revolutionary endeavour. Many of the American frontiersmen, Davy Crockett, Jim Bowie, Sam Houstan, Buffalo Bill Cody, U.S.Grant, 'Stonewall' Jackson and others came from the 'Scots-Irish' communities.

It was in the 18th Century that waves of Scottish Gaelic-speakers began to move across the Atlantic in the wake of the Jacobite defeats and the attempts to 'root-out' their communities. Migration increased with the 'Highland Clearances', which were as ruthless a plan for the destruction of the Scottish Gaels as Cromwell's attempt to extirpate the Irish nation. Many commentators have noted the significant lack of literature in Scottish Gaelic in Scotland for reasons that have already been dealt with. One of the positive aspects of this enforced migration was that, freed from the constraints of the terrible Anglicization policies, the Scottish settlers in America amply made up for the suppression of their language with a quantity of pamphlets, newspapers and magazines and books.

In 1776, the Provincial Congress of North Carolina published its declaration supporting the American Declaration of Independence in Scottish Gaelic, because of the large number of Scottish settlers in the State. North Carolina still holds the record for the first surviving Gaelic publication, printed at Fayetteville in the year 1791. It was a book of sermons by Dugald Crawford. Probably, many other items were published but the last known item published in the State was Paruid Grannd's ***Dain Spioradail*** in 1826. As no other Gaelic books or pamphlets survive after this, one is forced to the conclusion that the Scottish Gaelic community was being rapidly assimilated. Yet it is recorded that the last sermon preached in the language was delivered in Galatia, Cumberland County, in 1860; and the last *native* Scottish Gaelic speaker of North Carolina, J.Hector Smith, of Moore County, near Southern Pines, did not die until 1921.

An indication of how strong the language was in North Carolina is given by reports that American Negro servants learned the language in order to serve their masters. A story in a contemporary newspaper records an old Scottish lady arriving in North Carolina. She had been worried about tales of the hot climate on the journey. However, she was delighted when, stepping off the boat, she heard two men conversing in Scottish Gaelic nearby. She turned the corner of a pile of luggage to greet them and found two negroes chatting away. Her worst foreboding about the climate seemed true. She cried out in horror: *"A Dhia nan gras, am fas sinn uile mar sin?"* (O God of mercy, are we all going to turn black like that?).

It was in Nova Scotia, Canada, that Scottish Gaelic took root and has lasted as a living language to this day. The settlements of Prince Edward Island, Cape Breton, Pictous and Antigonish were made primarily during the 'Highland Clearance' period. The Scottish communities here were slow in publishing in their native language. Perhaps the settlers still laboured under the mental restraints of the anti-Gaelic attitudes suffered in Scotland. Once they began, however, there was no stopping them. In 1832, a reprint of a Scottish Gaelic translation of Dyer's *Christ's Famous Titles* was published on Prince Edward Island. In 1836, *Dain Spioradail* by Paruid Grannd and *Laoidhean Spioradail* by Dughall Buchanan were published in Montreál. Then, in 1841, *Iul a' Chriostaidh* by Father Ronald Rankin appeared. While these first publications were simply reprints of earlier works, a 'native' work was not long in appearing. The first Scottish Gaelic book to be both written and published in Canada was *Companach an Oganaich no An Comhairliche Taitneach* (The Youth's Companion, or The Friendly Counsellor) by Alexander MacGillveray, published in Pictou in 1836. It was a book of essays on a wide variety of topics and it became a bestseller among the Scots.

There now emerged a steady stream of works in Scottish Gaelic and, as early as 1840, a newspaper *Cuairtear na Coille* (The Forest

Traveller) was being published in Ontario. This was replaced in the 1850's by *An Fear-Teagaisg* (The Teacher). In 1851, John Boyd established the first Gaelic printing press in Antigonish and launched a monthly magazine entitled *An Cuairtear Og Gaelach* (The Gaelic Tourist). Boyd was Canadian-born and his magazine became the centre of Nova Scotian culture. But the fact that many children were acquiring English caused Boyd to issue a weekly newspaper, in addition to *An Cuairtear*, entitled *The Casket* which was half in Gaelic and half in English. Boyd recognized that English was becoming the dominant language in Canada and wrote:

> We're sorry that we must admit that Gaelic is drawing back every day and English strengthening her foundation more and more at every turn; so that there is every appearance that she will push the poor Gaelic into a tight corner unless it gets more support than it is getting.

Eventually, the Gaelic section of *The Casket* was dropped. Then, in the February 12th, 1920, issue of *The Casket*, Father Donald M.MacAdam restored a Gaelic column. Later, one of the professors at the St Francis Xavier University in Antigonish, Patrick J.Nicholson, took over the column and wrote it for twenty years, contributing what has become of exceptional value to Gaelic literary endeavour. *The Casket* is still published.

Not long after the establishment of *The Casket*, *Albannach Chanada* was launched from Toronto by Angus Nicholson. In 1871, Nicholson also launched *An Gàidheal* which found subscribers not only in Ontario, but also in Nova Scotia, Quebec, New Brunswick, Michigan, Illinois and North Carolina. Not long afterwards, Nicholas moved his publishing headquarters to Glasgow, Scotland. Toronto still has a Gaelic-speaking community and Comunn Gaìdhlig Thoronto (Toronto Gaelic Society) founded in 1887 is the oldest Scottish Gaelic society in North America. It holds an annual mòd (festival) and bimonthly *ceilidhs*.

In the 1880's, Alexander Maclean Sinclair, born in Antigonish in 1840, became prolific in publishing literary works such as *Clarsach na Coille* (Harp of the Forest), *The Glenbard Collection*, four volumes of Gaelic poems chronologically arranged from 1411 to 1875, gleaned from manuscripts he had managed to acquire in Scotland; two volumes of poems by members of the clan

MacLean; two miscelleaneous volumes of songs as *Filidh na Coille* (The Forest Poet); and *MacTalla na Tur* (Echo of the Towers), and edition of John Lom MacDonald's poems; and a volume of Alexander MacKinnon's poems. Sinclair also wrote a volume of history, pamphlets and articles. His labours were of remarkable value to Gaelic literature.

Jonathan G.MacKinnon was equally outstanding in his contribution to Gaelic in Canada. Born in Whycocomagh, Cape Breton, he launched an all-Gaelic weekly newspaper on May 28th, 1892, in Sydney, Nova Scotia. It was called *Mac-Talla* (The Echo). This weekly newspaper survived its first year and increased in size. After ten years of publication, MacKinnon was compelled to curtail the appearance of the newspaper to fortnightly. With advertising revenue still falling off, on June 24th, 1904, the last number of the newspaper was published. It had achieved twelve years of successful publication and no other Gaelic publication, not even in Scotland had ever held such a record. MacKinnon established an important milestone in Gaelic literature and the influence of *Mac-Talla* was an enormous one. Even after the demise of *Mac-Talla*, MacKinnon continued his labours, translating and publishing works by major writers such as Tolstoy, Thomas Hardy and others. He continued to write a Gaelic column for one of the Sydney newspapers and, in 1928, he started to edit a Gaelic monthly *Fear na Ceilidh* (The Visitor) which ran for two years. When he died on January 13th, 1944, he was a great loss not only to the Scottish Canadians but to Scotland and her culture.

Other attempts were made to emulate the success of *Mac-Talla*. The Scottish Catholic Society of Canada sponsored a magazine entitled *Mosgladh* (The Awakening) which appeared in 1922 and ran for five years when it was changed to a newspaper format and lasted a further five years. In 1925, *Teachdair nan Gàidheal* (The Gaelic Herald) was launched from Sydney by James MacNeill. It lasted for ten years but became irregular and eventually ceased publication. MacNeill then devoted his time writing a Gaelic column for one of the Sydney newspapers.

Scottish Gaelic began its decline in Nova Scotia as an inevitable result of the spread of English throughout Canada. As early as 1879, John A.Morrison, a Member of the Nova Scotia provincial parliament, urged the teaching of Gaelic in Nova Scotian schools. The language was still widely known in the province for him to be able to make that speech to the Parliament in Gaelic! Yet it was not until 1921 that the Nova Scotia Department of Education allowed Gaelic to be taught in schools as an optional subject, provided students elected for the study and the trustees found a qualified teacher. Many problems were placed in the way of education in Gaelic. Nevertheless, both St Francis Xavier University and Dalhousie University in Nova Scotia, and Knox and Queen's in Ontario, established Gaelic study courses and found many students who wanted to study the language.

In 1930, the Nova Scotia Department of Education sent out a questionnaire to teachers and ministers of religion in the Gaelic-speaking areas, asking their opinions on the question of a status for the language. In Cape Breton, the strongest Gaelic-speaking area, a Gaelic College was founded and opened by the Premier of Nova Scotia, the Hon.Angus L.MacDonald on July 26th, 1939. This gave encouragement to the language. About this time, a census showed that 32,708 people in Nova Scotia spoke Gaelic as their first language and, in 1950, the Nova Scotia Government appointed a Gaelic Advisor to the Education Department and C.I.N. MacLeod was the first to occupy this new post.

Nevertheless, Gaelic began a rapid decline and, by the late 1950's, it was discovered that only 7,533 people used Gaelic as their first language, while it was estimated that some 35,000 had some knowledge of it as a 'secondary language'. The Nova Scotian Government said that the rapid decline was due to the influx of English-speakers from other provinces, as well as the moving of heavy industry into previously rural areas. In 1984, the Cape Breton Gaelic Society reported that there were only 1,400 Gaelic-speakers left in the area. (The official Government census of 1971 gave the figure of 1,420 speakers.) An Comunn Gàidhlig Cheap Breatunn (Cape Breton Gaelic Society) was founded in Sydney in 1969 to "perfect members in the use of the Gaelic language, poetry, traditional legends, books and manuscripts; the vindication of the rights and character of the Gaelic people, and generally the furtherance of their interests whether at home or abroad". The Society publishes newsletters and occasional pamphlets and books, and its members contribute Gaelic columns to local newspapers.

The language no longer enjoys any legal status and is not taught in any schools in the area. Language courses do enjoy a relatively wide support throughout Cape Breton and are organized by various school boards, the Gaelic Society, the University College of Cape Breton, the Highland Village Society and the St. Anne's Gaelic College.

At the present time, there is still a Gaelic echo in Cape Breton. At a ceilidh, one may still hear a local singing:

'S e Ceap Breatunn tir mo ghraidh,
Tir nan craobh 's nam beanntan ard;
'S e Ceap Breatunn tir mo ghraidh,
Tir a's aillidh leinn air thalamh.

Cape Breton is the land of my love,
the land of trees and mountains high;
Cape Breton is the land of my love,
the loveliest land on earth!

Dr John Edwards, of the Department of Psychology, St Francis Xavier University, Antigonish, in his study *Attitudes towards Gaelic and English among Gaelic speakers in Cape Breton Island, Nova Scotia* (1982) presented a doleful outlook for the future. He found the language spoken in rural areas mainly by people over 50 years of age. "Those who now support the language, or who study it, or who join Gaelic organizations, are largely middle-aged. More general efforts in support of Scottish culture tend to be superficial, 'stagey' and, perhaps, somewhat distasteful...Scottishness becomes allied to commercial and tourist drives and, as Shaw (1977) notes, 'people praise Gaelic in English...' Dr Edwards concludes:

> In short, Gaelic in Cape Breton seems to be nearing its final chapter as an ordinary spoken language. Like other contexts, this one has been investigated too late, although the efforts of the Celtic Studies Department at St Francis Xavier university are most commendable, with valuable folklore information being carefully collected.

It is incredible to find that Scottish Gaelic seems to be far more healthy in Canada *outside* of Nova Scotia! According to the 1971 census on mother tongues, Ontario has the biggest Gaelic-speaking population of 6,000. Gaelic is still taught in Glengarry County, Ontario. The provinces of Alberta and British Columbia have 3,000 speakers each while Saskatchewan and Manitoba have Gaelic-speaking communities of 2,500 each. Only the province of Québec (so concerned about preserving the rights of French-speakers) fails to take any census figures on the large Breton, Irish and Scottish Gaelic speaking communities within the province. Scottish Gaelic was once the dominant language of the Eastern Townships of Québec, places like Compton County and Frontenac County, near Sherbrooke. Compton County was strongly Scottish Gaelic speaking in 1937 when the extent of the language there was recorded. Canada (excluding Québec) therefore returned a Gaelic-speaking population of 18,420 people in 1971.

It will be seen from this outline that, as considerable as the Celtic diaspora was, as extensions of Celtic culture those settlements which were made were rather meagre. Only in two places, Patagonia and Nova Scotia, have clearly identifiable Celtic-speaking communities survived into modern times. Those communities are now less healthy than the homelands from which they sprang. The Scottish Gaelic of Canada has given a significant contribution to the literary history of the language and one which anti-Gaelic commentators tend to ignore while pointing to the paucity of literature in Gaelic in Scotland, as a means of degrading the language. The lesson to be learned is that this paucity is a result of the centuries of vicious, anti-Gaelic control. While there has been some Welsh literary activity among the Patagonians, the contribution—compared to Scotland—has not been so marked. Apart from the emotional contributions of groups such as the Irish-Americans, the migrant Celtic communities have made negligible efforts in the support of the languages and cultures of their native countries, far less in aid of the struggle for political independence. When one makes a comparison with the efforts of the diasporic Jews in support of Israel, however one may view that State, the diasporic Celts have been sadly lacking. It is true that the 'exiled' Celts retain an emotional attachment for their homelands but it is usually an evocation of a 'never-never' world, and they are generally uncomfortable when confronted with the cultural and political realities of the 'home' situation. There are, of course, exceptions. There are individuals who remain committed to the cause of the communities they have left behind, but such people are few and far between. It is one of the great historical 'ifs' to reflect what might have been, if the diasporic Celts had been imbued with the same commitment to cultural identity and homeland as the diasporic Jews have demonstrated.

Chapter Nine
Celtic Unity

There has never been a time when the Celtic peoples were more aware of their common cultural heritage and similarity of national and social problems as in recent years. Is this 'Celtic consciousness' a new concept? Imperial policy—in particular, English imperial policy—has always been divisive, its aim is *divide et impera* (divide and rule). The policy has worked successfully throughout the English Empire and one must remember that it was among the Celtic peoples that the concepts of *divide et impera* were first practised and perfected by the English. That success almost forms a tradition among the Celtic peoples.

There may be some who will raise their eyebrows when I say 'English Empire' and not 'British Empire'. The Scottish people, in general, remain inordinately proud of having secured and ruled the Emprie for England. They would prefer the term 'British', to appease their national self-respect, if one can derive self-respect from the centuries of exploitation and misery which was a product of such empire. Scottish regiments and an Anglicized, Scottish civil service maintained the Empire in many countries. In some corners of the former Empire, the kilt and bagpipes are still seen as symbols of oppression. While it can rightly be argued that the majority of English people did not benefit from the Empire but only the ruling élite, nevertheless, the cultural ethos of the Empire was English; the imperial urge was an English one and England was undoubtedly the centre of the Empire. The Celtic countries were simply the first nations to be incorporated into the Empire and then used to supply troops for other colonial areas.

The ancient Celtic name of 'Britain' was revived by the English in the 18th Century, as a sop to Scottish national consciousness after the Union. *British* has come to mean *English* and, indeed, an etymological dictionary states that 'Britishness' means 'characteristics of the English'—not the Scots, Welsh or Cornish. Therefore, the Empire was English and the Celtic countries were the first exploited colonial outposts of that Empire. The only difference which marked the Celtic peoples off from their brothers and sisters in Nigeria, India or Malaya lay in the fact that, by dropping their language and culture, they could 'pass for English' and, by so doing, could theoretically benefit from the Empire. There is no denying that many *assimilados* did so. The shameful list of 'British' generals, colonial adventurers and administrators, all bearing Anglicized Celtic names, is not a small one. They were not benefactors to their own Celtic communities, but simply the mercenaries of England seeking, primarily, their own self-aggrandisement. *An té a rugadh i stábla ní capal é*, say the Irish. Everything born in a stable is not a horse.

Divide and rule is a concept as old as that of empire itself. The English were adept at its practice, using Sikh against Hindu and Moslem against both; using Turk against Greek; Arab against Jew; Ibo against Hausa and Yoruba against both; Assin against Ashanti; Protestant against Catholic...the list is endless. The result was always the same—conquest and exploitation.

In the case of the Celtic countries, there is a tendency to recall events such as the massacre of unarmed Dublin civilians in Batchelors Walk, 1914, by members of the Kings Own Scottish Borderers; or the time when a South Wales police detachment was sent to Cornwall to break the miners' strike of 1857; or the time when Scottish soldiers opened fire on demonstrators in Tonypandy, Wales, 1910; or the Irish troops who took part in the Clearances in Scotland. Even today, Scottish troops are given a particularly high profile in the insurgency war in Ireland, and Welsh troops have also been used. This is the divisive tradition that the makers of imperial policy would like the Celts to recall, creating scissions and animosities among them. Unity among the Celtic peoples has been, and is, a frightening prospect to England's political masters. Superficially, the policy of *divide et impera* has worked so well among the Celts that it can be wondered whether there is, in fact any contrary tradition.

The Scottish writer, Seumas Mac a' Ghobhainn, wrote in the *Stornoway Gazette*, in 1971, a poem entitled *Am Mart, 1971*, concerning the death in Ireland of three Scottish soldiers and an

IRA volunteer.

Ceathrar Ghàidheal óg
Air giúlan thun na h-uaighe
Air gualainn leathan nan companach
Ri fuam na piob-mhór
Fear aca fo bhratach Poblachd na h-Éireann
's an triúir eile fo bhratach dhearg nan Sasunnach
Is e sgeul aosda ceudna a rithsid
Leis an nambaid ársaidh
a' suathadh an lamhan neo chiontach
Air chul deascan liomharr
Fada air faibh bho'n bhlár.

Four young Gaels
borne to the graves
on the broad back of their comrades
to the sound of pipes
one under the flag of the Irish Republic
three under the red banner of England
it is the same old story again
with their enemies
rubbing guiltless hands
behind shiny desks
far away from the battlefield.

The poem demonstrates an awareness of the divide-and-rule ethos which is shared by all Celtic nationalists. Yet individual awareness of divisive policy is not the same as a tradition of Celtic co-operation and unity. Is there any real tradition of Celtic unity?

Certainly, in the ancient Celtic world, we find a remarkable sense of solidarity among the Celtic-speaking peoples. Thus could the senate of the Greek city state of Massila (Marseilles) ask the Celts of Gaul to speak to their fellow Celts of Galatia, in modern Turkey, and request them not to aid nor recruit mercenaries for Antiochus III in his war against the Greeks. The druidic priesthood, the religious and social concepts and the law system, were—with language—a unifying force among the ancient Celts. Henri Hubert, in his *The Greatness and Decline of the Celts*, 1932 states: "This solidarity of the Celtic peoples, even when distant from one another, is sufficiently explained by the sense of kinship, of common origin, acting in a fairly restricted world, all the parts of which were in communication". The unifying force of the common Celtic religion, managed by the druids, was replaced by a thousand years of the Celtic Church with its monks and scholars.

A sense of common Celtic identity emerges in the 10th Century in the Welsh poem *Armes Prydain* (The Prophecy of Britain), which appeals to the peoples of the Celtic world—of Wales, Cornwall, Cumbria, Strathclyde, Scotland, Mannin, Brittany and Ireland—to come together to throw back the English invasion of Britain. The poem appeared at the time when, in 927 AD, Athelstan destroyed a Celtic confederation of the Irish, Scots, Strathclyde Britons, Cumbrians and Cornish; and it was probably in support of this confederation that the poem was written.

When Robert Bruce regained independence for Scotland, defeating the English at Bannockburn in 1314, he also liberated Mannin from the English. His victories were greeted with joy by the Irish chieftains. Bruce sent envoys to them writing: "Whereas we and you and our people and your people, free since ancient times, share the same national ancestry and are urged to come together more eagerly and joyfully in friendship by a common language and by common custom, we have sent over to you our beloved kinsmen, the bearers of this letter, to negotiate with you in our name about permanently strengthening and maintaining inviolate the special friendship between us and you, so that with God's will your nation may be able to recover her ancient liberty". The Irish invited Robert Bruce's brother Edward to become King of Ireland and he was so crowned on May Day, 1316.

The victories of the Bruce family in Scotland, Isle of Mann and Ireland, caused the Welsh, led by Gruffydd Llwyd, to invite Edward Bruce to aid them in securing their freedom from England. Edward Bruce accepted on condition that he ruled Wales "as your prince (the last Llywelyn) formerly most fully used to exercise". But Edward Bruce was defeated and slain in Ireland, Gruffydd Llwyd's uprising was smashed and only Scotland retained its independence. Owain Glyndŵr of Wales made a treaty with Scotland against England in 1400-1408.

There was a great deal of intermingling among the Bretons and Cornish until the 16th Century, when the Cornish language was generally in decline. Bretons were found to be living in Cornwall in large numbers until the Reformation, which gave the final blow to Cornish. A singular Celtic form of wrestling has survived in

Cornwall, Brittany, Wales and even in Cumbria. In 1520, Henry VIII met Francois I at the 'Field of the Cloth of Gold', near Boulogne. It is recorded that, before the battle, the two kings allowed the Welsh and Breton wrestlers to hold a contest. Similarly, another chronicler mentions a wrestling contest between Cornish and Bretons in 1551. In 1927, a Cornish Wrestling Association was formed, since when there has been regular wrestling tournaments between the Cornish and Bretons.

Scots and Irish have always tended to band together, especially during the 18th Century uprisings in Scotland and, indeed, when the Scottish Friends of the People was formed to establish a Scottish Republic, delegations were sent to the United Irishmen and reciprocal delegations were received from Ireland. Thomas Muir, named as President of the Scottish Republic during the rising of 1797, was an honorary member of the United Irishmen. When the Young Ireland movement rose in 1848, Scotland also had revolutionary links with the movement. A National Guard was formed in Aberdeen and John Daly, a Glasgow revolutionist, told his followers: "We can best help Ireland by keeping the army in Scotland". In 1867, many Scotsmen supported the Irish Fenian movement and while England was using Scottish troops in suppressing the Fenian rising, the conduct of some politically aware regiments vindicated their use as imperial troops. For example, the 73rd Foot was a mainly Scottish, Gaelic-speaking regiment, and were politically sympathetic to the Irish. When they went into action against Colonel O'Connor's Fenian troops in Kerry, they deliberately allowed the Fenians to escape through their lines at night.

There was much co-operation between the Scots and Irish during the Land War period and the former Fenian leader, Irish Party MP, Michael Davitt, visited Scotland many times, advising on the setting up of a Scottish Land League. During 1916-21, S.Reeder commanded a Scottish Brigade of the IRA while Scotsmen such as Iain Mackenzie Kennedy, urged Scottish support for the Irish struggle. Kennedy, a committed republican and a musician, poet and Gaelic scholar, learned Irish and joined the West Cork Brigade of the IRA. He fought during the War of Independence and was killed in the Civil War in 1922. The great Scottish labour leader, John MacLean, who founded the Scottish Workers'

Republican Party, was a friend and supporter of James Connolly, the Irish Marxist leader executed after the rising of 1916. MacLean wrote *The Irish Tragedy: Scotland's Disgrace*, first published in 1920, but it is so forceful and telling that it has been reprinted many times since.

During 1919-21, many Welsh voices were raised in protest opposing the war against their fellow Celts of Ireland and among them was that of radical leader, Llywelyn Williams, who was shouted down at a Liberal Party Conference for condemning the atrocities of the 'Black and Tans'. Similar protests have been raised during the current war in Ireland. It was thanks to Welsh journalists, specifically the newspaper *Baner ac Amserau Cymru*, that the world was awakened to the nature of the French repression in Brittany and forced to desist. Similarly, the attempted repression of 1969 achieved world headlines due to the voice of Gwynfor Evans, MP.

It was a German scholar, Franz Bopp, in 1838, who clarified linguistic identification of the Celtic languages which was then consolidated by Johann Casper Zeuss's great work, *Grammatica Celtica* (Leipzig, 1853). Thus Celtic studies were put on a sound scientific basis and departments to study Celtic were established in many European universities. England dragged behind until Matthew Arnold's famous appeal (*The Study of Celtic Literature*, 1867) led to the foundation of a chair of Celtic Studies at Oxford.

Celtic Societies began to be formed. During the 18th Century, Breton delegations had attended Welsh Eisteddfodau, and it fell to the Bretons to organize the first Inter-Celtic Congress at St. Brieuc, in 1867. Various magazines began to make their appearance, such as *The Celtic Magazine*, *Celtic Monthly* and *Celtic Review*, which sought to raise a common Celtic consciousness. During the 1890's, a Celtic Association was formed and, in 1901, launched the first major pan-Celtic publication called *Celtica*. This seems to have foundered after 1903 and the Celtic Association also disappeared. It was in 1901 that a Celtic Congress was established which has been held annually ever since. In the early years, it was basically a body of academics and is today concerned with the maintenance of educational contacts between the Celtic peoples. During the 1960's, a Celtic Youth Congress took a more radical political line. Amazingly, the first pan-Celtic magazine of real influence was published from Toronto, Canada, in the 1950's by Pádraig Ó Bríon. This was called *Teangadoir* (The Linguist) and carried articles in all six Celtic languages. It ceased publication in May, 1960, after 30 issues.

In August, 1961, at Rhos, near Llangollen, North Wales, a group of people dedicated to the cause of political, economic and cultural independence for all the Celtic peoples, met to form a league which would establish links between the national movements of the six Celtic nations. Within a year of that gathering, the League of Celtic Nations (later shortened to the Celtic League) had flourishing branches in the four largest countries and, within a few years, in the two smaller countries. Those pioneers who met at Rhos were Alan Heusaff, from Brittany, who was to be elected General Secretary of the League, a post he has held with unflagging enthusiasm ever since; Pádraig Ó Conchúir, a Conradh na Gaeilge activist; J.E.Jones and Elwyn Roberts of Plaid Cymru (Party of Wales); and Seumas Philbin and Alan McCartney from Scotland. Initially, Alistair Graham's magazine *The Celtic Voice* presented a forum for the League but, by late 1962, the League launched its own publication entitled *Celtic News*. In its early days, the League had two aims: to foster cooperation between the national movements in the Celtic countries, particularly in an effort to obtain international recognition of Celtic national rights; and to share the experiences of the Celtic national struggles and exchange constructive ideas.

The foundation of the Celtic League was a major political step. Previous pan-Celtic movements had been merely cultural, such as the Celtic Congress. The League was dedicated to the concept, to paraphrase the words of Pádraic Pearse, of "a Celtica which is not only Celtic but free as well; a Celtica which is not only free but Celtic as well". The early days of the League were difficult for those trying to preach not only pan-Celticism on a cultural level but also on a political level. The movement, however, began to make headway. In June, 1963, it made its debut on the world stage by giving evidence to the European Commission on Human Rights, concerning the French persecution of the Breton language, and was also active in bringing attention to the Breton problem. In June, 1965, the League issued its first major publication, a book arguing the case for self-government for the Celtic countries which was used as the basis of a 62-page memorandum presented by the League to the United Nations Organization in November of that year. From 1963, the League, had sufficient membership and finance to start issuing an annual volume, containing a diversity of papers and articles on aspects of the Celtic struggle, in addition to the *Celtic News* periodical. This annual ceased to be published in 1973, and *Celtic News* was relaunched as *Carn*, a more professional, quarterly publication. Some of the branches began to issue their own branch publications, such as the periodical *Omma*, launched by the Cornish branch in 1971, and the *Celtic League Mannin and AMA Newsletter* by the Manx branch. The League also published an impressive 332-page volume in 1984, entitled *For A Celtic Future*, edited by Cathal Ó Luain, as a tribute to the work of Alan Heusaff.

Today, the role of the Celtic League is seen as follows:

> The fundamental aim of the Celtic League is to contribute, as an international organization, to the struggle of the six Celtic nations to secure or win their political, cultural, social and economic freedom. Our aim is not so much to maintain national characteristics against the pressures of assimilation and oppression by the occupying powers, as to create the structure of a new Celtic society.
>
> It is hoped that by fostering co-operation and by developing a consciousness of the common factors of solidarity and similarity that bind them, a formal association of the Celtic nations will one day emerge. Each nation, on its own, is weak compared with the imperialist powers that have for centuries controlled them. Only by uniting their efforts can the six Celtic peoples halt the economic and cultural decline which is endemic in all six countries.
>
> In view of the fact that each nation is conditioned by a different history, we must not expect uniformity of thought but allow diversity to express itself within the League, so that we may better recognize those areas of possible cooperation that would eventually form the basis of a common policy upon which the formal association of our nations may be realized.
>
> On an internal level, the role of the League complements that of the national organizations which work for their countries' right to become full, autonomous and sovereign nations. It is only if they have failed in their task that our branches would step in to help stimulate the re-organization of the forces of liberation at home.

There is a growing number of people in the Celtic countries who believe that the future of the six Celtic nations, after independence is achieved, might lie in forming a confederation between themselves, in order to give stronger expression to their common cultural and social heritage. In his autobiography, *Lucky Poet* (Methuen, 1943), Hugh MacDiarmid, poet and Marxist, advocated the establishment of Workers' Republics in the Celtic countries "and, indeed, make a sort of Celtic Union of Socialist Soviet Republics". MacDiarmid was an early advocate of pan-Celticism. In *The Welsh Republic* by C.Bere, published by the Welsh Republican Movement, Cardiff, in the late 1940's, it was stated that: "Federalism in Britain under English patronage would certainly not give the vital substance of freedom to the Welsh nation, only its ineffectual shadow. It is only to a continental or *Celtic federation of nations* that Wales can rightly belong and perhaps owe the moral duty to surrender some part of her sovereignty".

There is a school of thought in favour of the idea of forming cultural, political and economic links, along the lines of the Scandinavian model—Celtica. I mooted this idea in *The Creed of the Celtic Revolution* (Medusa Press), 1969. It is, of course, a long-term aim but it must be remembered that the Nordic Association started life in the same way as the Celtic League, and this led to the formation of a Nordic Council that was instrumental in creating the Scandinavian Treaty of Co-operation of 1962. Now, there is a common Scandinavian citizenship, an economic market and inter-government co-operation, especially on matters of social security, health and joint scientific research. There are Language Boards in each of the Scandinavian countries and, while each country has an independent defence force, there are agreements on joint defence. I have long believed that the Scandinavian model could be emulated by the Celtic countries after independence. The idea has been frequently discussed in Celtic League circles, with advocates such as Seumas Philbin and, writing in *Carn* in 1980, Tomás Ó Ciara.

The common Celtic identity has also been established through the medium of several pan-Celtic festivals which have become annual events. In the early years, delegations from sister Celtic countries would attend the great national cultural festivals such as the Eisteddfod Genedlaethol Frenhinol Cymru (National Eisteddfod) and the Urdd Eisteddfod (Youth Festival) in Wales; or the Mòd na Alban in Scotland; An t-Oireachtas in Ireland; and the Lowender Peron in Cornwall. Now, there are several specifically pan-Celtic festivals. Lorient, Brittany, has an annual Inter-Celtic Festival in August which has been attracting a quarter of a million visitors to a programme of Celtic music, song, dance and other cultural events. A Pan-Celtic Festival Week is held annually in May in Killarney, Ireland, which is now an important event in the promotion of Celtic music and song. On Mannin, Yn Chruinnaght, which was revived as a Manx annual cultural festival, welcomes participants from the other Celtic nations, so that it is now a pan-Celtic festival in character. An annual Celtavision Song Contest is firmly established in which song entries from the Celtic countries, sung in the Celtic languages, are performed, judged and televised throughout the Celtic world.

One of the most important visual demonstrations of Celtic consciousness occurred in 1980. when Michael Russell established the first Celtic Film and Television Festival on the island of South Uist. From this small beginning, it has grown into a widely recognized and important festival. The Fifth Celtic Film and Television Festival was held in Cardiff, Wales, in April, 1984, attracting 145 entries of which 44 were in the Celtic languages, including 29 in Welsh, four in Irish, three in Scottish Gaelic, five in Breton, two in Cornish and one in Manx.

Scrif-Celt '85, the first Celtic Book Fair, an exhibition and conference of contemporary writing and publishing in the Celtic languages, was organised in London by the London Branch of the Celtic League on April 13, 1985. This was significantly held to coincide with the International London Book Fair. It attracted the support of over 60 Celtic language publishers and organisations who demonstrated to the world the vitality of contemporary Celtic literary and publishing endeavours.

In October, 1983, an important step was taken by the United Nations Educational Scientific and Cultural Organisation (UNESCO) at its 22nd Session of General Conference in Paris, when approval was given to funding a Project for the Study and Promotion of Celtic Cultures. It had been in November, 1965, that the Celtic League had presented its first memorandum on the state of the Celtic languages and culture. In 1983, UNESCO, recognizing the problems faced by the Celtic nations, instituted a programme for research and, more importantly, for ways of promoting the languages and cultures. Among the projects listed were a comparative investigation of the teaching of the Celtic languages; the possibility of establishing a travelling exhibition illustrating the extent of Celtic culture across Europe, in earlier times, and its contemporary position; the establishment of awards for writers in the Celtic languages; a television co-production of programmes designed to develop a consciousness of the Celtic heritage; and the provision of a 'Celtic Kit', comprising maps, charts and cassettes for educational purposes in Celtic countries and elsewhere. A *Celtic Cultures Newsletter* was launched by UNESCO to give details of the developing project. Whilst the programme of projects falls short of the urgent measures needed to stop a further decline in the languages, it is, at least, the first faltering step in the international arena. The United Nations, through UNESCO, has recognised the principle of promoting the Celtic languages and their cultures. This principle should not be lost sight of because, for the very first time in their history, the Celtic peoples have international approval for the teaching and promotion of their own languages.

In 1981, the Canadian publishers McClelland and Stewart, published a volume entitled *The Celtic Consciousness*, edited by Professor Robert O'Driscoll, director of the Celtic Studies Department at Toronto University. Containing 55 essays, 350,000 words and 170 illustrations, this was not merely an academic work on Celtic history but it also dealt with the emergence of modern Celtic nationalism. The book provided a title for the remarkable phenomenon which had been developing during the 20th Century—Celtic consciousness! It would be churlish to say that the tremendous growth of this Celtic awareness was due solely to the activities of the Celtic League; nevertheless, a substantial part of the growth during recent decades has been directly due to its pioneering efforts in promoting that consciousness.

Pan-Celticism is a growing concept in the world. Canada boasts a Canadian Celtic Congress and a Canadian Celtic Arts Association which have organized many pan-Celtic conferences and festivals. The Celtic Arts Association issues a small quarterly journal. In the United States of America, a glossy magazine called *Keltica* is issued by the Society of Inter-Celtic Arts and Culture from 96

Marguerite Avenue, Waltham, Massachusetts 02154, USA. The society organized its first Inter-Celtic Congress in Boston in July, 1985. In Australia, *Tir na nÓg* (Land of Youth) is the title of the quarterly journal of the Australian Celtic Association, published from 17 York Street, North Fitzroy, NSW 3068. A Celtic Council of Australia was formed at a public meeting in Sydney on March 24, 1982, to develop the self-awareness of the Australian Celtic community and is now seeking to establish a chair of Celtic Studies at an Australian university or universities. Its convenor is Peter Alexander, 125 Bradfield Road, West Lindfield, New South Wales 2070. Australia holds communities from all the Celtic speaking groups (even Cornish and Cornish language classes are held in New South Wales). Recently *An Teachdaire Gàidhealach* was relaunched in Australia, named after the early 19th Century Gaelic newspaper, and is obtainable from GPO Box 5289, New South Wales 2001.

In 1968, Gwynfor Evans, then a Plaid Cymru MP, writing as President of the Celtic League, said:

> Today, the sixteen million people of the Celtic countries should be exerting a great influence in the world, but the part they play on the world stage in no way matches the promises of their history and gifts. It should be possible to compare their contribution to civilization and world-order with that of the four Scandinavian nations, but to name them together is enough to illuminate the disappointing performance of the Celts. Our attitude to ourselves as national failures has been one of unmoved complacency or self pity...
>
> When one asks why these nations of ours are not living full, vigorous, confident national lives, the answer is surely obvious; it is that their people, apart from Ireland, have not made an effort to equip themselves with the institutions of nationhood. They failed to make the effort because, until recently, they lacked a proper sense of the importance of nationhood generally and their own in particular. In consequence, they have no power to create their own conditions of life, no power of choice, of decision, of initiative, of action. They cannot cause things to happen; things always happen to them. Their fate is to be at the mercy of events outside their control. That is, they lack national freedom, without which there can be no sustained development. This is why, in field after field, their life exhibits the shortcomings and mediocrity of provincialism, lacks the dignity and brilliance which could be theirs.

Yet, in 1985, there is not only national awareness but a Celtic awareness and a sense of unity which is a tangible force, uniting those sixteen million people of the Celtic nations in new attitudes and with a new hope for the future.

Chapter Ten
Celtic Nationalism

If one were naive, one might believe that there is no need to convince anyone of the moral right of the Celtic nations to self-government, or that their languages should have status within the Celtic national territories. Self-determination and the right to speak one's own language in everyday life, in education at all levels, in courts of law and in public or in assembly, are fundamental human rights recognized by the United Nations' Charter, the Universal Declaration of Human Rights and the European Convention on Human Rights. According to such grandiose charters, there should be no national problems among the Celtic peoples. But what is right for a conqueror is not right for the conquered. Therefore, one has to produce arguments as to why these nations should have cultural freedom and political independence.

There has been a great deal written about the Celtic demands for independence, especially the economic arguments, and there was a time, during the 1970's, when the media were ascribing economics as the sole reason for 'nationalism'. Admittedly, listening to some members of the Scottish National Party at that time, one could well have formed the impression that the only argument for separation from England was an economic one. I do not propose to argue economics: I am a fundamentalist.

Let us start, then, by asking what nationalism is? Like the word 'love', it is frequently misused and misunderstood. A great variety of types claim to suffer from it: German Fascists, Afrikaaners, Spanish Falangists, American Anti-Communists, Vietnamese, Greek-Cypriot Unionists, Israeli Zionists, Palestinians...and most certainly the French and the English.

We have to understand clearly that there are two types of nationalism. There is the nationalist who believes in his country, right or wrong; who believes that his nationality is superior to all others; who tries to impose his language and culture on other people, stamping out other nation's nationality and, in the case of the Celtic countries, incorporating them as uniform units in a big state. Such a nationalist is, of course, an imperialist and is essentially racist. Then, in reaction to imperialist nationalism, we have the second type of nationalist who strives to prevent his people's language and culture from being destroyed; who tries to prevent his people from being economically exploited by the imperialist; and who strives to return his national community to a position of political independence.

As a socialist, I have long held that the advocacy of freedom of a nation from cultural, political and economic exploitation by another nation, is inseparable from the achievement of a true socialist society. National and social freedom are not two separate and unrelated issues: they are two sides of one great democratic principle, each being incomplete without the other.

Because the Celts tend to talk much about their nationality, the English and French have been quick to assume that Celts believe their nationality is superior. English and French people have the ability to take their nationality for granted because no one threatens it. That is not so with the Celts. A person may not be conscious of his foot until someone treads on it but, once that happens they are hardly conscious of anything else, and will keep referring to the pain in their foot until it goes away. I think George Bernard Shaw put it more succinctly in his preface to the play *John Bull's Other Island* (originally written in 1904):

> A healthy nation is as unconscious of its nationality as a healthy man is of his bones. But if you break a nation's nationality, it will think of nothing else but getting it set again. It will listen to no reformer, to no philosopher and no preacher, until the demand of the nationalist is granted. It will attend to no business, however vital, except the business of unification and liberation.

While some of the better informed and intelligent sections of the English and French nations are sympathetic to the Celtic problem, the Celtic peoples can hardly expect them to be more supportive than that in their predicament. The English and French are placed in the position of robust, healthy persons, never knowing a day's sickness in their lives, trying to understand the problem of a fragile and sickly person. Not only that, but one must remember that they are also the *cause* of the person's sickness.

So, what is Celtic nationalism about? Singing anthems? Waving flags? Seeking control over merely 'historic' territory? No, of course not. The fundamental principle of Celtic nationalism is concern for the welfare of the individual against cultural, political and economic exploitation. Nationalists, whilst of differing political ideologies, agree on one main point—that it is the inalienable right of a people to make their own decisions, and not to have decisions imposed upon them by other nations.

In the war of propaganda against Celtic nationalism, cynical politicians or silly, unthinking people, have denounced Celtic nationalism as racialism. We have already seen that the 'race' concept is utter nonsense. A Celt is one who speaks, or is known to have spoken in modern times, a Celtic language. Two great Celtic nationalists were John and George Maxwell, who were champions of the Scottish Gaelic language. They were negroes. Their father had been adopted by a Gaelic-speaking sea captain and his wife whose home was in Cape Breton. He grew up and married, with Gaelic as the language of his home as, indeed, it was then the language of Cape Breton. His sons, John and George, were therefore second-generation, Gaelic-speakers, and strong exponents of the language and of Celtic independence. John died in Malagawatch in the early 1930's and George died in Whycocomagh in 1936. Then there was Othmar Remy Arthur, who died in the late 1960's in a car crash in Kildare and is still remembered with affection in Ireland. A West Indian, he settled in Dublin, learnt the language and was a familiar figure at music festivals, singing songs in Irish. In the 26-County state, there are 30,000 people who are Jewish in religion, many of them in the forefront of political life and active in the language struggle. We have noted that the present President of Israel, Chaim Hertzog, was born in Belfast and educated in Dublin and is also an Irish-speaker who is as much an Irishman as an Israeli. In Wales, Cardiff's Butetown is one of the oldest black communities in the United Kingdom. The inhabitants of Butetown are as Welsh as the inhabitants of any other district in the same City. One could extend the list indefinitely. Celts are marked off from their neighbours by language and culture, and for no other reason.

Claims of Celtic racism are nonsensical and particularly cynical, coming from peoples of nationalities who have preached, and still preach, a most virulent racism towards the Celts. For example, not long ago the London *Observer* admitted: "Over many centuries and until quite recently, the English treated the Irish, the Scots and the Welsh, much as the Germans treated their Slav neighbours—with a mixture of ruthlessness and mockery." Lord Acton, an English historian, could write arrogantly:

> The Celts are not among the progressive, initiative races, but among those which supply the material rather than the impulse of history, and are either stationary or retrogressive...the Celts of these islands...waited for a foreign influence to set in action the rich treasures which in their own hands could be of no avail...

The London *Times* could remark, without turning an anti-racial hair:

> The Welsh language is the curse of Wales. Its prevalence, and the ignorance of English have excluded, and even now exclude the Welsh people from the civilization of their English neighbours...Not only the energy and power, but the intelligence and music of Europe have come mainly from Teutonic sources, and this glorification of everything Celtic, if it were not pedantry, would be sheer ignorance. The sooner all Welsh specialities disappear from the face of the earth the better.

Honoré de Balzac encapsulated French attitudes towards the Bretons in his novel *The Chouans* when he wrote:

> ...they strive to preserve the traditions of the Celtic language and customs; thus their lives retain deep traces of the superstitious beliefs and practices of ancient times. There the feudal customs are still respected. There the antiquarian finds druidical monuments still standing, and the genius of modern civilization stands aghast at the thought of penetrating immense primeval forests. Incredible ferocity, brutal obstinacy, but unswerving fidelity to one's oath; utter ignorance of our laws, our manners, our customs, our new coins, our language, but patriarchal simplicity and heroic virtues unite to make the inhabitants of these country districts poorer in intellectual combinations than the Mohicans and redskins of North America, but withal as grand, as crafty and as unforgiving.

When the Celts seek to defend their languages and cultures against such ignorant attacks, then it is claimed that it is they who are being racialist!

Racism, especially against the Irish, with its weary attendant collection of anti-Irish jokes, has been especially prevalent during the past fifteen years. Even self-proclaimed liberals, (in particular, Bernard Levin) have been guilty of writing some of the most venomous and mischievous racist attacks on the Irish. Sir John Junor, editor of *The Sunday Express*, could calmly write in his leader column of October 28, 1984: 'Wouldn't you rather admit to being a pig than to being Irish?' In spite of voiciferous indignation from the Irish community in Britain, Sir John refuses to apologise nor does he see his remark as 'racist'. It is a comment on Irish mentality when one thinks of the reaction there would have been had the remarks applied to the black British community. Such racist attacks on the Celtic peoples is not just a question of the general ignorance and apathy of the English and French nations about their near neighbours. It is endemic of the mistaken views that both those nations hold of themselves and of the historic role of their country in the world. A gigantic exercise in self-delusion has especially helped to preserve English pride and self-regard through the centuries. Actions taken for reasons of political and economic expediency—the slave trade, the ruthless attempted extirpation of other nations, the long toll of atrocities, the appropriation of vast tracts of other people's countries—have been justified by claims of religious, cultural and racial superiority. As a result of this, the English people have been unable to see themselves as others see them. Perhaps the day will come when the historical myths of the English ruling class will no longer be accepted by the English people in general; when the notion that the English Empire was 'great', or was established for reasons other than the profit and self-interest of a small élite, or that the English are in any way superior to any other nation on this Earth, will finally be confined to the dustbin of archaic legend. In her excellent study, *Nothing but the same old story—the roots of anti-Irish racism* (Information on Ireland, 1984), Liz Curtis writes:

> These myths have served the English ruling class well over the centuries, clouding the harsh reality of exploitation and colonization. Today, these myths help them to maintain their unjust occupation of part of Ireland, to use the black English people as scapegoats for the failure of the system, and to amass great wealth at the expense of the peoples of the Third World. These myths must be challenged and destroyed if we are to achieve freedom and justice for Ireland, and build England, Scotland and Wales into just societies, no longer dependent on the exploitation of people either within or outside their borders, and with social and economic equality for all.

Racism is not, and never has been, part of Celtic national

philosophy. It is inevitable in a conflict against colonial powers that a certain number of symbolic generalizations manifest themselves. Considering the bitterness of the historical reality, utterances by Celtic nationalists are surprisingly moderate and level-headed. The English and French peoples are not hated, but English and French rule in the Celtic coutries is; imperialism and the imperialist ruling class and their tools are the objects of enmity. Indeed, Celtic nationalists can and do sympathize with the English and French working classes who are oppressed by the same interests as they are. Between the exploited Celtic peoples and the exploited English and French should thrive a greater knowledge and understanding of one another's problems. Regretfully, it is the English and French who generally tend to chauvinism and are imbued with racial attitudes where Celtic problems are concerned because of centuries of acceptance of imperial propaganda.

Celtic nationalism is part of a world movement; a reaction to a growing, world sickness. All over the globe, there is a nascent new individualism rising in revolt against the mass society of our day.. The revolt is against the tremendous drive of 'Big Power' politicians towards a world state, a world government and a world language and culture. Unity through uniformity, where there are no 'national' barriers. This is the simplistic way of seeking world peace and co-operation by an attempt to destroy natural differences between communities. This is the ultimate and fallacious dream of a *Brave New World* and perhaps the most crude imperial concept ever proposed. Celtic nationalism, along with the struggle of other small nationalities, in seeking to achieve cultural, political and economic freedom, is a reaction to this idea.

Throughout this book there has been an emphasis on language and its attendant culture. We have observed that it is only by language that the Celtic peoples are defined. The concept is not unique. A Basque person, for example, is called an *Eskualdun* in Basque—literally 'one who possesses the Basque language'. There is no other definition. Imagine the reaction to someone speaking no other language but Russian arriving in London and claiming to be English and one can begin to have an idea of the importance of language definition in the majority of people's minds.

Yet why are small, linguistic-cultural communities important? It is often said that language is merely a means of communication. If it were true, then the development of the vast range of different languages spoken throughout the world would have been one of the great catastrophies of human history. However, language is more than a material means of communication. Culture is that very distinct quality of living that is to the community what personality is to the individual. The main medium of mental cultivation, or culture, is language, and diversity of language is absolutely necessary for a rich diversity of culture. Martin Brennan wrote:

> If this ever-growing uniformity of the material side of our life is not offset by a rich cultural diversification, then man will face an awful crisis of a deadly sameness and monotony of life, a frightening prospect of utter boredom of spirit which would deprive him not merely of the will to achieve but the very desire to survive.

The more the individual, the community and the nation, feel that they have something particularly their own to contribute to mankind, the more they will respect themselves and respect other people; the more they will be heartened to develop the unique set of values that they possess. It would seem that diversification of language and culture is the product of a very fundamental law of human nature. Critics have claimed that languages are barriers, but barriers need not be purely negative things—they can be creative. Barriers to reproduction between originally interbreeding sections of plant and animal species have been the means of enabling these to speciate and produce the present rich variety of living forms. At the cultural level, the practical barrier of language enables different groups to develop, diversify and enrich their own inherited cultures, instead of having their individuality dissolved in a flat, colourless uniformity.

The language and culture of a people are that people's very basis for being. Language is a product of many centuries of cultural development, a vehicle of all the wisdom, poetry, legend and history which is bequeathed to a people by its forebears. Rough hewn, chiselled and polished with loving care, it is handed down as a beautiful work of art—the greatest art form, I would venture; the noblest monument of man's genius.

The repression of minority languages and cultures, such as the Celtic group, is caused partly by cynical expansionist policies, and partly by a lack of understanding of the values enshrined in the languages of such minority groups. It is generally believed that a language that does not possess a rich literature is a poor vehicle of expression. Eduard Sapir commented:

> The most primitive South African Bushman expresses himself with the help of a rich symbolic system which in essence is quite comparable to the language of a cultured Frenchman...Many primitive languages have a richness of form, a wealth of possibilities of expression which surpasses anything known in languages of modern culture.

Therefore, even if the Celtic languages were simply primitive and lacking in literature, as the English and French actually believe them to be, then they would still be worth struggling for. But the centuries of propaganda from England and France which has sought to dismiss the Celtic languages as 'peasant dialects', 'gibberish' and 'merely a patois', are demonstrated to be nothing more than invented justifications for the systematic destruction of those languages and culture. Knowledge of the Celtic languages provides an access to a great wealth of literature which, with the exception of Greek and Latin, is older than the literature of any other European people and which maintains a continuity from the early mythological and heroic cycles.

Language, thought and culture, are inseparable. Language and thought are two aspects of the same thing. To change one's language is tantamount to changing one's mentality. The linguistic philosopher, Benjamin Lee Whorf, wrote:

> We are inclined to think of language as a technique of expression and not to realize that language, first of all, is a classification and arrangement of the stream of sensory experience which results in a certain world order, a certain segment of the world that is easily expressible by the type of symbolic means that language employs. In other words, language does, in a cruder but also in a broader and more volatile way, the same thing that science does.

In the countries where language and tradition have been suppressed or relegated to second-class positions, the members of the ethnic group are correspondingly deprived and degraded. In what remains of Celtic society, the Celts find that they are in an environment which is hostile, where they are taught that their status as Celts is of no importance, and that they have no contribution to make to that society unless they become English or French. Their own culture holds no significance and therefore the only useful role in life is to swiftly change their nationality.

Is it a wonder that Celtic society produces a fantastically high percentage of alcoholics? One Breton hospital recently estimated that two-thirds of its admissions were alcoholic cases. Celtic society also produces the biggest percentage of prostitutes in the United Kingdom and France. Celtic society has a correspondingly high percentage of social misfits. French and English commentators are swift to see this social pattern as part of the Celtic character, rather than its being the result of centuries of degradation of the Celt, and the imposition of an alien language and culture while the native language and culture were vilified.

Fortunately, the system of physical punishment of children who spoke Celtic languages in schools has now been stopped. The beatings, the wearing of symbols of disgrace, including the hanging of a human skull around the neck of five to seven-year-old children in a Lewis School in the middle of this Century, the financial fines imposed by the more 'humane' school-teachers, have ceased now. It does not require a great deal of imagination to realize what sort of product would emerge from this 'education' system. One cannot wonder at the diffident, clannish and slightly hostile attitude of the average Scottish Gaelic-speaker today towards strangers—even to those who, by their willingness to learn some Scottish Gaelic, have shown they are in sympathy with the well-being of the Scottish Gaelic-speaking peoples. To suffer the traumatic experience, at the age of five years-old, of being pitched suddenly into an absolutely hostile environment, where the only language the children know is forbidden and harsh punishment is imposed if a word of it is uttered, has resulted in the terrible environmental sickness of Scottish Gaeldom. Tormod MacLeòid recalled in 1965:

> As an infant of five, newly arrived in the classroom, I was confronted with a young lady, who seemed to me to be a goddess, but remote. We had no common language. I knew no English, but she spoke no Gaelic. Learning the Roman alphabet might seem to be a task equal for all normal infants, but the task is made difficult for the child who received instruction and explanation in a foreign language which he does not know.

Such a hostile environment naturally produces a general inferiority complex. This inferiority reveals itself in the way many Celts who are native speakers of their languages will pretend ignorance to outsiders, insisting on speaking English or French no matter how scanty their knowledges of those acquired languages. One such instance revealled itself when the Scottish journalist, Seumas Mac a' Ghobhainn, wrote to a native Gaelic-speaking school teacher asking about the state of the language in his area. The native speaker replied, to this enquiry written in Gaelic, with a reply written in English; and even Mac a' Ghobhainn's name was rendered into English, not just in Anglicized phonetics as MacGowan, but translated as 'James Smith'. Had the Italian composer, Guiseppe Verdi, been addressed by an Englishman as 'Mr Joseph Green', I am sure that the musician would simply have forgiven the man for his crass ignorance. Yet for a Scottish Gaelic-speaker to address another Scottish Gaelic-speaker in such fashion, not in any attempt at studied insult but in the belief that such behaviour was normal, is indicative of a deep mental sickness towards the fact of nationality.

The neutralization of Celtic culture and history has led to many anomalies in these islands. Scots will insist that there are two nationalities in Scotland, just as Irish Protestants in the north of Ireland insist they are ethnically different from Irish Catholics. For many years, there were some who felt that Monmouth was an English county and not a Welsh one.

Many still believe that Cornwall is just as English as Kent. Bizarre ideas as to who the Celts are—that the Cornish are descendants of the wrecked mariners of the Spanish Armada, that the Welsh are a lost tribe of Israel, and that part of Scotland is inhabited by a strange unknown 'race' called the Picts—permeated through popular consciousness. Such general ignorance is summed up by the fact that the United Kingdom's Trades Union Council's former general secretary, Len Murray, on a Trades Union Day of Action held on St. David's Day, March 1, 1984, could blandly tell his cohorts to remember that St. David of Wales slew Goliath!

The Celtic societies are culturally sick. The cure for this sickness is well-known and has been successfully carried out in many other countries. It consists in reviving the native languages, with their literatures, their histories and traditions, and being able to gain full control over the cultural, economic and political life of the national community. Only by this path will the Celtic nations regain their identities, and only then will each feel a oneness with its past and a confidence in its future. Winston Churchill, that arch-imperialist, once said: "A nation which forgets its past can have no future". Be it remembered that he was more keen than most Englishmen that the Celts should forget their past. Tacitus, the Roman historian, also summed it up nearly 2,000 years ago: "The language of the conqueror in the mouths of the conquered is ever the language of the slave".

There has been much written about the mechanics of language-restoration and those who criticize the idea, claiming that language-revival is unworkable, merely demonstrate their own insularity. The Hebrew language's revival—that impressive restoration of a language dead for 2,500 years as a normal, modern, everyday tongue is frequently quoted. One can point to many other examples which have stronger parallels with the Celtic situation. Such examples as Albanian, Armenian, Czech, Danish, Estonian, Faroese, Finnish, Icelandic, Indonesian, Korean, Latvian, Lithuanian, Norwegian, Polish, Rumanian, Slovakian, Slovenian and Ukrainian, were sketched in *The Problem of Language Revival* (Club Leabhar, Inverness, 1973) by myself and Seumas Mac a' Ghobhainn. Language-revival and reconstruction has and can work.

I have never made any attempt to disguise the fact that, in supporting the national struggles of the Celtic peoples, I do so as a socialist. The majority political ideology among Celtic nationalists inevitably tends to be a radical socialist one, although there are fringe elements of bourgeois liberalism. Right-wing ideologies find little support among Celtic nationalists for a Celtic nationalist who advocates 'conservatism', capitalism and monarchism would be the equivalent of a German Jew electing to preach National Socialism in Hitler's Germany.

One of the saddest things, both in England and France, is the attitude of the socialist movements towards the Celts. It is true that some elements of those movements see the Celtic struggle as an essential part of the anti-imperial struggle but, generally, the socialist movements in those countries are every bit as imperialist as the right-wing. In this respect, the Celts often provide their own worst enemies.

Neil Kinnock, elected to lead the United Kingdom's Labour Party in 1983, is a 'geographical Welshman' bearing a Scottish name. He has several times demonstrated his strange desire to destroy every vestige of Celtic separateness from England. The Welsh still remember his campaign against Gwynedd County Council's language policy in education; others recall that it was Neil Kinnock who helped to arrange the referendum on devolution in such a way that, while the majority of Scots voted for a Scottish Assembly, it was still denied them. At least, Lloyd George held some consciousness of his Celtic heritage, and cherished his native language to some extent, but Neil Kinnock has no such pretensions. He is a non-Welsh speaking, avowed Anglophile who panders to the theory of the majority of England's socialists, that Celtic nationalism is contrary to socialism, a retrogressive ideology and quite reactionary. Such socialists have often been asked how they can continue to let one nation dominate another, and pretend that it is not imperialism because the dominating nation purports to have a 'socialist' government? Some of them even argue that socialists should not sympathize with oppressed nationalities, or with nations resisting conquest, for the sooner national boundaries are overthrown the better.

Geoffrey Bell, in his superb study, *Troublesome Business: The Labour Party and the Irish Question* (Pluto Press, 1982), has documented the history of the attitude of mainstream English socialism towards the Irish struggle, in which he concludes that the attitudes and relationships of the Labour Party to Ireland "have been neither honourable, internationalist nor socialist". The same comment applies to its attitudes to the other Celtic nations and one can agree with Bell's conclusion that, to future historians, "Labour's definition of socialism will remain the most curious of all".

But the English socialist's attitude towards the Celts in their national ambit is not so different from the French socialist's attitudes towards the Bretons, or, indeed, the other small nationalities within the French state. In a book published in the USSR in 1984 by the ethnographer S.Bruk, a distinction was made between the French, and the Bretons, Basques, Alsacians, Flemings, Catalans etc, who comprise the nationalities of the French state. On February 17th, 1984, M.Marchais, Secretary-General of the French Communist Party, wrote a protest to the

Secretariate of the Communist Party of the USSR.

> France is one country, one nation, one people...We protest indignantly against such ridiculous and odious allegations...For us, as for all the citizens of our country, every man and women of French nationality is French...Every attempt using hazardous criteria which borders on racism in an ill-defined way, seeking to define as not purely French such and such members of the French community, is offensive to the national consciousness. Nobody here can accept that, our Party least of all.

Again one asks the question: who are the racists—the persons who want to maintain their particular nationality or those who seek to liquidate it? It is obvious that M.Marchais is not concerned with the Breton 'national consciousness' as only the French 'national consciousness' counts within the multi-national French state. Such chauvinism opens the way for a frightening repression of the Bretons and other nationalities within the state, should the French Communist Party gain power with such an ideology. The Communist Party of France seems to have conveniently forgotten the teachings of V.I.Lenin himself on the national question, which was that national freedom was a principal condition for his ideal of a socialist world. Writing in 1917, Lenin stated: "The principal condition of a democratic peace is the renunciation of claims of annexation. This must not be wrongly understood in the sense that all powers should recover what they have lost, but according to the only true meaning, which is that every nationality without exception in Europe and in the colonies should obtain freedom..." Unfortunately, it is a human condition for people to claim to be followers of this philosopher, or that religious leader, without bothering to adhere to their teachings.

It was the Irish Marxist leader, James Connolly, executed for his part in the 1916 uprising, who said that nations which submit to conquest or who abandon their languages in favour of those of their oppressors do so not because of altruistic motives, or love of the brotherhood of man, but from a slavish, cringing spirit. Such a spirit could not exist side by side with the socialist ideal. "I cannot conceive of a socialist hesitating in his choice between a policy resulting in such self-abasement and a policy of defiant self-reliance and confident trust in a people's own power of self-emancipation by a people,' he wrote in *The Harp*, in April, 1908. He considered "the free expression of nationality to be as desirable in the interest of humanity in general as the free expression of individuality is to the nation."

For Connolly, as with the majority of Celtic nationalists: "True patriotism seeks the welfare of all, and is inconsistent with the selfish desire for worldly wealth which can only be gained by the spoliation of less favoured fellow mortals". Writing in *Workers' Republic*, July 7th, 1900, Connolly gave a clear picture of what his nationalism involved, one that is still shared by today's Celtic nationalists.

> Ireland without her people is nothing to me, and the man who is bubbling over with love and enthusiasm for 'Ireland', and can yet pass unmoved through our streets and witness all the wrongs and suffering, the shame and degradation wrought upon the people of Ireland, aye, wrought by Irishmen upon Irishmen and women, without burning to end it is, in my opinion, a fraud and a liar in his heart, no matter how he loves that combination of chemical elements which he is pleased to call 'Ireland'.

Connolly declared the internationalism of the Celtic nationalists when he wrote in *Workers' Republic*, August 5th, 1899:

> We mean to be free, and in every enemy of tyranny we recognize a brother, where ever his birth place; in every enemy of freedom we also recognize our enemy, though he were as Irish as our hills. The whole of Ireland for the people of Ireland—their public property, to be owned and operated as a national heritage, by the labour of free men in a free country.

The Celtic peoples have strong socialist traditions in which they reject bureaucratic, authoritarian, imperialist, state socialism; and recognize that the principles of a true socialist society must be particular to, and suited for, the needs of each peoples.

Henry Simons has already written that world peace does not lie in the destruction of little nations, but in the destruction of large multi-national states who are the real monsters of imperialism and mercantilism. In that statement, he was merely echoing Aristotle's *Politics* and St. Augustine of Hippo's *City of God*. Arnold Toynbee linked the fall of civilization, not to the fight among nations but to the rise of the multi-national states and empires. From Henry Simons, in political science, to Kathleen Freeman, as an historian, from the economist Justice Brandeis, to the sociologist Frank Tennenbaum, the universal cause of modern social difficulties has been lain at the doorstop of the multi-national states and the 'overgrowth' of societies. The solution to problems such as economic misery, war, loss of individual freedom, is not in international unions and unifications, but in the dismemberment of the world's multi-national states; in the ending of the last vestiges of imperialism. Professor Leopold Kohr, writing in *The Breakdown of Nations* (London, 1957), was one of the first theorists this century to condense the values of 'smallness' into a comprehensive social analysis, and furnish a philosophical framework for the individualism which is rising in revolt against mass, centralized existence.

The Celtic struggle is an integral part of the world struggle to create a society in which humankind is able to survive the appalling modern pressures and grow towards a society which will be truly civilized, free from the day-to-day pre-occupation with material concerns, and therefore firmly on the path to a spiritual awareness. Celtic nationalists recognize that the way to a sound internationalism lies through the recognition, not the repudiation, of the fact of nationality. The solidarity of the peoples of the world must rest upon a pact of national units associated in a common purpose and destiny.

After centuries of the most ruthless colonization and oppression, the Celtic peoples still survive although, out of the sixteen million people who populate the Celtic areas today, only two-and-a-half millions speak a Celtic language. Nevertheless, the Celts have not gone lemming-like into the abyss in the wake of such peoples as the Etruscans. They survive as the 'bad conscience' of English and French imperialism and, perhaps, in that fact, lies the motive behind the savage mockery and contempt which is generally levelled at them.

Under continuing pressures, it might not be long before the Celtic peoples do disappear, for even if self-government is attained within the near future, the native governments might lack the will and ability to carry out a constructive, linguistic restoration. The Irish and the Manx possess some degree of statehood but, whilst they have gained *states*, they are losing the *nations*. If the languages die, and fade beyond all possibility of revival, then the term 'Celtic' would only stand a chance of survival as a geographical expression and the Celtic peoples would then be extinct.

This, then, has been a brief outline of the history, struggles and the aspirations of the Celtic peoples. It is a story which should find an echo of sympathy in the hearts of all those who have struggled, and are struggling, against imperialism in all its insidious forms in every corner of the world.

Further Reading

I have presented a primer for general reading and not an academic study, therefore I have dispensed with footnotes. Most references are given in the text. However, for those interested in further study, and in current events in the pan-Celtic world, the following will be useful:

Carn, the quarterly periodical of the Celtic League.

General Reading

The Rise of the Celts, Henri Hubert, Kegan Paul, London, 1934.

The Greatness and Decline of the Celts, Henri Hubert, Kegan Paul, London 1934.

The Celts, edited by Joseph Raftery, Mercier Press, Cork, 1964.

The Celts, Nora Chadwick, Pelican Books, London, 1970.

Literature in Celtic Countries, J.E.C.Williams, University of Wales Press, Cardiff, 1971.

The Celtic Realms, Myles Dillion & Nora Chadwick, Cardinal, London, 1973.

Pagan Celtic Britain, Anne Ross, Cardinal, London, 1974.

Women of the Celts, J.Markle, Gordon Cremonesi, London, 1975.

ALBA (Scotland)

Scottish Nationalism, H.J.Hanham, Faber & Faber, London, 1969.

The Scottish Insurrection of 1820, Peter Berresford Ellis and Seumas Mac a' Ghobhainn, Gollancz, London, 1970.

The Lion's Tongue, Kenneth MacKinnon, Club Leabhar, Inver-

ness, 1974.
MacBeth: High King of Scotland 1040-57, Peter Berresford Ellis, Muller, London, 1981.

BREIZH (Brittany)

La Bretagne écartelée, Yann Fouéré, Nouvelles Editions latines, Paris, 1962.
Langue et Litterature Bretonnes, Francis Gourvil, Presses Universitaires de Frances, 4th ed. 1976.
Le Breton: Langue Celtique, Yann Brekilien, Nature et Bretagne, 1976.
La langue bretonne face a ses oppresseurs, Jorj ab Herve-Gwegen, Nature et Bretagne, 1983.

CYMRU (Wales)

The Dragon's Tongue, Gerald Morgan, Triskel Press, Cardiff, 1966.
The Welsh Extremist, Ned Thomas, 2nd ed. Y Lolfa, Talybont, 1973.
The Welsh Language Today, Meic Stephens, Gomer Press, Llandysul, 1973.
To Dream of Freedom, Roy Clews, Y Lolfa, Talybont, 1980.

ÉIRE (Ireland)

A Literary History of Ireland, Douglas Hyde, new edition, Ernest Benn, London, 1967.
The Fortunes of the Irish Language, Daniel Corkery, Cultural Relations Committee, Dublin, 1954.
A View of the Irish Language, ed. Brían Ó Cuív, Stationery Office, Dublin, 1969.
The Great Silence, Seán de Freíne, The Mercier Press, Cork, 1965 reprinted 1968, 1978.
Hidden Ulster, Pádraig Ó Snodaigh, Clodhanna Teo, Dublin, 1973.
A History of the Irish Working Class, Peter Berresford Ellis, revised edition, Pluto Press, London, 1985.
Northern Ireland: The Orange State, Michael Farrell, Pluto Press, London, 1976.

Ireland: The Propaganda War, Liz Curtis, Pluto Press, London, 1984.

KERNOW (Cornwall)

The Cornish Language and its Literature, Peter Berresford Ellis, Routledge, Kegan Paul, London, 1974.
The Death of Cornish, Peter Pool, Kesva an Tavas Kernewek, Cornwall, 1976.
Kernewek Hedhya: Report on the state of the language, Cowethas an Yeth Kernewek, 1984.
The Life of Cornish, C.Fudge, Dyllansow Truran, 1982.

MANNIN (Isle of Man)

Isle of Man(n), R.H.Kinvig, University of Liverpool Press, Liverpool, 1975.
The Study of Manx Gaelic, R.L.Thomson, Proceedings of the British Academy Vol. LV, 1969.

Useful Addresses

The Celtic League: Alan Heusaff, General Secretary, 9 Bóthar Cnoc Síon, Dromchonarch, Baile Átha Cliath 9, Éire. (addresses of the League's branches in the individual Celtic countries, and in America and London, may be obtained from the General Secretary).

Celtic language movements:

Alba (Scotland)
An Comunn Gàidhealach, Abertaff House, Inverness, Scotland.

Breizh (Brittany)
Stourm ar Brezhoneg, Iwan Kadored, ar Visenn, 56000 Gwened, Breizh

Cymru (Wales)
Cymdeithas yr Iaith Gymraeg, Pen Roc, Rhodfa'r Môr, Aberystwyth, Cymru.

Éire (Ireland)
Conradh na Gaeilge, 6 Sráid Fhearchair, Baile Átha Cliath 2, Éire.

Kernow (Cornwall)
Cowethas an Yeth Kernewek, 29 Midway Drive, Uplands Park, Truro, Kernow.

Mannin (Isle of Mann)
Yn Cheshaght Ghailckagh,. 23 Straid ny Keeilley, Purt ny h-Inhsey, Mannin.

Nova Scotia (Canada)
An Communn Gàidhlig Cheap Breatunn (Cape Breton Gaelic Society), 126 Woodlawn Drive, Sydney River, Nova Scotia, B1S 1H9, Canada.

Y Wladfa, Patagonia, Argentina
Unfortunately, the author has been unable to discover any movement seeking to keep alive the language in this Welsh-speaking area of the New World.

Language books, songbooks, cookbooks, art books, policital books. . .

. . . poetry, posters, greetings cards, diaries, T-shirts . . .

TALYBONT CEREDIGION CYMRU SY24 5AP
e-mail ylolfa@ylolfa.com
internet http://www.ylolfa.com
tel (01970) 832 304
fax 832 782
isdn 832 813